THE BONDAGE OF THE WILL

MARTIN LUTHER

MODERN PURITANS

PUBLISHER'S INTRODUCTION

Thanks for picking up a copy of The Bondage of the Will by Martin Luther. We hope this timeless work stirs your heart and helps you grow in your walk with the Lord.

If you enjoy this book, please share it with a friend, leave a positive review on Amazon, and explore more modernized and updated Puritan books at modernpuritans.com.

PREFACE

A BRIEF BIOGRAPHY OF MARTIN LUTHER

I think it's important to give the reader some context about the circumstances under which this work was written. To do this, I'll provide a quick overview of Luther's history and its connection to Protestantism.

Martin Luther was born in 1483 in Isleben, Saxony. His father, who had worked in the Mansfield mines, later became a proprietor in them. This allowed him to educate his son with both a pious father's care and a wealthy father's generosity. After providing him with basic education in some lower-level schools, he sent Martin to the University of Erfurth at a young age. There, Martin excelled in classical learning, eloquence, and philosophy, and earned his Master of Arts degree at the age of twenty.

His parents had planned for him to become a lawyer, but after dedicating himself to studying civil law for a while, Martin suddenly left it behind and joined a convent in Erfurth. In the convent, he became known for his hard work, self-discipline, and conscientiousness, but he also struggled with intense fear of God. He was often sad and sometimes experienced extreme mental anguish.

During these difficult times, Martin sought advice from his vicar-general, Staupitius. Staupitius comforted him by suggesting that he didn't know how useful and necessary this trial might be for him. He told Martin, "God does not exercise you for nothing. You will one day see that he will employ you as his servant for great purposes."

The historian notes that the event greatly honored Staupitius' wisdom, and it's clear that a profound and genuine conviction of sin, which led Luther to explore the truths of Scripture and seek the path to peace, was the driving force behind his actions. This understanding of Luther's mindset is the only way to truly grasp the motives that guided him in his public life.

It wasn't until his second year living in the monastery that Luther stumbled upon a Latin Bible in the library, and for the first time, he realized that significant portions of the Scriptures were being kept from the people. During that same year, when he fell ill, an older monk in the convent provided him with great comfort by directing his attention to the valuable belief, "I believe in the remission of sins." Luther later said that Staupitius had spoken to him like an angel when he taught him that "true repentance begins with the love of righteousness and of God." However, the old monk guided him to the source of this love. There may be, and indeed is, a longing for righteousness and a search for God that paves the way for this love. But there can be no genuine righteousness achieved or love felt for it and for God until we are aware of His forgiveness.

The wise old monk explained to him that this belief didn't just imply a general faith - for even the devils had that kind of faith - but rather, it was God's command that each individual should apply the doctrine of the forgiveness of sins to their own specific situation. He pointed Luther to the writings of Bernard, Augustine, and St. Paul as evidence of this. With incredible passion, Luther devoted himself to studying the Scriptures and the works of Augustine. He later read other theologians, but he remained steadfast in his loyalty to Augustine until the very end.

In 1507, Luther received holy orders, and the following year, he was appointed as a Professor of Divinity at Wittemberg, thanks to the recommendation of his friend Staupitius. This allowed Luther to prove his own predictions about himself. It was during this time that he formed a connection with Elector Frederic of Saxony, which proved to be very helpful in his future struggles. Frederic was deeply concerned about the reputation and success of his new school, and Luther exceeded his expectations as both a philosophy teacher and a public minister. Luther was a natural orator, skilled at moving people's emotions, and had an exceptional understanding of the elegance and power of his native language, which made him the wonder of his age.

In 1510, Luther was sent to Rome on important business for his order. He performed his duties so well that he received a doctorate upon his return. While in Rome, he observed the way religious worship was conducted, noting its grandeur, haste, and political nature. He was grateful to return to his convent, where he could pray sincerely and passionately without being mocked. Luther then began a public exposition of the Psalms and Paul's Epistle to the Romans, studying Greek and Hebrew diligently. He refined his taste and expanded his knowledge by taking advantage of the philological work of Erasmus, to whom he always acknowledged his great debt.

Luther rejected the restrictive teachings of Aristotle and the Schoolmen, and instead of just tearing down existing ideas like a satirist, he sought to build a scriptural theology on the ruins of a paganized Christianity. The true light of understanding gradually dawned on his mind: he went from suspecting error to being convinced of its presence. As he was forced to reject these errors, he was led step by step into the truth.

So, he was deeply engaged in studying, thinking, teaching, and preaching with a conflicted mind. Once he had been given some unique opportunities to understand the true state of religion - among both clergy and laity in his own country - he couldn't help but focus on the topic of INDULGENCES. He hadn't approached it as a theory; he wasn't aware of the true nature, basis, components, or consequences of the issue.

As a confessor, he had to deal with admissions of sin; as a priest, he had to prescribe penances. The penitents refused to comply because they had dispensations in their pockets. What a masterpiece of Satan's work was this! It's not "Sin no more, lest something worse happens to you;" but rather, 'sin as much as you want, as long as you can pay for it.'

Luther wouldn't absolve them. The bold-faced Tetzel became furious and ordered his pile of wood to be set on fire, intending to strike fear into anyone who dared to think of being heretics. For now, Luther simply said with great gentleness from the pulpit that 'the people might be better employed than in running from place to place to obtain INDULGENCES.'

He was certain it was wrong; he would attempt to stop it; he would try with proper procedure, seeking help from the archbishop and bishop for a solution. He was so unaware of the main players, their assistants, and those even further down in the hierarchy involved in the trade, that he asked his own archbishop to put an end to it!

Look at how God operates. Ambition, vanity, and excess are used to expose the horrors of the Papacy, so that God can reveal Himself through His actions towards it. The magnificent temple, which had previously been built to amaze people rather than for the praise and worship of God, must continue to be constructed - even though not a single bit could be taken away from Leo's pomp, sensuality, and splendor, despite his treasury already being empty. Reckless necessity leads him to a solution which, while it exposes his own character and the principles of the government he oversees, would likely prompt at least some to question the authority by which they were asked to tolerate such atrocities.

This method wasn't new, as Julius had used it before Leo. However, it had never been so widely and blatantly practiced as in this instance. It involved profiting from religion by selling merits for money—not only by pardoning but even legalizing the contempt and defiance of God through the distribution of certain extra riches of Christ and his saints, to which the Pope has the key. The price demanded varied with the buyer's circumstances, so that people of all ranks could benefit. In fact, all classes of people were made to contribute to ecclesiastical corruption, while the notorious Dominican Tetzel could claim that he had saved more souls from hell with his Indulgences than St. Peter had converted to Christianity through his preaching.

Luther investigated, studied, prayed, and called on his rulers. Eventually, receiving no help but only silence or warnings from authorities, he published his ninety-five theses or doctrinal propositions on the subject. These spread with a remarkable impact and effect throughout all of Germany in just fifteen days.

Tetzel responded with one hundred and six theses, which led to sermons in reply and counter-reply. Luther was so dutiful, sincere, and confident in the truth that he sent his publications to his superiors in the church—his diocesan and his vicar-general—asking the vicar-general to forward them to the Pope. The issue was now out in the open. New opponents emerged, and Luther was thorough and restrained in his responses. Eventually, Leo was provoked. He had praised Brother Martin for his excellent intellect and attributed the dispute to monastic jealousy—a rivalry between the Dominicans and the Augustinians. But now, within sixty days, Luther had to appear in Rome to defend himself. In fact, he was already condemned as an unrepentant heretic without trial in the apostolic chamber in Rome— even before the summons reached him.

Through the help of his influential friend, the elector, Luther managed to get a hearing in Augsburg (if you can even call it a hearing), which only allowed him to admit his crime and recant. However, this was the kind of justice and judgment Luther faced from Cajetan.

After submitting as much as he could without actually writing the six letters (REVOCO) that would have resolved everything - even though there were other important issues besides the Indulgences - Luther left his arrogant and dismissive judge with an appeal that he made sure was officially recorded: "from the Pope ill-informed, to the same most holy Leo X, when better informed."

During his various meetings in Augsburg, both written and verbal, Luther firmly stood on his belief in scripture over all papal decrees. It was his triumph on this occasion that he defended this belief even in the face of the usurper's representative. A humble monk, as the cardinal condescendingly called him, respectfully followed and acted on the same principle that two apostles had used before him: "We ought to obey God rather than men." (Acts 5:29)

Cajetan didn't gain any respect in Rome for his negotiations in Augsburg. The papal advisors complained that he had been harsh and ungenerous when he should have offered wealth, a bishopric, and a cardinal's hat. These were the temptations they thought would sway Luther! (Romans 12:20) When he returned to Wittenberg at the end of 1518, Luther considered leaving Germany for France. However, the elector stopped him and urgently asked Emperor Maximilian to step in and help settle the controversy.

Meanwhile, Luther renewed his appeal to the Pope. Surprisingly, this was followed by a new bull in favor of Indulgences, confirming all the old abuses and not even mentioning Luther's name. In his current state of mind, still clinging to the Pope's authority, this document was timely. It made it impossible for Luther to retreat. Maximilian's death in early 1519 increased the elector's power to protect Luther during the interregnum and led to more lenient measures in Rome. A polite Saxon knight replaced the domineering Dominican.

"Martin," he said, "I thought you were some reclusive old theologian, but I find you to be a person full of life. Moreover, you have such popular support that I couldn't force you to come with me to Rome even with the help of 25,000 soldiers."

Luther was resolute, though softened. He had no objection to writing submissively to the Pope. At that point, he still recognized the Pope's authority, and it was a principle for him to show respect to his superiors and obey "the powers that be," Rom 13.1 in lawful matters if lawfully constituted.

The famous debates at Leipzig took place in July 1519. Here, Luther, who had been denied a safe conduct if he tried to appear as a debater, was finally allowed to defend Carolstadt's half-defended cause and speak for himself against one of the most learned, eloquent, and bitter papal opponents. Eckius, Luther's former friend, had come to earn laurels for himself and strength for the Papacy. But it was God who granted victory to the truth and used this occasion to provide Luther with many capable allies. Melancthon's approval of Luther's doctrine and his personal attachment to Luther were the results of this encounter.

"In Wittenberg, Melancthon was probably well acquainted with Luther's lectures on theology. But it was in the citadel of Leipzig that he heard the Roman Catholic beliefs defended by all the arguments that ingenuity could devise. There, his suspicions grew about the evils of the existing hierarchy, and his righteous spirit was stirred to imitate, in the grand objective of his future inquiries and efforts, the tireless endeavors of his zealous and daring friend."

It was here that the issue of papal supremacy first became a topic of debate. The act of granting indulgences implied the right, but the principle was now introduced by Eckius, with malicious intent, to cast scandal upon Luther, who at the time "saw men, but as trees, walking" (Mk 8.24). Luther even defended the Pope's supremacy, though on weaker grounds. He attributed it to human-based reasons: divine permission and the consent of the faithful. Although Eckius' thirteen propositions and Luther's opposing ones mainly focused on papal authority, they also covered other subjects. Many significant and widely relevant issues were brought up and debated during the discussion.

On all the debated topics, Luther demonstrated a mind that was receptive to the truth, as in the example just mentioned. However, it is uncertain whether he was fully enlightened to any truth at this point. Even on justification and free will, although he held the essence of what he later taught, he did not use the same arguments or defense methods. Here is his own account, as provided in the preface to his works:

"My own case," he says, "is a notable example of the difficulty with which a man emerges from long-standing erroneous notions. How true is the proverb, custom is a second nature! How true is Augustine's saying that habit, if not resisted, becomes necessity! I had taught divinity both publicly and privately with great diligence for seven years, to the point where I could recall almost every word of my lectures from memory. But in reality, at that time, I had only just begun to understand and believe in Christ. I had only recently learned that a person must be justified and saved not by their actions, but by their faith in Christ. And finally, regarding the Pope's authority, although I publicly argued that the Pope was not the head of the church by divine right, I still struggled with the idea that the entire papal system was a creation of Satan. I didn't see it that way, but stubbornly fought for the Pope's right based on human reasoning. I was so deceived by the example of others, the title of the Holy Church, and my own habits. Because of this, I've learned to be more understanding towards devoted Catholics, especially if they're not well-versed in religious or even secular history."

After the debate, Luther calmly reviewed his own thirteen propositions and published them with brief explanations and evidence, mainly relying on Scripture and church history to support his conclusions. These intellectual battles of the past were the foundation for the reawakening church. The people listened, and the people read. And so, according to Luther's favorite principle, the stone that will destroy the Antichrist was cut out without hands.

In 1520, Miltitz advised Luther to write a second letter to the Pope. As Luther's understanding of the truth grew, he found it challenging to write this letter honestly, and it's debatable whether he succeeded in his attempt. He had already told his friend that he strongly believed the Pope was the real Antichrist. Luther said, "The lives and behavior of the Popes, their actions, their decrees, all agree most wonderfully to the descriptions of him in Holy Writ." So, how could he still approach the Pope as his authorized leader and desired protector, flatter him, and propose terms of mutual silence?

It's true that the tone of his letter changed compared to his previous one. He pointed out many of the wrongdoings in the Pope's government, explicitly refused to recant, and insisted on his essential principle: "perfect freedom in interpreting the word of God."

He is also particularly wise, fair, straightforward, and powerful in warning the Pope against the grandiose words his flatterers use to praise him: "O my people, those who call you BLESSED lead you astray." However, we would prefer to see more honesty and fewer compliments, for example, not so subtly separating the person from the office, the man from his court; withholding wishes and prayers for good when he began to believe that only curse and destruction could follow. The only reasonable defense is that his mind was not yet FULLY made up about the Pope. He had doubts; he thought he was obligated to go to the utmost in efforts to reconcile; such an appeal would be a test. In evaluating the correctness of this action, it is clear that everything depends on the amount of enlightenment that had reached his mind at that time. But, having written to Spalatinus as he did earlier in the same year, and later writing his treatise on the necessity of reformation in June, and his Babylonian Captivity in August, it is hard to imagine that, in the intervening time, he would have maintained a mindset that, consistent with simplicity, could dictate his, or any letter of accommodation to Leo.

Eventually, however, having thoroughly tested his David, and having convinced him of his foolishness, the Lord completely removed it from Luther while sealing up his enemies in theirs. Never was there a more evident example of Jewish blindness and hardening than in the Conclave's decisions at this time. — "He has blinded their eyes and hardened their heart" Joh 12.40 — Leo refuses to be appeased. After a three-year delay, when Lutheranism had grown to a size and strength that no fire can burn, the condemnatory bull is issued on June 15, 1520, in Rome. And after a brief period of mysterious silence, it is published in Germany.

The text discusses how 41 propositions were extracted from Luther's writings, all deemed heretical. The reading of his books was forbidden, and they were ordered to be burned. Luther was excommunicated, and secular princes were asked to help arrest him. However, Luther was ready for this, as he had formed a judgment about the papal usurpation and was willing to suffer martyrdom for the truth if necessary. The conflict had officially begun.

Luther responded by publishing two tracts. In one, he treated the bull ironically, questioning its authenticity but still calling it the "execrable bull of Antichrist" and urging the emperor and Christian princes to defend the church against the Papists. In the other tract, he seriously addressed the 41 condemned articles, defending the authority of Scripture and encouraging everyone to study it without relying on the interpretations of others.

After responding to the bull, Luther demonstrated his defiance by burning it, along with the papal decretals and parts of the canon law related to pontifical jurisdiction. This act was not done out of anger but rather from a place of calm conviction. He then selected 30 articles from the burned books, published them with brief commentary, and asked the public if he had shown them less respect than they deserved. The last two articles included one stating that the Pope has the power to interpret Scripture and teach as he pleases, and no one is allowed to interpret it differently.

Article 30, etc., states, "The Pope does not derive authority from the Scripture, but the Scripture derives authority, power, and dignity from the Pope." The speaker claimed to have more of a similar kind. If we assume his cause was just, then his bold actions were undoubtedly right. His situation called for decisive measures. He was either a candidate for burning at the stake or a defender of the oppressed. What kind of defender? Not by the sword of a knight-errant, but by actions that showed his sincerity and arguments that proved he had a valid reason.

During this time and the two years prior, he published countless works. He knew his life was at risk, so he valued the limited time he believed he had. The cause of Christ, which he felt was entrusted to him, was to be upheld, expanded, and ultimately made victorious only by the nonviolent sword of the Spirit. He would wield that sword with all his strength, without stopping, weakening, or growing tired. His primary hope was in the word of God, presented simply and clearly. He added short practical and experiential writings (appealing to common sense and Scripture), but the explained word was his foundation. This is why he put so much effort into the Epistle to the Galatians, which he first published in 1519. After fifteen more years of research, during which he lectured on the subject, he revised, corrected, expanded, and reissued it in 1635. His devout, hardworking, and philosophical historian says:

"I have read and pondered this treatise many times, and after much thought, I am convinced that, as it was one of the most effective means of reviving the light of Scripture in the sixteenth century, it will, with God's blessing, be able to do the same in any age when people are willing to consider the divine truth and when souls are troubled by a sense of their own sinfulness. I'm not sure if this will be appreciated by anyone other than those who are serious, humble, and truly sorry for their mistakes. These are the only people who will find the crucial topic of justification worth accepting. The AUTHOR had deeply explored the human heart and understood its inherent flaws. He had spent a long time trying to find peace of mind through following rules and doing good deeds, but it was only when he discovered the spiritual aspect of justification that he found relief from his intense anxiety. He was chosen by Providence, not just among other reformers, but in a more extraordinary and superior way, to teach humanity this essential religious belief after it had been hidden for over a thousand years. Compared to this, all other subjects of debate seem insignificant! The main point is that we are not justified by our actions, but by our faith in Christ."

I can't resist sharing a quote from this truly spiritual work:

"This teaching about faith must be presented in its purest form. As a believer, you are so completely united with Christ through faith that you become one with him, as if you were the same person. You cannot be separated from Christ; instead, you remain so closely connected to him that you can confidently say, "I am one with Christ." This means that his righteousness, his victory, his life, death, and resurrection all belong to me. On the other hand, Christ can say, "I am that sinner." In other words, my sins, death, and punishment belong to Christ because he is united and connected to me, and I am connected to him. Our faith joins us together so closely that we become one flesh and one bone. We are part of his body, his flesh, and his bones. In fact, the connection between Christ and me is even stronger than the bond between husband and wife, who are considered as one flesh. This faith, therefore, is not at all an ineffective quality; in fact, it has such great excellence that it completely confounds and destroys the foolish ideas and imaginations of the Sophists, who have come up with numerous metaphysical theories about faith, charity, merits, and qualifications. These things are so important that I would love to explain them more thoroughly if I could."

Luther faced many opponents in his battles. His bold statements were clear, logical, and decisive, and his responses to those who attacked them were quick, strong, and complete. He didn't avoid, delay, or hold back. His admirer, the historian, feels the need to apologize for Luther's intensity and harshness. I don't agree with the need for an apology. God, who created Luther, gave him his language. His language was suitable for his situation, his time, and his audience. Such writings were needed and would be read; they stirred up the powerful and were understood by the common people. Luther's own description of himself, given later, is worth more than a thousand apologies. He says,

"I am born to be a rough debater. I clear the ground, pull up weeds, fill up ditches, and smooth the roads. But to build, to plant, to sow, to water, and to beautify the countryside belongs, by the grace of God, to Melancthon."

If Luther had a spirit of bitter hatred and cold-hearted malice towards his opponents, then he should be condemned. But we all know that harsh words can be spoken without any malicious intent, and a smooth tongue can often hide a poisonous spirit. I am more inclined to take issue with his vanity than with his irritability.

The obligations that Charles V owed to Frederic were significant enough to ensure some level of protection for Luther. Charles V didn't really care about Luther's opinions, even though his own biases likely leaned towards the old system. He was more concerned with the political implications of the situation. It was clear that the elector's friend, Luther, should not be condemned without a fair hearing. So, after much negotiation and correspondence, it was agreed that Luther would appear at Worms.

Frederic, being a wise protector, managed to get Charles to expressly renounce the principle that "faith is not to be kept with heretics." Several princes co-signed Luther's safe conduct, and Luther boldly preached his way to Worms, as if to confront as many devils as there were tiles on the houses of the chosen city.

Luther's defense at Worms has sometimes been disappointing, and he himself seemed to feel that he had been too cautious and vague. Later, when he spoke of his boldness (shortly before his death), he questioned whether he should have been so daring at that time and gave credit to God for his courage. Many historians have celebrated this fact in relation to his determination to proceed to Worms, despite the strong discouragement he faced along the way.

It's believed that God, who created man's mouth and gives him wisdom, and who has promised for such occasions, "I will give you a mouth and wisdom which all your adversaries shall not be able to challenge or resist" (Luke 21:15), guided Luther's speech with perfect wisdom during that challenging time. The speech he delivered was appropriate for the situation and the time. However, the question remains: was it the speech we would have expected from Luther?

We acknowledge that there may never have been such a moment, possibly since the days of the Apostles. All the grandeur of Caesar was before him. But, it must be admitted that there is more of the influence of Frederic, Spalatinus, and Melancthon in Luther's speech than of Paul before Felix or Peter and John before the council.

Listen to his own words:

"I have serious doubts (he says in a letter to Spalatinus a few months later) and my conscience is deeply troubled because, following your advice and that of some other friends, I held back my spirit at Worms and didn't act like an Elijah, confronting those idols. If I were ever to face that audience again, they would hear very different words from me." And again:

"To please certain friends and not to seem unreasonably stubborn, I didn't speak up at the Diet of Worms. I didn't stand up to the tyrants with the strong determination and energy that a defender of the Gospel should have! Also, I'm tired of being praised for the restraint I showed on that occasion."

The dean thinks it's all due to humility, but I have no doubt that there was a lot of well-founded and conscientious self-criticism in these admissions. However, he stood by his principle: the free use of the word — the Scripture is for everyone, and everyone has the right to interpret it freely. He would only change his mind if convinced by Scripture, but not otherwise. When told that he needed to clearly state whether he would or would not retract his views, Luther immediately said, "My answer will be straightforward and clear. I don't feel obligated to believe either the Pope or his councils, because it's obvious that they have not only made mistakes but also contradicted themselves many times. So, unless I'm convinced by Scripture or clear reasoning, my belief is so solidified by the scriptural passages I've presented, and my conscience is so committed to following the word of God, that I can't and won't take back anything — because going against one's conscience is neither safe nor innocent."

There's something especially moving about the words that follow:

"Here I stand, I can't do otherwise. May God help me. Amen."

People tried many times to convince him privately, but in the end, he decided to stick to the word, saying, "rather than give up the word of God, when the case is quite clear: I WOULD LOSE MY LIFE."

In just three hours after his last meeting with the Archbishop of Treves (who, despite being a devout Roman Catholic, had shown a strong inclination to help him), Luther received an order to leave Worms. He was only granted twenty-one days of safe passage and was not allowed to preach on his journey home. A bloody edict was then secretly pushed through the diet: many of the members had already left Worms before it was voted on. The enactment ceremony took place in the emperor's private quarters; the decree was backdated, as if it had been passed on the 8th instead of the 21st, and Aleander, the Pope's representative and Luther's accuser, who had been quite troubled by the immense consideration and respect shown to Luther, received it as a sort of consolation and sedative from the emperor, so that he could draft the sentence.

As expected, Aleander wrote the edict with great bitterness and hostility. The first part states that it is the emperor's duty to protect religion and eliminate heresies. The second part describes the efforts made to bring the heretic back to repentance. The third part strongly condemns Martin Luther. The emperor, with the advice of the electors, princes, orders, and states of the empire, decides to carry out the Pope's sentence, as the Pope is the proper guardian of the Catholic faith. He declares that Luther must be considered excommunicated and a notorious heretic, and forbids anyone from receiving, supporting, or protecting him under penalty of high treason. He orders that after the twenty-one days allowed to him, Luther should be pursued wherever he may be, or at least be arrested and held prisoner until the emperor's wishes are known. He directs the same punishment for all of Luther's followers or supporters, and orders their goods to be confiscated unless they can prove they have left his side and received absolution. He forbids anyone from printing, selling, buying, or reading any of Luther's books, and instructs the princes and magistrates to burn them.

However, this grand decree was never carried out. Charles was too preoccupied, entangled in complex and conflicting politics, and too dependent and needy to take revenge for the Pope in Germany at the time. In 1522, a diet of the empire held in Nuremberg agreed to a conclusion that Luther saw as an abrogation of the decree. In 1523, a second diet held in the same place, after some significant differences of opinion, reached a similar decision. The Lutherans were divided between hope and fear, experiencing ups and downs over the following years. In 1526, when bad outcomes were expected, the diet of Spires, after much disagreement, ended favorably. However, the Pope's anger was only postponed.

In 1529, a second diet at Spires almost established the overlooked Edict of Worms. The aggressive way it was conducted led to a protest from the Lutheran states and princes (from which we get the name "Protestants") and resulted in the famous defensive alliance of Smalcalde. The Augsburg decree in 1530 only confirmed the need for this alliance.

Even the most moderate statements of belief and careful behavior had no calming effect; force was being prepared, and it had to be countered with military cooperation. However, it's not by human strength or might that the Lord wins battles. That powerful alliance, which could bring 70,000 men to the battlefield under the leadership of John the Constant, to face only 8,000 of the emperor's men, quickly dissolved like winter snow. In 1547, the emperor conquered everything, captured the two main Protestant leaders, and displayed them to their followers. He established his Interim, killed the Protestant witnesses, and claimed to be the master of the "Man of Sin" (2 Thessalonians 2:3) in his control over the Lord's people.

But look! In three and a half years, the witnesses "whose dead bodies have been lying in the street of the great city, which spiritually is called Sodom and Egypt, where also our Lord was crucified" (Revelation 11:8) - even in that Germany which has been called the highway of Europe - are seen standing on their feet again. The deceitful and scheming Maurice is used to bring deliverance to the Protestants. The emperor in turn becomes a fugitive, filled with panic, and is extremely close to being captured by those he once held captive. Finally, the unexpected Treaty of Passan legalizes Protestantism and ensures a place in the symbolic heavens for the revived witnesses.

In 1546, Luther was taken away from both the disasters and victories of these later events due to a quick illness and early death. Exhaustion and stress had weakened his naturally strong and healthy body, and he passed away as an old man at the age of sixty-three.

The storm that had gathered around Luther's head at Worms was initially repelled by a clever strategy of the elector, which he likely shared secretly with the emperor himself. By staging a fake arrest while Luther was on his way back to Wittenberg, Frederick was able to hide him in Wartburg Castle, where he provided for him for ten months. He would have continued to do so for the rest of Luther's life if he had allowed it. In this hiding place, which Luther called his "Patmos" and compared himself to St. John who was exiled to that island by Domitian, he experienced many visions from God that guided his future ministry.

Luther showed some impatience during his time in hiding. He complained that his kind captor fed him too well, causing him to eat and drink too much, and making him feel dull and sensual. However, the truth seems to be that he thrived on activity and excitement. He didn't enjoy hunting as much as lecturing to hundreds of young men and preaching to thousands.

During this time, however, God nurtured Luther and made him wiser in the art of caring for his followers. Although he may have felt dull and heavy, he was not idle. Dressed as a horseman, he wrote many tracts, improved his knowledge of Greek and Hebrew with the goal of translating the Scriptures, and actually completed his German translation of the New Testament, publishing it that same year. These accomplishments were certainly not the result of laziness or indulgence!

During this period, one of Luther's most elaborate original works was his response to Latomus' defense of the Louvain divines. Seckendorff describes it as a confutation filled with solid learning and sound divinity, making it impossible to reply without resorting to obvious nitpicking or outright impiety. He claims that even if Luther had never published anything else in his life, this single work would be enough to compare him to the greatest divines in the church's history.

At the time of writing, Luther only had the Bible as a reference. Yet, he managed to interpret key passages from the Prophets and the Apostles, debunking the misleading interpretations of sophistical commentators with such skill and erudition that the true meaning of the inspired writers becomes clear to any devout and attentive reader. He dedicated the work to Justus Jonas, who had recently been appointed president of the College of Wittemberg, offering it as a sort of congratulatory gift.

In the dedication, Luther expresses his hope that Jonas, who is now responsible for teaching the harmful decrees of Antichrist, will be guided by the Spirit of God to do his duty – that is, to unteach everything related to Popery. He encourages Jonas to remain strong and courageous, not fearing Baal-peor, but believing in the Lord Jesus, who is blessed forevermore. Amen.

In this treatise, Luther defends himself against accusations of insincerity for having submitted to the Pope and the accepted opinions for so long. He expresses his regret for doing so, his gratitude to the Lord Jesus Christ for the insight he gained into the Scriptures – which he considers far superior to the scholastic divinity of the time – and his firm belief that the Pope is the Antichrist prophesied throughout the sacred writings.

He says he doesn't care if people accuse him of not being moderate. As for sedition, it's the same thing the Jews accused Christ of. The main issue at hand, he argues, is "THE NATURE OF SIN."

"If the quotes I've used from St. Paul don't actually mean SIN in the way we understand it, then my whole argument falls apart. But if that's not the case, then Latomus' objections don't hold up. He criticizes me for saying that no human action can withstand God's judgment. I say he should be scared to argue the opposite. Let's say someone could actually claim they've done a good deed that fully follows God's command. That person might tell God something like this: 'Look, Lord, with your help, I did this good thing. There's no sin in it, no flaws, and it doesn't need your forgiveness. So, in this case, I'm not asking for it. I want you to judge this action fairly and without bias. I'm confident that, since you're just and true, you can't condemn it. So, I take pride in it before you. Jesus' prayer teaches me to ask for forgiveness for my wrongs. But for this action, I don't need mercy to forgive sin; I need justice to reward my good deed.'"

This kind of arrogant, un-Christian thinking comes from the pride of the scholastic system! The idea that human actions can be sinlessly perfect isn't supported by the Bible. It's based on a few quotes from the Church Fathers, who don't even agree with each other. And even if they did agree, their authority is still just human.

We are instructed to test all things and hold onto what is good (1 Thessalonians 5:21). This means that all doctrines should be examined through the lens of the sacred Scriptures. There are no exceptions, not even for Augustine, Jerome, Origen, or an antichristian Pope. Augustine, however, supports my perspective on this issue.

I have my reasons for referring to the issue you describe as "sin" rather than using the milder terms "defect" and "imperfection." I would like to ask those who agree with Latomus if they are not creating an unrealistic ideal, similar to the Stoics' concept of a wise man or Quintilian's idea of a perfect orator. In other words, are they not describing a fictional character that has never existed and never will? I challenge them to find someone who would claim their own work is without sin.

Your way of speaking leads to dangerous misunderstandings about the nature of sin. You give credit to human abilities when it should be attributed to divine grace alone. This approach makes people overconfident in their vices and undervalues the significance of Christ's mystery. As a result, gratitude and love for God are diminished.

There is an immense outpouring of grace involved in converting sinners, but you seem to overlook this. By considering human nature innocent and misinterpreting or distorting the Scriptures, their meaning is almost lost in the Christian world.

I don't feel the need to apologize for sharing these enlightening excerpts. "The subject of this debate is of utmost importance (if anything can be called important), as it involves God's glory, the necessity of Jesus Christ's grace, the practice of genuine humility, and the comfort of troubled consciences."

Luther ends his book by noting that he has been accused of treating Thomas Aquinas, Alexander, and others unfairly and ungratefully. He defends himself by saying that those authors had caused much harm to his own mind, and he advises young theology students to avoid scholastic theology and philosophy, as it could ruin their souls. He expresses significant doubts about whether Thomas Aquinas was even a good man, but he has a better opinion of Bonaventura. Luther claims that Aquinas held many heretical opinions and is the main reason for the prevalence of Aristotle's doctrines, which destroy sound doctrine. He asks, "What is it to me, if the Bishop of Rome has canonized him in his bulls?"

As valuable as this work is, it cannot compare to the truly Herculean and apostolic labor that was interrupted by performing it. Luther says, "You can hardly believe how reluctantly I allowed my attention to be diverted from the quiet study of the Scriptures in this Patmos, by reading the sophistical quibbles of Latomus." And again: "I really begrudge the time spent in reading and answering this worthless publication, particularly as I was EMPLOYED IN TRANSLATING the Epistles and Gospels into our own language."

We, who can easily read a chapter in the Bible whenever we want, tend to forget the effort it took to provide us with that Bible in our native language and the risks we faced to have the freedom to read it with our own eyes and handle it with our own hands. Especially in times when, through God's clear guidance, versions of the Scriptures are circulating throughout the entire known world in more than 140 languages and dialects, and it is rare to find someone who even has the desire, let alone the ability, to limit the circulation of the sacred volume. We are ill-prepared by our own feelings and experiences to appreciate the gift of a Bible that is now, for the first time, available in the vernacular tongue.

But Luther had to fight not only for the right to read but also to work so that they might have something to exercise that right on. Luther easily foresaw the significant consequences that would come from a fair translation of the Bible in the German language. Nothing would shake the foundations of ecclesiastical despotism more effectively; nothing was more likely to spread the knowledge of pure Christian doctrine. As a result, he was eager to speed up the work, while his opponents dreaded its execution more than any heresy that the church's greatest enemy could commit.

So, he had started and was preparing himself for the completion of his work by studying the original languages more closely when he was interrupted by Latomus. This was a project that required the silence and seclusion of his Patmos for its initiation and beginning, but it couldn't be satisfactorily completed without more resources than he had there.

"I find," he says, "that I have undertaken a work that is beyond my strength. I won't touch the Old Testament until I can have the assistance of yourself and my other friends at Wittemberg. If it were possible for me to be with you and remain hidden in a cozy room, I would come. And there, with your help, I would translate the whole thing from the beginning so that eventually there might be a version of the Bible suitable for Christians to read. This would be a great work of immense importance to the public and worthy of all our efforts." This challenging task was finally accomplished: the New Testament, as I have already mentioned, was published in 1522; the Old Testament was completed in parts until it was finished in 1530.

"In this work, he was greatly assisted by the labor and advice of several of his friends, particularly Jonas and Melancthon. The entire performance itself was a testament to the incredible work ethic that characterized this reformer."

The impact of this work was quickly felt in Germany. A huge number of people could now read the precious word of God in their own language, and they could see for themselves the solid foundations of the Lutheran doctrine. The Lord provided them with a powerful tool, like Ithuriel's spear, to be used by the masses. It's no surprise that the Catholics were upset and burned the books. After all, what has kept the Papacy in power if not ignorance of THE BOOK? And what will ultimately destroy it, according to Luther's insightful and enlightened prediction, is the knowledge of the Book.

"The kingdom of Antichrist, as predicted by the Prophet Daniel, must be broken WITHOUT HAND; meaning that the Scriptures will eventually be understood by everyone, and people will speak out and preach against the tyranny of the Papacy using the word of God. This will lead to the MAN OF SIN being abandoned by his followers and dying on his own. This is the true Christian way of destroying him. To achieve this goal, we must put in all our efforts, face every danger, and endure every loss and inconvenience."

It's surprising that in our time, there are individuals - or should I say, many people - who belong to the Catholic Church and are passionate about spreading the Scriptures in their country's spoken language. One of these individuals, standing tall above the rest, has been responsible for distributing over 300,000 copies of his own German translation, as well as many thousands of Luther's version.

To judge the quality of Luther's translation, one would need not only a deep understanding of Hebrew and Greek but also of the German language. It was certainly elegant and clear, and it was far better than any other scriptural publication that had been known to the people before.

It's likely that this work had its flaws, but it's safe to assume that it was mostly accurate and reliable, given the strong understanding, biblical knowledge, and diverse expertise of the author and his collaborators. It was a highly appreciated gift for those who were finding their way out of ignorance. When other reformers in different countries followed this example, the accessibility of real scriptural knowledge increased significantly, especially considering the impact of the printing press.

Emser, a plagiarist who supported the Pope, first tried to discredit Luther and then attempted to outdo and replace him. However, his "correct" translation was essentially just a copy of Luther's work (since he was known to be ignorant of the German language), with a few changes that favored Roman Catholic beliefs. As a result, people read Luther's work under Emser's name, and Luther was grateful, saying with sincerity, "Regardless of whether it's done with false motives or true ones, Christ is being preached, and I'm happy about that, and I will continue to be happy." (Philippians 1:18)

Luther didn't enjoy being confined to solitude for ten months, often showing signs of impatience. He thrived on taking action and found it difficult to remain idle. He expressed his feelings by saying, "For the glory of God's word and to strengthen both myself and others, I'd rather be burned alive than live here half-dead and useless. If I die, it's God's will, and the Gospel won't suffer at all. I hope you'll take my place, just like Elisha succeeded Elijah!"

I wish he hadn't written that last sentence to his friend Melancthon. Nevertheless, after ten months, the situation in his beloved Wittenberg, combined with his own preferences, made it clear that it was in the best interest of the church - and therefore, God's will - for Luther to risk his life and safety by leaving his hiding place and returning to his public role in the then-budding center of Protestantism.

Melancthon lacked energy and strength, while the elector lacked courage and determination. Carolstadt had become chaotic, and the people were like lost sheep without a shepherd. The enemy was taunting them, saying, "There, There." Realizing that brief, secret visits were no longer enough, Luther decided to take a risk. He knew the elector well enough to act first and apologize later. So, he left Wartburg and wrote his noble letter to the elector while on his way from Borna.

In that letter, he honestly explained his motives and expectations, freeing Frederic from any responsibility for his safety and expressing his complete trust in divine protection. With no real or even pretended safeguard other than God, he continued his journey.

Luther wrote, "I want you to know that as I return to Wittenberg, I believe I am under a far more powerful protection than anything the elector of Saxony can provide. To be clear, I don't want your protection. I never thought to ask for your defense. In fact, I believe that you should receive support and protection from Luther's prayers and the good cause he is fighting for. This is a cause that doesn't need the help of the sword. God will take care of it without human assistance. I declare that if I knew you intended to defend me by force, I wouldn't return to Wittenberg. This is a situation where only God should guide, and people should wait patiently for the outcome. The person who trusts God the most will bravely defend both themselves and others. Your faith in God is weak, so I cannot rely on you for my defense and hope of deliverance."

If I had to choose the most remarkable moment of Luther's life, I would say it was at Borna.

All the generosity, bravery, and determination that he showed later were simply the actions of the spirit he had clearly received at that time. This was the result and effect of the Lord's most complete and vivid revelation of Himself to Luther's soul. This allowed Luther to fully trust in God. He made this decision at Wartburg and announced it at Borna. His return to Wittenberg brought healing, confidence, and peace to his scattered, anxious, and doubtful followers.

Luther's valuable life was preserved for the church for 24 years after his return to Wittenberg. During these years, he first had to build, which he found more challenging than tearing down. He then had to protect, expand, maintain, and perpetuate his new establishment. He had to guard against the greed of the secular authorities without making church officials wealthy. He needed to find knowledgeable teachers for the people without supporting lazy individuals. He had to turn the uneducated into educators and eliminate extravagance without compromising decency. Often, he was unsure of what to advise, and frequently he had to settle for what he considered second-best. The printing press was his primary tool for both fighting and educating. His publications covered a wide range of topics, and he had deep thoughts and knowledge, as well as substance and importance, for all of them.

We must remember that throughout this time, he was like a ship sailing through a storm. He was not only excommunicated (he had excommunicated others in return), but also an outlaw under the ban of the empire. Anyone who dared could have captured and handed him over to the authorities. Is this not the man whom the Lord holds with His right hand, protects as the apple of His eye, and provides for even in the midst of his enemies? (Psalms 17:8; 23:5)

Luther's professed enemies were not his worst. The elector's cautiousness, the fear of his allies, the people's madness, the desire for change, envy, debate, and his own stubbornness were more harmful to him than his opponents like Eckius and Aleander, the Conclave, and the

Emperor. Luther's character can be understood from this brief look at his history. He was generous, broad-minded, self-disciplined, studious, selfless, fearless, and wise. "He feared God; he feared none else."

Early in life, Luther experienced a deep understanding of his own sins, accountability, helplessness, and powerlessness. Melanchthon tells a story about Luther being so overwhelmed by thoughts of divine vengeance that he was almost frightened to death. On one occasion, Luther was so terrified during a theological debate that he went to a neighbor's room, lay on the bed, and prayed aloud, repeating the words: "He has enclosed all under sin, that he might have mercy on all." (Galatians 3:22)

This sensitive conscience made Luther receptive to the divine word. We have seen how God placed it in his path. For a long time, it only brought terror to him. "THEREIN is the righteousness of God revealed," (Romans 1:17) led him to blasphemy. Eventually, God had mercy on him, opened his eyes, and showed him that the righteousness of God mentioned there is not His own essential righteousness, which makes Him hate and punish sin, but a substance He has provided to cover sinners.

This understanding, which had been a stumbling block for Luther, became his entrance into paradise. Over time, God revealed the mystery of this righteousness more clearly to him. He showed Luther that Jesus Christ was this righteousness in person, and that to enter into Him and put Him on by faith was to be righteous before God. Christ's merit was complete for justification; nothing needed to be added or could be added to it by a sinner, and it was received by faith alone.

So far, the Lord had given him clarity of vision, though not complete, and He provided it quickly. After this, He allowed Luther to make mistakes, even until the end of his days. Now, since "it pleased God, who had set him apart from his mother's womb and called him by his grace, to reveal his Son in him, he immediately did not consult with human beings;" Gal 1.15-16 "he couldn't help but speak about the things he had heard and seen;" 1 John 1.3 "he was willing not only to be arrested but also to die in Jerusalem for the name of the Lord Jesus" Acts 21:13-33.

God granted three unique gifts to this chosen witness, which define his testimony: an extensive understanding of the Scripture, an exceptional ability for complex and intricate reasoning, and a remarkable skill in communicating with everyday people.

To demonstrate the first point, you can refer to all of his works, including his translation of the Bible, if that's not convincing enough. For the second point, consider his debates with Eckius, Latomus, and Erasmus, particularly the treatise that follows. And for the last point, look at his numerous writings and sermons, especially his address to the common people during the outbreak of the peasant war. His commentary on the Galatians provides examples of all three points.

This was the man whom the Lord chose and used as the most prominent, active, and effective partner in achieving the Reformation! However, it's strange that people only focus on one aspect of God and only the surface of that aspect when His entire being is revealed. The Reformation was God's act - an act only surpassed by those of Calvary and the Red Sea in displaying His power and might. He accomplished it by working through both Luther and his enemies, such as Charles, the Elector, Leo, Cajetan, Campeggio, Prierias, Hogostratus, and the whole group of aggressive opponents who wanted to silence and burn those who criticized Babylon, as well as through Jonas, Pomeranus, and Melancthon.

In fact, if we want to truly understand this event as a display of God's power, we must examine not only the good and evil workers, both visible and invisible, but also the steps He took to prepare for His mission and the various elements He used to carry it out. We need to consider the capture of Constantinople by the infidels, which led to the spread of Eastern scholars throughout Christendom; the barbarians developing an interest in literature, and the invention of the printing press making it easier to acquire knowledge; and the various agents and conflicting interests that fueled their activity.

We must see rival princes and previously submissive vassals now starting to question their rulers. We must see a dominating Charles, a chivalrous Francis, a lustful and greedy Henry, a bombarding Solyman, a reckless Leo, a calculating Adrian, a hesitant Clement — German freedom, Italian compliance, Castilian independence, Flemish lightheartedness, French loyalty, Genoa's fleet, and Switzerland's mercenaries, Luther's determination, Frederic's aloofness, Melancthon's disheartenment, and Carolstadt's impulsiveness — all created, stirred, and mixed by God as a sort of moral chaos. Out of this, in His perfect timing, He commands knowledge, liberty, and peace to emerge for His captives in Babylon. Luther describes himself, as we have seen, as a rough debater: debate was his element; from his first appearance in public, his life was spent in it. I hope my reader has learned not to despise or even fear debate. It has been, from the beginning, the Lord's chosen weapon for revealing His truth, just as evil has been its own great developer. What are Paul's and John's Epistles if not argumentative writings? What was the Lord's entire life and ministry if not a debate with the Jews? Luther knew its uses well, and he had experienced its peaceful results: it provokes inquiry, silences the critics, and strengthens the believers. However, there were three debates out of his many that he would have preferred to avoid, as they were against former friends. In the first, he was mostly right, but not without question; in the second, he was entirely wrong, without question; in the third, he was completely right, without question — without question, I mean, not regarding any public trial that has been held and judgment given, but before the court of sound reason.

Andreas Bodenstenius Carolstadt, who was unheard, unconvicted, and banished by Martin Luther. What! Had Luther become a persecutor? Did he, who should have been a martyr himself, make martyrs of others? Not quite, but he was accused of doing so, and there were appearances against him! Honest Carolstadt - there is some debate about whether he truly deserves this name - was a turbulent man. Although he was a learned man and still a professor at Wittemberg, he let it be known that he despised learning. He had no real enthusiasm for Luther's "broken WITHOUT HANDS." Carolstadt placed himself at the head of a few inexperienced and hot-headed recruits and ranted about the papal abuses that still remained among them. He proceeded to remove these abuses WITH HANDS, by breaking images and throwing down altars. This disorderly spirit was what prompted Luther's return.

Luther said that the account of what had happened at Wittemberg had almost driven him to despair. Everything he had suffered so far was comparatively just a joke and child's play. He could not lament enough or express his disapproval of those tumultuous proceedings. The Gospel was in great danger of being disgraced because of this. Carolstadt fled before him. He became a divisive preacher at Orlamund, was banished by the elector, and eventually restored through Luther's intercession. However, their reconciliation lacked warmth. In the end, Carolstadt retired to Switzerland, where he served as a pastor in a community that better aligned with his own beliefs. He died in 1531.

Carolstadt was one of Luther's earliest defenders, but he later became his rival and enemy. They engaged in a sort of fratricidal war for several years after Luther's return from Wartburg, through conferences, sermons, and treatises. Among these treatises, Luther's "Address to the Celestial Prophets and Carolstadt" is the most significant. It is undeniable that Luther was not the author of Carolstadt's banishment, even though he fully approved of it. In fact, upon Carolstadt's submission, Luther made great efforts to have him restored. He could not succeed with Frederic, but he did succeed with John.

Still, I have found him quite unpleasant, random, and unfairly sarcastic in his opposition to Carolstadt. I also thought he was unjustifiably dismissive and exclusive in his interactions with the Munzerites, and maybe too confident in denying any influence of his teachings on the peasant war. That's why I said "not without question." But upon closer examination, I see clear evidence that Carolstadt was indeed what Luther accused him of being - unpredictable, extreme, dishonest, and inconsistent in his beliefs. He was also a preacher and practitioner of rebellion, and he had joined forces with Munzer and his followers, earning a place among the so-called Celestial Prophets. I find clear evidence that Stubner, Stork, Cellery, Munzer, and the others were a group of deceitful hypocrites, full of anger and false claims of divine favor, which they never explained or defended.

Luther's method for identifying false prophecies and false claims is also worth noting, as it is effective and practical. However, it might be based too much on his own personal experiences (I'm referring to his test of conversion). Furthermore, I find Luther's teachings so clear in emphasizing the importance of civil obedience that it was impossible for the peasants, or those who used them as a cover, to claim that Luther had encouraged their rebellion. It was also crucial for accurate doctrine that he disavow and express his disgust for their mistakes. So, aside from the part of the debate concerning his views on the sacrament, Luther was in the right. And on that topic, even though Carolstadt reached the correct conclusion, his arguments were so weak, inconsistent, and dishonest that he undermined his own success.

In the second of these controversies, which was initially started by Carolstadt but eventually taken up by more capable individuals, Luther was unfortunately mistaken. He was wrong in both his beliefs and the way he defended them. This serves as a poignant reminder of the limitations of human understanding, as we can only see as far as God allows us to. It is not always beneficial or in line with God's glory for us to fully comprehend everything as it truly is. Instead, we should be mindful of our origins and the limitations of our knowledge, as stated in Isaiah 51:1.

Is there any exception to this observation among human teachers and writers? Can we name even one whose work does not bear this mark, reminding us that we are reading a human's creation and not God's?

Luther believed that the actual substance of the Lord's body and blood was present in the bread and wine of the Eucharist, alongside the original substance of the bread and wine. This belief contains all the absurdity of the Catholic doctrine of transubstantiation, as well as an additional inconsistency: that the same substance can simultaneously be of two different types.

Now, even though the word of God asks us to accept many things as true that go beyond our senses and logical reasoning, it never asks us to believe in something that contradicts them. Can you find a specific passage, chapter, or verse in the Bible that asks us to believe in an obvious contradiction? This point applies not only to the more complex aspects of faith, like the coexistence of three equal persons in one divine essence, Jesus Christ being both God and man, and the presence of divine and demonic forces within the human soul, but also to the simpler truths about God's moral attributes, which have been distorted and confused by neglecting this principle.

For example, Martin Luther struggled to reconcile his understanding of God's moral attributes with his representation of truth and went so far as to claim that we don't know what these attributes are in God. However, if qualities like justice, faithfulness, purity, grace, mercy, and truth aren't fundamentally the same in God as they are in his moral creatures, then we can't know, believe, or feel anything accurate about him. How these attributes coexist with each other and with God's actions is a separate issue, but it's a clumsy, false, and harmful approach to solving difficulties by denying basic principles. If our very understanding of moral qualities is challenged and taken away, then we cease to be moral beings.

The belief in consubstantiation, then, contradicts both our senses and reason. Four of our senses argue against it, while only one can claim to support it. If the disciples heard Jesus affirm it and if we hear it from their writings, then our sight, touch, taste, and smell all tell us that it's just bread and nothing more that we're biting into.

A body can only be in one place at the same time. Therefore, the Lord's body, which is at the right hand of God, cannot be in any place where the sacrament is administered, let alone in multiple places at the same time. This is just like how the bread Jesus held in his hand when he instituted the sacrament couldn't be in the same place as his hand. Luther talked a lot about the ubiquity of the Lord's body, but what does that really mean? Aren't we explicitly taught that the Lord's body is in one place for a while?

"So then, after the Lord had spoken to them, he was received up into heaven, and sat on the right hand of God;" Mark 16:19

"Who has gone into heaven, and is on the right hand of God." 1 Peter 3:22

"Who is even at the right hand of God." Romans 8:34

"Sit on my right hand, until I make your enemies your footstool." Matthew 22:44

"Whom the heavens must receive until the times of restitution of all things." Acts 3:21

Moreover, what ends all debate is that, in reality, Jesus now has no such body and blood to give.

"There is a natural body, and there is a spiritual body." 1 Corinthians 15:44

"Flesh and blood cannot inherit the kingdom of God." 1 Corinthians 15:50

Jesus did indeed turn his spiritual body into a natural one by miracle for a few moments at various times after his resurrection, so that he could give credibility to his witnesses, "even to those who ate and drank with him after he rose from the dead." Acts 10:41. But ever since then, his ongoing, ordinary existence has been in a body that no teeth could chew and no lips could enclose.

Luther's main focus was on the words, "This is my body." He took his sound and just principle of interpreting Scripture literally, not metaphorically, where possible, to a false and even ridiculous extreme in this case. This was in opposition to his own admitted exception: "unless an evident context and some absurdity which offends against one of the articles of our faith in the plain meaning, constrain us to such interpretation." (See Part IV, Section III, p. 239 of the following work.)

Is this the only example of such a form of speech? Circumcision, which is usually referred to as the symbol of the Abrahamic covenant, is called the covenant in some places; the two stone tablets are called the covenant; the lamb is called the Passover; the rock struck in Horeb is called Christ (1 Cor 10:4). Moreover, if the bread is transformed into his body, then the cup should also be transformed into a testament; "this cup is the new testament" (Luke 22:20). And when we have eaten this flesh and drunk this blood (if such an act were possible)

What has carnal chewing and swallowing done for us? It's as if flesh could nourish the spirit, or as if Christ's flesh were spirit (though Luther believed that it was so). Luther's insistence on this belief weakened his overall credibility as a logical thinker and undermined the authority of his arguments. In this debate, he appeared like an orator who could passionately argue about anything, even something as trivial as a broomstick. He used his great mental powers to make forceful appeals and crafty illustrations to support this unfounded belief.

It's not that Luther knew or thought he was defending a falsehood. His only excuse is that he was honest – indeed, honest until his dying hour. Although he may have regretted the intensity of his spirit and language against his opponents, he never conceded on his doctrine. He declared it during a severe illness in 1526 and continued to preach and write about it until the end.

Luther regretted the spirit he had shown in this debate, and rightfully so. He defended his belief aggressively, calling names and demonizing his adversaries. At the very least, his opponents were just as pure, learned, and hardworking as he was, if not as commanding in their presence, as exalted in their sufferings, or as successful in their endeavors. Tearing apart the unity that should have existed between Switzerland and Germany was more his doing than theirs.

This bitter controversy, regrettable for many reasons but not without its direct and indirect benefits, began in 1524 and continued up to and beyond Luther's death. The churches that bear his name still hold on to his dogma.

In the last of these debates, I declare that he is completely right. By right, I mean in terms of his conclusion and his opponent - although he presents some arguments that could have been left out, and he doesn't always demonstrate a complete understanding and proper use of his tools.

Erasmus, who was about sixteen years older than Luther, had provided some assistance to the reformers. This was mainly by making it easier to learn ancient languages through his successful studies in literature, but also by using his unique talent for ridicule to mock some of the more blatant wrongs of the Catholic Church. It's not that he was genuinely concerned about these issues; he was a man born to make people laugh - he loved a good joke - and monks and friars provided him with material he couldn't resist. So, like Lucian and Porphyry, without really intending to, he paved the way for a better faith by mocking much of the old one. He was offended by the idea of being considered a skeptic, and many people today think it's unfair to label him as such. But isn't anyone who takes their soul lightly a skeptic? And aren't the majority of professing Christians just a group of such people who, if put to the test, would act out what Luther said sarcastically: "God has not given everybody the spirit of martyrdom."

Erasmus had somewhat aligned himself with the reformers by speaking highly of them, especially Luther, and agreeing with many of their beliefs. In 1520, when the papal bull was being prepared and eventually released, he had written and spoken in strong support of Luther:

- "God sent him to reform humanity."

- "Luther's ideas are true, but I wish he was more gentle in his approach."

- "Luther's cause is controversial because he attacks both the monks' livelihoods and the Pope's authority."

- "Luther has great natural talents; he's skilled at explaining complex literary points and reigniting the true essence of evangelical doctrine, which has been nearly snuffed out by trivial academic debates. Many highly respected, knowledgeable, and religious people appreciate Luther's books. The more someone is known for their moral integrity and gospel purity, the fewer issues they have with Luther's ideas. Even those who disagree with his teachings praise his character. It's a shame that such a gifted person is driven to desperation by the monks' furious protests."

When urged by the Pope's representatives to write against Luther, he replied, "Luther is too great for me to confront. I don't always understand him. But to be honest, he's such an exceptional man that I learn more from a single page of his books than from all of Thomas Aquinas' writings."

However, as the reformation movement progressed, Erasmus didn't move forward with it but instead retreated. His primary motivation was vanity and a love for praise from others, particularly from influential figures like princes, high-ranking church officials, and esteemed individuals. He wanted to be highly regarded, especially for his extreme moderation, as befitting a man of letters. He aspired to be an Atticus of his time. Wholeheartedly joining the reformers wasn't the way to achieve this goal. The movement's leaders looked down on them, and, even more frustratingly, they wouldn't make him a prominent figure within their ranks.

The quote from Horace goes, "Among all, the star of Julius shines, like the moon among the lesser fires." But he wasn't that moon; Luther was that moon. So, what could he do but sulk and clearly distance himself from them, letting the princes know they were mistaken if they thought he was one of them? In doing so, he could skillfully achieve two things at once: get back at them for disregarding him and make room for the sun and stars to shine on him. He admitted this in his response to Luther:

"Up until now, I haven't written a single word against you; otherwise, I could have gained a lot of praise from important people. But I saw that it would harm the Gospel. All I've tried to do is dispel the notion that you and I are in complete agreement and that all your teachings can be found in my books. Efforts have been made to plant this idea in the minds of the princes, and it's still difficult to convince them that it's not true."

Luther would have been happy if things had stopped there. Erasmus had done everything he was meant to do, but he shouldn't become their enemy. He was a skilled sharpshooter - some of his shots would hit, irritate, and discourage. However, there were lower-ranking members in Luther's group as well as in the Pope's, and they didn't pay enough attention to maintain Luther's position. They would go beyond it. They mocked the satirist, hinted quite openly about his true nature, and belittled him to his superiors. Luther tried to lessen the impact of their attacks, but it was too late: the enemy had already gotten to him.

Henry VII of England had begged, Pope Adrian VI had pleaded in two letters, Duke George had demanded, Tunstall had implored, and Pope Clement VII had convinced - and all the while, the pain from the wasps' stings still lingered.

Luther makes one last effort to calm Erasmus with great patience (but without compromising honesty), including some subtle hints about the true state of their cause. However, as Erasmus himself admitted, it was done politely.

'I won't criticize you for acting like a stranger to us in order to stay on good terms with the Papists, who are my enemies, or for being too harsh in your judgments of us.' ...'The entire world must gratefully acknowledge your incredible talents and contributions to the field of literature, which have allowed us to read the sacred Scriptures in their original languages. I never wanted you to abandon or neglect your own unique abilities and join our side.' ...

'I wish that Hutten's COMPLAINT had never been published.' ...

'I share your concern about the anger and hatred directed towards you by so many distinguished individuals. I can only imagine how much distress this must cause you, as even someone with your level of virtue, which is purely human, cannot be completely unaffected by such challenges.'...

'What can I do now? Tensions have escalated on both sides, and if I could play the role of a mediator, I would ask that they stop attacking you so fiercely and let your old age find peace in the Lord. In my opinion, they would act this way if they took into account your limitations or the enormity of the disputed issue, which has long been beyond your abilities. They should be even more considerate of you, given that our cause has progressed to the point where we don't even fear an all-out assault from Erasmus – we are far from being intimidated by any of his criticisms.'

'Our prayer is that the Lord may grant you a spirit worthy of your immense reputation; but if that doesn't happen, I beg you, if you can't support us, at least remain an observer of our intense struggle and don't side with our opponents. And please, don't write any more essays against us – if you agree to this, I promise not to publish anything against you.'

All efforts are in vain: to protect his wealth, to express his gratitude for what he has already received, and (unless he is treated cruelly) to earn more, his promises must now be fulfilled, and the Diatribe is released. He talks a lot about the significant risk of publishing it:

"No printer in Basel would dare to take on his or any work that contained a word against Luther."

He informs Henry VI (to whom he had sent part of the manuscript for approval) that "The die is cast; my little book on Free Will is published: a daring act, believe me, if the current state of Germany is taken into account. I expect to be attacked; but I will find comfort in the example of your majesty, who has not been spared from their insults."

His conscience is revealed when he says to Wolsey, "I have not chosen to dedicate this work to anyone, lest my critics should immediately claim that in this matter I had been paid to please the powerful. Otherwise, I would have dedicated it to you or the Pope."

His main motivation is evident when he talks about the significant impact he anticipated from his publication. He writes to Tunstall:

"The little book is out; and although written with the utmost restraint, it will, if I am not mistaken, cause tremendous upheaval. Pamphlets are already being thrown at me."

Such was the origin of the Diatribe; the creation of an irritable, discontented, and vain man who had meddled with both sides, satisfied neither, but was now determined which side he would support; yet he still aimed to maintain his favorite image of moderation. It is the work of a great scholar, but not a profound thinker; of "one who had skimmed the surface of his question, but had not delved into its core;" of someone who knew what is in the Bible but did not truly understand the Bible.

The text is quite imposing but not solid. It criticizes and praises, but doesn't disprove what it condemns or establish or define what it approves. Yet, this is a work that many people, even those who claim to be serious about their faith, will defend and maintain in opposition to Luther's views. In fact, many who consider themselves Calvinists or Calvinistic (I'm not a fan of labels – I prefer to focus on character and principles rather than sects or parties) are actually, in their hearts and minds, supporters of free will. They try to oppose the testimony of Jesus Christ, the Son of God, with their own flawed human reasoning, creating their own version of God by mixing bits of Scripture with their own imagination. Instead, they should be studying and learning from the true and living God revealed in the Bible. I agree with Luther's assessment that this work is tedious, confusing, deceptive, false, and harmful.

Luther was initially hesitant to respond to it, but eventually decided to do so for reasons he explains in the introduction of his letter. If he was going to address such a work by such a person on such a topic, he had to do it with all his might, just as he has done. So, if you want to see Luther, you can see him here.

Erasmus responded with two separate treatises under the name of Hyperaspistes, meaning 'defender with a shield.' The first, as he tells us, was written in just ten days so it could be ready for the upcoming Frankfurt fair (a major event for both literature and commerce at the time). It was a passionate and rushed piece, in which he didn't give himself time to think. The second was a much longer and more carefully crafted work, in which he was completely unrestrained and serious. If he could have, he would have shown no mercy to Luther and crushed him completely. But, as they say, "the gods had other plans."

This second book is quite long and tedious, but the tediousness that every reader will complain about isn't so much due to its length, but rather the confusion that runs throughout it. The writer manages to stay engaged despite the excessive wordiness, thanks to their ongoing hostility and resentment. However, the reader becomes tired and disoriented from being led down unclear paths one after another, never reaching a clear and satisfying conclusion. Paying close attention to a long series of confusing and jumbled ideas can wear out the intellect, just as trying to focus on hard-to-see objects can exhaust even the best eyesight.

Luther didn't respond to this double-edged criticism. He knew that Erasmus was fighting for victory, not truth, and he had better things to do than write books just to repeat unanswered arguments. There was nothing in the Hyperaspistes that hadn't already been addressed in his Bondage of the Will, just as there was nothing in the Diatribe that hadn't been brought up and refuted many times before. Therefore, the Letter or Treatise presented to the public should be seen as containing Luther's complete, final, and, as he believed, unrefuted and indisputable judgment on the state of the human will.

According to Erasmus, the human will is in a state of liberty; according to Luther, it's in a state of bondage. This is the subject and position that Erasmus brought up for debate, and Luther accepted the challenge.

The esteemed Locke, whose name I always mention with reverence and gratitude, has shown that the question is improperly stated. He says that the will is essentially just a power of the human mind or the person; freedom is also a power of the person.

So, asking if the will is free is like asking if one part of a person controls another part of them. It's similar to asking if their sleep is fast or if their virtue is square - freedom doesn't really apply to the will, just like speed doesn't apply to sleep or squareness to virtue. The right question to ask is not whether a person's will is free, but whether the person themselves is free. Locke says that a person is free only as far as they can choose to do something or not do it, based on their own thoughts and desires. Freedom is the ability to act or not act as we wish.

However, if people still want to ask if the will is free, the question should be changed to: is a person free to exercise their will? This can refer to either the act of using their will or the outcome of that act, which is the thing they choose. Regarding the act, Locke says that in most cases, people don't have freedom because once they think about doing something, they have to make a decision. As for the outcome, Locke says that people can't help but have freedom: they want what they want and are happy with what makes them happy. To question this is to assume that one will controls another will, and so on, forever. It's important to note that Luther also agrees with Locke on this point, saying that a forced will is a contradiction and should be called "non-will" instead of "will."

The scholars that Luther and Erasmus learned from made a distinction between the will's overall ability and the will when it's being used or put into action.

Their question was not, "is there free will?" but rather, "is there free choice?" In reality, this distinction doesn't make much of a difference. What were they actually debating? It's not about an inactive ability, but rather about how that ability functions when it's used. How else can we understand its nature and properties? Luther's insight is as sharp as Locke's in this matter.

Erasmus, when defining free will, describes it as the power of the human will that allows a person to choose things related to their salvation or to turn away from them. In essence, he's suggesting that there's something in between the will and its actions. However, Luther, when examining this definition, argues that there can't be any such middle ground. He uses language so similar to Locke's that it prompted the following comment from his historian:

"Luther, with as much sharpness as if he had studied Mr. Locke's famous chapter on power, replies, etc."

"But what is meant by this power 'applying itself and turning away itself,' unless it's the very act of willing and refusing, choosing and despising, approving and rejecting; in short, unless it's the will performing its very function? I don't see it. So, we must assume this power to be 'a something interposed between the will itself and its actions:' a power by which the will itself carries out the act of willing and refusing, and by which that very act of willing and refusing is brought forth. It's not possible to imagine or conceive anything else here." (See Part iii. Sect. ii. p. 132.)

However, this false distinction actually helps to resolve the whole issue. The incorrect question they've been asking is, "Is the will free?" The right question to ask would be, "Is the understanding free?" In other words, does a person's will have all the information it needs when making a decision on any given matter? A misguided understanding will lead to a wrong conclusion, even though that conclusion is made without any coercion.

Now, I believe this is the true situation: the NATURAL person, with their understanding clouded, is disconnected from God's life due to their ignorance and the blindness of their heart. Additionally, they are controlled by the devil, who works to maintain and increase their blindness. As a result, they make decisions based on incomplete and false information. The same observation applies to the SPIRITUAL person, to the extent that they are not fully spiritual and allow their flesh (through which the devil influences them) to impact their decision-making, all in the name of the greater principle of "God's glory in their real good."

It's actually the judgment, perception, or understanding, not the will, that is truly in bondage. This is because the faculty that presents objects to the decision-making faculty does so inaccurately, either by hiding what should be shown or by presenting a false or distorted appearance of what is and should be there. This idea helps explain the paradox that the will is both free and not free. In everyday language, the will is free because it cannot be forced; however, it is not free because it operates in the dark. Therefore, it might be more appropriate to call it "blind-will" rather than "bond-will," which is Luther's term.

This idea can also explain other mysteries and paradoxes, such as Paul's struggle in Romans 7, Pharaoh's hardening, our own daily experiences, and even the entire system of God's governance over a world of moral beings. Only the considerations that God presents to us can truly form the basis of our judgments and decisions regarding our actions. In other words, our free will is subject to His influence, and through our perceptions, His will becomes ours. However, I have used the language of the participants in this discussion, which is also the language of everyday life.

I talk about the will as being free or in bondage, and I use the term "Freewill" to describe a supposed power in humans, separating it into a distinct substance and often personifying it.

Let's agree then, that the question isn't worded correctly: the proper inquiry isn't whether a person's will is free, but whether the person is free; or rather, as we just saw, whether their perception is clear and complete. Still, the core of the debate remains unchanged, and its importance is still significant. Essentially, we're trying to determine the moral state of humans; and the considerations, even the expressions used in many parts of the discussion, show that we're not just debating an abstract question about the will, but investigating our human nature. What could be more important than this subject? What can be understood if this remains unknown? What kind of Christ would an ignorant believer in Freewill have? (See Part 1. Sect. 5, 6, 7, 8). The truth is, ignorance of the real state of humans is at the root of all religious ignorance. And it's clear that the Lord's dealings with his people involve bringing them to know, use, and enjoy Him through deep, detailed, self-emptying, and self-humbling self-knowledge. How can this happen if we don't recognize the depths of powerlessness and wrongdoing, as well as the blindness and hostility we've willingly fallen into?

This treatise's unique approach is to explore the current state of the human soul using only scripture and scriptural reasoning, without any abstract philosophical investigation beyond what's absolutely necessary for writing and reading about it intelligibly. Luther was not ignorant of metaphysics.

He had been extensively trained in Aristotle and the schoolmen. If he didn't use such weapons, it was because he looked down on them; I should rather say, it was because, according to his own testimony as mentioned earlier, he found them harmful. Erasmus sometimes forces him to engage in this kind of debate, where he proves that he could have skillfully used such weapons if he had considered them to be appropriate for the sanctuary. Someone who was a thoughtful observer and a skilled judge said of him, 'Even in the metaphysical complexities, which couldn't be entirely avoided in this deep inquiry, he greatly outperformed Erasmus.' But those who have truly submitted themselves to the authority of Scripture and have a deep understanding of the Father's testimony about Jesus will feel that, as this subject is the most important one that can engage the human soul, this method of investigating it can alone be expected to yield a satisfying conclusion. They will be glad, therefore, that someone like Erasmus—a man well acquainted with the text of Scripture (as Luther testifies of him, "who thoroughly examined all our works"—Part 3. Sect. 6. note e)—should have issued his challenge in the form of an appeal to the canonical Scriptures only; and that someone like Luther, who had delved quite deep into the mines of that volume, should have accepted and brought it to a resolution.

The order of the argumentation is clearly outlined in the Table of Contents that follows and is also mentioned at the beginning of each Part and Section. So, I'll just briefly mention that after a short Introduction, Luther follows the order of Erasmus' work (which, despite being somewhat scattered, provides a guide for navigating its complexity). He first examines Erasmus' Preface, then his Proem, then his testimonies, then his supposed refutation, and finally establishes his own position with direct proof. He concludes the entire work with an emotional appeal, and each Part also ends with a heartfelt touch. Many people think that Luther lacked tenderness, but the once-cloistered, and later married and fatherly monk, could indeed be gentle, compassionate, and childlike.

The format of the treatise is in the form of a letter to Erasmus, which is why I've chosen to divide it into Parts rather than Chapters. Dividing a letter into chapters seems a bit strange, even though we're used to it in our organization of the Scriptures. However, it's important to remember that this division has no authority and has led to some misunderstandings. Locke even suggests that those who want to understand Paul should disregard it. My only advice regarding these Parts is that readers shouldn't be discouraged by some of the less engaging debates in the first Part. While I don't find them uninteresting, the work becomes more engaging as it progresses. I hope readers will find this to be true and remember that we must first find a way to approach the walls before we can storm them.

As for Luther's writing style, I can't really compliment it. The sentences are long, the ideas are numerous, and the words are often crude and arranged in a discordant manner. However, there is always meaning in what he says, even if that meaning isn't always immediately apparent or clear.

He can be quite eloquent at times, and other times, he's more straightforward. His language reflects who he is as a person. He's more like Hercules with a club than Achilles with a sword, and he's more of a Menelaus than an Ulysses. He's always strong, sometimes playful, and occasionally subtle. He never leaves any room for his opponents to escape, often dragging them through their own arguments.

The strengths of this treatise include a strong stand for truth based solely on God's testimony, without mixing in human opinions (see Part 2, Sections 1-12). This foundation is cleared of any objections (Part 2, Sections 13-14). A significant part of God's truth is firmly established (see Part 3, Part 4, Part 5), and much of it is also indirectly stated or implied, proven, or left to clear and obvious inference. As a result, one can confidently say, "Give me Luther, and I will give you THE TRUTH."

However, Luther hasn't provided us with a clear answer, neither in this treatise nor anywhere else. The flaws in his theological system are evident in this, his best work, as well as in his other writings. I use the term 'theological system' because truth is a vast, unified whole, not a collection of disconnected and disjointed propositions. This whole consists of many parts that, while distinct, are so closely intertwined and connected that it's nearly impossible to truly understand any one part without understanding each and every part, as well as the entire whole.

Those who claim there is no system in the Bible should explain what they mean by "aletheia" (the truth). They should also explain why this term should be used to describe the counsel or plan that God is carrying out through Christ, why it should be a name for Christ, and why it should be a name for God.

If God is the ultimate truth, the true one; if Christ is His image; if the plan or system of divine actions within Him is the image of that image; if the Gospel or teaching of God's kingdom is the message that declares that plan; then it's easy to understand why one term can be applied to all these different subjects. They are all, in various ways, the truth. It's not a valid argument to say, 'this respected person didn't see it there,' or, 'that respected person didn't see it there.' It may still be there, and if it's not, then God hasn't achieved His goal in revelation, which is not to reveal a statement, but to reveal Himself. Everyone should study the Bible in a way that helps them know God through it — which they can't do unless they understand what's written there, within themselves, and grasp it as a whole. At the same time, they should be cautious: they should form their understanding not by ignoring or suppressing any part, but by giving a fair, well-thought-out, and verified meaning to each and every part of the testimony.

The shortcomings of this treatise, then, are the shortcomings of Luther's theological system. He wasn't able to see that all of God's interactions with creatures can be traced back to one grand plan, created, ordained, and carried out to achieve one grand purpose; that this grand purpose is the manifestation of God; that this plan is, in all its aspects (not just in the part related to human redemption, but every bit of every part), based on, guided by, and completed in and through Christ — the eternally predestined and, in time, truly risen God-Man (see Part 2, Section 8, note R; Part 3, Section 32, note S). Even less was he able to discern the structure and components of that plan through which God is accomplishing this goal: that Adam — meaning not just the individual Adam, but everything created in him, including the entire human race — is the main and central subject of God's self-revealing actions (see Part 3, Section 28, notes T, V, X; Section 37, note L, etc.).

Although he had some understanding of the mystery of Christ's identity (see Part 1, Section 3; also Section 16, note n) - that He was truly God and man, an equal member of the Trinity, made human through the Virgin's impregnation by the Holy Spirit - he didn't fully grasp the mystery that Christ's identity is formed by uniting a human person, the spiritualized man Jesus, with His divine identity. He has been acting in this combined identity, inspired not by His own divine nature, but by the Holy Spirit, from the very beginning. He first existed as the glorified God-man in a hidden, predestined way, until the time of His ascension. Since then, He has openly and continuously done the Father's will, not His own, through the inspiration of the Holy Spirit, not His own divine nature. In this way, He demonstrates the Trinity in every action He performs, which is, in fact, every action of God.

Furthermore, His human identity was incredibly unique, being both a son of Adam and a son of God at the same time. The Holy Spirit's impregnation gave Him a pure soul, while the daughter of Adam gave Him a sinful body. In this way, He became the sinless sinner. He, who knew no sin, was made sin for us (2 Corinthians 5:21) and was tempted in every way as we are, yet without sin (Hebrews 4:15). The same Holy Spirit that created Him sinless also kept Him without sin amidst all the temptations of the world, the flesh, and the devil, until He died to sin once (Romans 6:10) and His mortality was swallowed up by life (2 Corinthians 5:4).

In this deep mystery of Christ's identity, the key aspect is the 'union yet distinctness' - both in terms of his divine and human nature, and in terms of his oneness with us. Luther wasn't able to fully grasp this concept. (See previous references in Part 2, Section 8, note R; Part 3, Section 22, note 3; also Part 5, Section 22, note L; Section 28, note O.) Additionally, although Luther understood that humans are born guilty (which he attributes to being born from Adam, see Part 5, Section 20), and that our nature is entirely tainted from birth, making us both vile and powerless (a fact he assumes and discusses throughout his treatise, but see especially Part 4, Section 10), he didn't fully comprehend the mystery of the creation and fall of every individual in the human race, both male and female, in connection with Adam. (See Part 4, Section 10, note Z; Part 5, Section 20, note P.)

Furthermore, while Luther recognized that there are chosen and rejected people, with God predestining some for eternal life and others for eternal death, he didn't have a deep understanding of the covenant relationship with Christ, the appropriateness of His work, and consequently, the chosen people. This understanding would make God just in differentiating between them, even though the original and eternal separation goes beyond justice, reaching the level of sovereignty that is only limited by omnipotence.

So, not only was he left without any understanding of God's plan and purpose due to his lack of knowledge, but he also couldn't grasp the concept that reconciles the spiritual mind to the severity of God's decisions. How else would God's ultimate goal be achieved? He even had to give up on the idea of God's justice (which is truly and clearly flawless in this process) and instead resort to the harmful lie that we know nothing about God's justice and must remain ignorant until "THE DAY" reveals it. If justice, truth, and all other moral virtues are not essentially the same in God as they are in us and according to our spiritual understanding of Him, then everything is in chaos: we know nothing about God, and His revelation is pointless.

Furthermore, while he was able to grasp some aspects of the freedom and completeness of a sinner's justification through Christ, it was impossible for him to fully and accurately understand it due to the ignorance already mentioned. He didn't see the eternal justification that individuals received in Christ Jesus before the world began, with God promising to raise them up as accepted ones because of Christ's death. He also didn't clearly understand what made up their atonement in time or the state they were brought into as a result. They have been treated as if they had earned a state of gracious acceptance, in which they can produce, as God enables them, and actually do produce, fruit for God.

⌣ | ⌣

He didn't realize that even though their crown is a free crown, the Lord has arranged it in such a way that it's fair for God to distinguish between the righteous and the wicked. There's a mindset in the righteous that corresponds to how God reveals Himself in His new-creation kingdom, while the wicked only harbor hostility towards Him.

Although Luther had some understanding of the Holy Spirit's influence, his other areas of ignorance prevented him from truly grasping its nature. He didn't realize that the gift of the Holy Spirit is actually the gift of His personal presence and action, which is a unique, super-creation gift given through Christ. This gift is given according to God's will and timing, and is provided when it's best for His people and withheld when it's better for them not to have it.

This gift doesn't contribute to a sinner's justification in the strict sense, but it does enable those who are justified to demonstrate their righteousness. When I say it doesn't contribute, I mean that none of their actions performed through the Spirit contribute even the slightest bit to their acceptance. They are freely foreknown, predestined, called, justified (meaning they receive absolution from all sin without cost), and glorified, while it's the Holy Spirit who enables and even compels them to believe. This belief shows their obedience to God's command and marks them as those for whom Christ died according to the Father's will, which is also the will of the sacred and equal Trinity.

Luther's lack of understanding on this topic led him to claim that Adam had the Spirit, that the Spirit fulfilled the law for us, and that the Jewish church wasn't justified by the law because they didn't have the Spirit (see Part 4, Section 10, note Z; Part 5, Section 10, note Z) - as if the Spirit of grace was something we naturally or legally possessed! Additionally, while he recognized the Law as a condemning principle, he didn't grasp its true nature, form, and purpose - that it was an added, temporary, and symbolic element, whose glory was meant to fade away (see Part 3, Section 24, note I; Part 5, Sections 10-13). This lack of understanding led him to impose the Law back on God's people, instead of getting rid of it for good; he added burdens with one hand that he had barely removed with the other.

Luther also failed to grasp the distinct nature and purpose of Law-obedience and Gospel-obedience. He didn't realize that the obedience to the Law he essentially demanded, even if not explicitly, is not only an attempt to earn life instead of living out the life already given, but also a denial of who God is and how He reveals Himself to us while we claim to believe in and serve Him.

These are some of the main FLAWS in Luther's theology: 63, which he displays, as expected, in this detailed treatise. I believe I have fairly addressed both his strengths and weaknesses. My goal has been to provide the most accurate translation of his entire text, including every word and syllable. His strengths, which should be evident if I have succeeded in my efforts, are made even more noticeable by clarifying each point of his argument and labeling them clearly with numbers 1, 2, 3, etc.

I have tried to counteract his errors and shortcomings by presenting THE TRUTH in each case. My explanations are thorough, but I don't think they are overly long-winded. I have aimed for conciseness, and in some cases, I may have achieved the result of forced brevity, making the text unclear. However, I hope this is not often the case.

You might have already noticed that if I were to publish Luther's work, it must be accompanied by NOTES. I genuinely believe that without them, his work would be not only difficult to understand but also incomplete and misleading. So, I've stuck to two basic principles throughout: 'in the text, it's all about Luther and nothing else; but in the notes, I express my own thoughts, whether they agree with or contradict his.'

Now, you might wonder why I would even bother publishing Luther's work when I consider his ideas to be both incomplete and incorrect. Well, I have a few reasons. Despite its flaws and mistakes, I believe this is a truly valuable, impressive, and noteworthy piece of writing.

I'm publishing it because:

1. I think the subject matter is extremely important.

2. I don't know of any other valuable work on this crucial topic that uses the same kind of reasoning.
3. Luther's name carries weight with some people, and I hope it will attract readers.
4. When he's right, he's very right and very persuasive.
5. Even his mistakes and shortcomings can shed some light on the correct ideas and help pave the way for a better understanding of the truth.

The wise Paley once said that if he could make his students aware of the exact nature of a problem, he was halfway to solving it. I hope that by showing readers the kind of God, Christ, and salvation that Luther presents, they will seek a better understanding.

I've mentioned that Luther's name is like gold, and I hope it will bring in readers. But don't think that I'm relying on Luther's reputation to support the truth. Far from it. Just as he rejected the authority of others, I reject his authority and that of any other uninspired teacher.

The fair and legitimate use of human authority is to grab people's attention. When an important man of God speaks, it's worth listening to and considering. But if he were here now, he would say, "Weigh my words against the teachings of Scripture; only accept what I say if it aligns with God's oracles." We should respect the opinions of a godly, God-raised, and God-owned man, but remember that he is still a fallible human. This man carried his fallibility with him to the grave, and it remains not only in his writings but also in the minds of his blindly-devoted followers who agree with him wholeheartedly. "To the law and to the testimony." Good! But that appeal will not guarantee the knowledge of THE TRUTH. Not everyone who studies the Scriptures knows THE TRUTH. It is the Scripture, as we believe it to be revealed to us by the Holy Spirit, that guides our spirit. While we must show respect and obedience to the decisions of a lawfully established human tribunal—even submitting to its punishments, which could destroy our worldly possessions and our flesh—our spirit recognizes no constraints except those imposed by the Spirit.

I present this work, both in regard to Luther and my own part in it, for the reader's thoughtful, patient, and eager consideration. I ask you to compare what is written here with the Scriptures and to bring a prayer with you as you do so: "Lord, help me understand your word; keep me from hastily rejecting anything in this book, even if it contradicts my preconceived opinions; and enable me to welcome, digest, hold fast, and enjoy what is true in it!"

I've already mentioned that my goal was to create a faithful translation, and I believe the Lord has granted me my wish. It goes without saying that this has been a challenging task. Any scholar knows that translation work is incredibly delicate. In every language, there is a specific word that corresponds more accurately to the given one, but it can often take hours of contemplation to find that word. This has been a significant part of my struggle.

Luther's work, more than most, required this level of attention, as he uses many emphatic and unique words. Additionally, his meaning isn't always clear. He also wrote in a dead language, and although he tried his best and was even thought to have had help from the elegant pen of Melancthon, he was not a particularly skilled writer. Furthermore, he uses countless proverbs, some German and some classical.

As a very knowledgeable friend of mine, whom I consulted for help, kindly wrote to me, "The Germans, you know, are great proverbialists, and many of their allusions are now lost. I have searched a great variety of authors, on a similar inquiry (he was kind enough to do so now), but in vain." I, too, have done some research and asked many questions, but have learned nothing. For example, the Wolf and the Nightingale (p. 79), the beast that eats itself (p. 196), and the palm and the gourd (p. 373). My greatest confusion has come from his mixing of old and new, which sometimes led me to follow him like a will o' the wisp, thinking I had a lantern to guide me, only to find myself left in darkness.

I'm afraid my notes might be criticized by two types of readers, both of whom will consider many of them unnecessary. All I can say is that none of them have been included without careful thought and intention. I wanted to prove my accuracy to the learned and provide assistance to the unlearned so they could understand me. The learned must tolerate my tedious dullness, while the unlearned must put up with my Latin and Greek.

Regarding my theological views, I might come across as more assertive and confident than even Luther himself to some people. Let me clarify my position here. I don't claim to be infallible, and I only want my statements to be measured against the Scripture. However, I want to offer my readers the full advantage of the certainty and thoughtfulness with which I've developed, held, and shared my opinions. To do this, I'll avoid using hesitant phrases like "if I'm not mistaken," "I believe it will be found," or "I would venture to affirm." Topics like these require a decisive mindset from the teacher, and if they don't want to encourage doubt in others, their words must convey the unwavering confidence they feel. Moreover, there's a power and significance in truth that both inspires and demands boldness.

Before parting ways with my readers, I'd like them to recognize their debt to the late, esteemed Dean of Carlisle, Dr. Isaac Milner. It's his completion of his brother's valuable history that has provided me with the majority of my information about Luther. His work is a result of extensive research, where he examined numerous original documents and gathered insights from sources that previous historians had left untouched. In doing so, he has defended, illuminated, and celebrated the fearless leader of the Reformation.

AFTERWORD ON PLATO AND AUGUSTINE

I have made an effort to help those who may not be knowledgeable or have access to books by providing some information about the various individuals mentioned in this work. There are two main writers I want to focus on: one is Plato, and the other is Augustine. Their fame, as well as Luther's frequent references to them (particularly Augustine), makes it necessary for me to discuss them.

1. Plato, who was indeed a great thinker, did not seem to be well-liked by Luther. Luther was very aware of the harmful effects of Plato's writ-

ings, as they encouraged a sense of arrogant self-reliance and contributed to the corruption of the truth by presenting distorted versions of its splendor and attractiveness. In Part IV, Section 52, Luther dismisses Plato's "Chaos," and in Part II, Section 5, he criticizes Plato's "Ideas." Despite this, Plato had some incredible ideas about God - where he got them from is another question. He contemplated God's nature, will, power, and actions, as well as striving for a connection with God and making efforts to improve and uplift the morals of his fellow citizens. Like others who theorized about God without divine guidance, Plato believed that both matter and God were eternal, although he granted God authority over matter and credited Him with shaping the world and bringing it into existence.

Without a doubt, it's quite a peculiar mix he creates - the world having a soul, even a compound soul; humans with their two souls, and secondary causes surrounding a seed of immortality with a material body! But in his 'chaos,' as wild as it is, and the universal soul that was immersed in it, which brought order through its movement, we can see a trace of distorted truth. In his 'ideas,' or 'first forms of things,' we find something even closer to reality - the eternal God designing, establishing, and bringing forth everything that exists. And in his ideal world, where God reigns supreme compared to the visible system and its sun, we get a faint glimpse of the unseen glory and the peace found in the unending contemplation of the resting God.

I'm not trying to bring people back to Platonism, but rather to show them that even the pagan Plato had a deeper understanding and appreciation than many who have been exposed to the true light. I want to help them realize that revelation and tradition have spread much further than they might be aware of, so it shouldn't seem strange if even non-believers are dealt with based on a level of knowledge we might have mistakenly thought they didn't have access to.

The concept of a Trinity, more or less distant from the purity of the Christian faith, has been found to be a central principle in all the ancient schools of philosophy and in the religions of almost all nations. Traces of an early popular belief in it can even be seen in the appalling rituals of idolatrous worship. If reason wasn't enough for this significant discovery, what could be the source of information other than what the Platonists themselves suggest: "a theology delivered from the Gods," i.e., a revelation. This is the explanation that Platonists, who were not Christians, have given for the origin of their master's teachings.

But how could those who lived before Christianity and had no knowledge of the Mosaic teachings obtain their information? Even though some early Church Fathers may have believed otherwise, there is no evidence that Plato or Pythagoras knew about the Mosaic writings. Additionally, the concept of a Trinity can be traced back to an earlier time than Plato, Pythagoras, or even Moses. Their information could only come from traditions based on earlier revelations, from the scattered fragments of the ancient patriarchal belief system - the belief system that was universal before the first idolaters deviated from it. Despite the gross and enormous corruptions of idolatry, this belief system could never be completely erased.

"What Socrates said, what Plato wrote, and what the other pagan philosophers from various nations discussed, is nothing more than the twilight of revelation after the sun of it had set in the race of Noah." (See Horsley's Letters to Priestley, pp. 49, 50.)

I find it surprising that Luther would mock Plato so harshly, especially since his beloved Augustine acknowledged his debt to the philosopher.

"And first, as you showed me how you resist the proud and give grace to the humble, and how great your mercy is shown in the way of humility, you provided me with some of Plato's books translated into Latin through a person filled with philosophical pride. In these books, I read passages about the divine word similar to those in the first chapter of St. John's Gospel, where his eternal divinity was displayed, but not his incarnation, his atonement, his humiliation, and the glorification of his human nature. For you have hidden these things from the wise and prudent and revealed them to babes, so that people might come to you weary and burdened, and you might refresh them... Thus, I began to form better views of the divine nature, even from Plato's writings, just as your people of old took the Egyptians' gold because whatever good there is in anything, it all belongs to you."

At the same time, I managed to avoid the negative influences in those books and didn't pay attention to the Egyptian idols. His historian comments on this, saying, "There's something divinely spiritual about the way he was saved. It's quite remarkable that the Platonic books were the initial trigger, although I think the Latin translation he read had incorporated some scriptural elements, following the style of the Ammonian philosophers."

So, it appears that Plato could provide some guidance to Augustine, even though he himself was far from enlightened. However, we can see that there was truth, and discerning truth, mixed in with his falsehoods.

2. Augustine's mistakes were similar to Luther's, but they were amplified by his lack of understanding of the doctrine of justification. It's said that he had the basic components of this doctrine, but he never managed to put them together.

His story was truly remarkable. After a wild youth filled with excessive partying and indulging in the beliefs of the Manichees, he eventually found himself serving vanity, lust, pride, and atheism. However, he eventually submitted to the true God and embraced His Son. This unique experience prepared him to become a strong advocate for grace, especially against the rise of Pelagianism during his time.

Gradually, he began to use his own experiences to interpret Scripture. As his biographer notes, St. Paul's doctrine of predestination was not something he initially embraced for its own sake, but it eventually became an important part of his beliefs. He defended it passionately, though not in its entirety, against its opponents. In fact, how could he defend the concept of grace (referring to the gift of the Spirit) without it?

According to his biographer, Augustine's understanding of predestination was actually deepened by the controversy surrounding Pelagianism. This demonstrates that not fully knowing the foundation and structure of truth means not fully understanding any aspect of it. His biographer praises him for his moderation, which in this case is another term for his lack of knowledge. However, the truth is that not fully understanding predestination, which is the core "of the mystery of God, and of the Father, and of Christ," meant that he didn't fully understand justification, redemption, the state of humanity, or the grace that he so passionately defended.

The grace of the Spirit (properly called) is just a part of God the Father's grace, given to us in Christ Jesus before the world began. Even with that part, which he spoke about so passionately, he didn't fully understand its source, path, and end. It's one thing to ask why this beloved person was left in ignorance and used that way; it's another thing to accept that he was.

The truth is, both he and his respected partner Luther show that the understanding of divine truth develops over time. Augustine knew things that Cyprian didn't, and Luther knew things that Augustine didn't. So why should the growth of knowledge stop with Luther, Calvin, and Cranmer?

Even though Augustine didn't grasp the full extent of grace, he still celebrated its unconditional nature. With his background, how could he teach anything else? The unique beauty of the Gospel is that it teaches humility and gives God the honor He deserves. Augustine's personal experiences made him especially suited to share this message. He understood human limitations and knew that there was no goodness within himself. As a result, he was perfectly equipped to explain the total corruption and rebellion of human nature, which he knew to be true.

Humility is at the heart of Augustine's teachings. He showed people what it means to be humble before God, doing so with genuine simplicity and profound seriousness. In this regard, no other non-biblical writer has surpassed or even matched him in any era.

Few authors can equal Augustine's ability to describe the inner struggle between the flesh and the spirit. He portrays this conflict in a way that only those who have deeply experienced it can understand.

The Pelagian claims of perfection forced him to emphasize that even the most humble and holy individuals must battle against sin throughout their lives.

Augustine enjoys discussing two practical subjects: charity and heavenly-mindedness. He excels in both areas, and his writings consistently demonstrate a focus on the afterlife and deep, humble love. These themes influenced his actions from the moment he converted.

Despite the darkness that surrounded him, God made Augustine a light for the church. For over a thousand years, his writings nurtured the light of divine grace in individuals during a time of widespread superstition. His works were considered second only to the sacred Scriptures and guided those who feared God. There is no other example in history of such widespread benefit to the church from one person's writings.

Augustine is often referred to as "Beatus Augustinus," and his words were considered authoritative by Luther, Calvin, and other leaders of the Reformation. Even eleven hundred years after his death, a quote from Augustine was often enough to end any dispute.

INTRODUCTION

Martin Luther, etc.

To the esteemed Mr. Erasmus of Rotterdam,

Martin Luther sends greetings and peace in Christ.

REASONS FOR THE WORK:

In responding so late to your Diatribe on Freewill, my respected Erasmus, I have gone against both the general expectation and my own habits. Up until now, I have seemed eager not only to seize any opportunity to write when it came my way, but even to actively seek them out without being provoked. Some might be surprised by this new and unusual patience (as it may be) or fear of Luther's, who has not been stirred from his silence even by the many speeches and letters exchanged among his adversaries, congratulating Erasmus on his victory and celebrating with a triumphant cheer.

So, this Maccabaeus, a stubborn defender, has finally found a worthy opponent that he doesn't dare to speak against! However, I don't blame these men at all. In fact, I'm more than willing to give you credit, something I've never done for anyone else. I acknowledge that you're not only much more eloquent and talented than me (a recognition we all rightfully give you - even more so for someone like me, a barbarian who has always lived among barbarians), but you've also managed to dampen my enthusiasm and desire to respond to you, making me feel weak before the battle even begins. You've achieved this in two ways: first, by skillfully arguing your case with such incredible self-control from beginning to end that I can't help but not be angry with you; and secondly, by somehow managing, through luck, coincidence, or destiny, to not say anything new on this important topic. In fact, you argue for free will with much less conviction than previous philosophers, yet you attribute much more to it (I'll discuss this in more detail later). It seemed completely unnecessary for me to respond to your arguments, which I've already refuted many times, and which have been utterly defeated and shattered by Philip Melancthon's unbeatable 'Common Places.'

In my opinion, his work not only deserves to be immortalized but even canonized. When compared to it, your work seemed so inferior that I genuinely felt sorry for you. You were contaminating your elegant and clever writing with such poor arguments, and I was quite upset with your unworthy content for being presented in such a beautifully eloquent style. It's like carrying house or stable sweepings on people's shoulders in golden and silver vases!

It seems you were aware of this yourself, considering the difficulty you had in deciding to write on this occasion. Your conscience must have been warning you that no matter how eloquently you tried to present the subject, it would be impossible to hide its true nature from me. I would see through all the fancy wording you used to cover it up – and I say this as someone who may not be the most polished speaker but, by the grace of God, is not lacking in knowledge.

I don't hesitate, like Paul, to claim the gift of knowledge for myself and confidently withhold it from you, while I attribute eloquence and genius to you and willingly keep them away from myself, as I should.

So, I've been thinking: if there are people who haven't delved deeper into our writings or firmly upheld them (supported by so many Scripture proofs) to the point of being swayed by Erasmus' insignificant or worthless arguments, even if they are presented attractively, then those people aren't worth receiving a response from me. For no amount of words or writings would be enough for such individuals, even if thousands of books were repeated a thousand times. It's like trying to plow the seashore, sow seeds in the sand, or fill a leaky barrel with water. We have provided plenty for those who have learned from the Spirit through our books, and they completely disregard your work. As for those who read without the Spirit, it's no surprise if they're easily swayed. Even if God turned all His creations into tongues, it wouldn't be enough for them. So, I've almost decided to leave these people, who were misled by your publication, with the crowd that praises you and declares your victory.

You see, it's not the number of tasks I have, the challenge of the task, the extent of your eloquence, or any fear of you that's holding me back from responding to you. Instead, it's my sheer disgust, indignation, and contempt—or, to be honest, my considered opinion of your Diatribe—that has kept me from answering you. Not to mention the fact that, like you, I stubbornly persist in my beliefs.

You always make sure to be evasive and ambiguous. You're even more cautious than Ulysses, flattering yourself that you manage to navigate between Scylla and Charybdis. While you want people to think you haven't really said anything, you still act like you've made a statement. How can anyone have a proper discussion with someone like that, unless they have the ability to catch Proteus? With Christ's help, I'll show you what I can do in response to this, and what you've gained by pushing me to it.

But there's a good reason for me to answer you now. My loyal brothers and sisters in Christ are urging me, as they believe many are expecting a response from me. After all, your authority, Erasmus, shouldn't be taken lightly, and the true Christian doctrine is at risk in the hearts of many people. I've also realized that my silence has been quite ungodly, and I've been tricked by my own wisdom or wickedness into neglecting my duty, which makes me responsible for both the wise and the unwise. This is especially true when so many of my fellow believers are asking me to step up and address the issue.

Our journey to understanding isn't satisfied with just an external teacher. In addition to those who guide us from the outside, we also desire the Spirit of God to teach us the doctrine of life within our souls - a thought that has greatly influenced me. However, since the Spirit is free and moves not where we want but where it chooses, I should have followed Paul's advice to "be instant in season, out of season," because we don't know when the Lord will arrive. What if some people haven't yet experienced the Spirit's teachings through my writings and have been discouraged by your arguments? Perhaps their time hasn't come yet.

Who knows, maybe even you, my esteemed Erasmus, could be visited by God through someone as humble and fragile as myself? It's possible that I might reach you at the right moment (I sincerely hope so, through the Father of Mercies and Christ our Lord) with this treatise and gain a dear brother in you. Although your thoughts and writings on the subject of free will are misguided, I am deeply grateful to you for strengthening my own beliefs by showing me how even someone as talented as you can argue so passionately for free will and yet achieve so little. This clearly demonstrates that the concept of free will is a complete falsehood, as it only seems to worsen the more it is defended, like the woman in the Gospel.

I would be eternally grateful if, through me, you come to know the truth, just as I have become more certain of it through you. However, both of these outcomes are gifts of the Spirit, not the result of our own efforts.

So, we need to ask God to open my mouth and your heart, as well as the hearts of everyone, and to be present as a Teacher among us, speaking and listening within our souls. Once again, I ask you, my dear Erasmus, to be patient with my blunt way of speaking, just as I am patient with your lack of knowledge on these matters. God doesn't give all His gifts to one person; we don't all have the ability to do everything. As Paul says, "There are distributions of gifts, but the same Spirit." (1 Corinthians 12:11) So, it's important that we use our gifts to help each other and carry the burdens of those who lack certain gifts, using the gifts we have received ourselves. In doing so, we fulfill the law of Christ (Galatians 6:2).

PART ONE
ERASMUS' PREFACE REVIEWED

SECTION 1: ASSERTIONS DEFENDED.

I'll start by quickly going through some parts of your Preface, in which you criticize our cause and promote your own. First, you've already criticized me in other writings for being so certain and unyielding in my assertions. In this Preface, you say that you're so displeased with my assertions that you'd be willing to join the Skeptics on any topic where the unbreakable authority of the divine Scriptures and the Church's decrees would allow you to do so. In fact, you always willingly submit your own judgment to that of the Church, whether you understand what she prescribes or not. You prefer this attitude.

I believe that you're speaking with a kind heart that loves peace, but if someone else were to say the same thing, I might argue against them, as I usually do. However, I wouldn't even let you, despite your good intentions, hold on to such a mistaken belief.

It's essential for a Christian to be comfortable with making assertions, as one cannot truly be a Christian without them. To clarify, by "assertion" I mean consistently adhering to, affirming, confessing, maintaining, and unwaveringly persevering in our beliefs. I think this is the true meaning of the word "assertion," both in Latin and in our current times.

However, I want to emphasize that we should only make assertions about things that have been revealed to us by God through sacred writings. We don't need Erasmus or any other teacher to guide us in uncertain or unimportant matters, especially when it comes to making assertions that are not only foolish but even disrespectful. These are the very disputes and conflicts that Paul condemns more than once.

I don't assume that you're talking about these types of assertions here, unless you're using a ridiculous debating tactic where you pretend to discuss one topic but actually discuss another, or if you're arguing with the recklessness of a disrespectful writer that the concept of free will is uncertain or unimportant.

As Christians, we don't associate with skeptics and academics, but we do welcome those who are even more determined in their beliefs than the Stoics. The Apostle Paul often emphasizes the importance of having a strong and unwavering belief in our conscience. In Romans 10, he refers to this as "confession," saying, "and with the mouth, confession is made unto salvation." (Rom 10:10) Jesus also says, "Whoever confesses me before others, I will also confess before my Father." (Mat 10:32)

Peter tells us to be ready to explain the hope that we have within us (1 Peter 3:15). And honestly, there's no need for a lengthy explanation – the importance of asserting our beliefs is well-known and celebrated among Christians. If you take away our assertions, you take away Christianity itself. The Holy Spirit is given to us from heaven so that we can glorify Christ and confess our faith, even to the point of death. If that's not asserting our beliefs, I don't know what is!

The Spirit is so committed to asserting the truth that it actively confronts the world and exposes its sins, as if challenging it to a fight. Paul instructs Timothy to "rebuke, and to be persistent even when it's inconvenient." (John 16:8; 2 Tim 4:2) But how effective would someone be at rebuking others if they didn't firmly believe and consistently assert the truth themselves? I'd say they're not fit for the job.

I feel a bit silly spending so much time discussing something that's as clear as day. What Christian would tolerate the idea that our assertions don't matter? That would be the same as denying the importance of religion, piety, and all the teachings of our faith. And if you think assertions are pointless, then why do you make them yourself?

You say, "I am not pleased with assertions, and I like this temper better than its opposite." But it seems like you're not really talking about confessing Christ and his teachings here. Thanks for the hint, and to be kind to you, I'll step back from my right to judge your intentions for now and save that for another time or topic. In the meantime, I suggest you watch your words and writing, and avoid using such expressions in the future. Because even if your thoughts are pure, your words (which are supposed to reflect your thoughts) aren't. If you think the issue of free will isn't important to understand and isn't part of Christianity, then you're speaking correctly, but your judgment is disrespectful. On the other hand, if you think it's important, then you're speaking disrespectfully but judging correctly. But then, there's no need for all these big complaints and exaggerations about useless arguments and disputes – what do they have to do with the issue at hand?

SECTION 2: ERASMUS SHOWN TO BE A SKEPTIC

But what about your words where you talk not just about the issue of free will, but about all religious teachings in general – saying that if the unbreakable authority of the divine writings and the decisions of the Church allowed it, you'd join the Skeptics because you're so unhappy with assertions. What a tricky way to say that you really respect the Scriptures and the Church, but you wish you were free to be a Skeptic. What kind of Christian would say that? If you're talking about unimportant teachings about things that don't really matter, what's new about that? In those cases, who wouldn't want the freedom to be a Skeptic?

Indeed, what Christian doesn't freely use this license to condemn those who are completely devoted to a particular belief? Unless, as you seem to imply, you think most Christians are the type who have worthless doctrines, yet still argue and fight over them! If, on the other hand, you're talking about essential beliefs, how terrible is it for someone to say they want the freedom to assert nothing in such cases? A Christian would rather say, "I am far from enjoying the skepticism, and wherever my human weakness allows, I not only want to firmly stick to God's word, asserting what it asserts, but also wish to be as confident as possible in matters that aren't essential and fall outside the scope of what Scripture says. For what is more miserable than uncertainty?"

Moreover, what should we make of these words you added: "to which in all things I willingly submit my judgment, whether I understand what they prescribe or not?" What are you saying, Erasmus? Isn't it enough to submit your judgment to Scripture? Do you also submit it to the decisions of the Church? Does the Church have the power to decide what Scripture hasn't? If so, what happens to our freedom and ability to judge those who claim to have authority, as Paul writes in 1 Corinthians 14:29, "Let the others judge"? It seems you don't want anyone to judge the Church's decisions, but Paul commands it. What is this new devotion and humility of yours, that you take away from us (at least by your example) the ability to judge human decisions and blindly submit yourself to people? Where does the Bible require this of us? Furthermore, what Christian would so carelessly treat the commands of Scripture and the Church as to say, "whether I understand what they prescribe or not"?

You're saying that you submit yourself, but you don't really care if you truly understand what you're professing or not. However, a Christian is in trouble if they don't confidently grasp the things they're supposed to believe in. I mean, how can someone believe if they don't understand? You're calling it "apprehending" when someone confidently accepts a statement and doesn't doubt it like a skeptic would. Otherwise, what could anyone truly understand in any aspect of life if "apprehending something" means "perfectly knowing and discerning it"? Plus, there wouldn't be a situation where someone could understand some things and not others at the same time, within the same context. If they've understood one thing, then they must have understood everything. For example, we need to understand God before we can understand any part of His creation.

In short, what you're saying seems to be that it doesn't really matter what anyone believes, as long as there's peace in the world. When someone's life, reputation, possessions, and good standing are at risk, they can just go along with whatever others say, like the guy who said, "They affirm, I affirm; they deny, I deny." You're basically saying that Christian teachings are no better than the opinions of philosophers and ordinary people, and it's pointless to argue, fight, and insist on them because it only leads to conflict and disturbs the world's peace. "What is above us, is nothing to us." You're trying to act as a mediator who would end our disagreements by condemning both sides and convincing us that we're fighting over trivial and pointless things. That's what your words amount to, I believe. And I think you know what I'm holding back here, my friend Erasmus.

However, let's just move past what I've said for now. I'll let your spirited attitude slide, as long as you don't show it any further. Be careful of the Spirit of God, who knows your inner thoughts and feelings, and isn't fooled by fancy words. I'm saying all this to discourage you from accusing our cause of being stubborn and inflexible in the future. By doing this, you're only revealing that deep down, you're like Lucian or some other cynical character who doesn't believe in God and secretly laughs at those who do. Let us be assertive, eager to make assertions, and take pleasure in them. But for now, you can continue to support your skeptics and academics until Christ calls you one of them. The Holy Spirit isn't a skeptic; it hasn't written uncertain statements or mere opinions on our hearts, but rather, assertions that are more certain and deeply rooted than life itself and everything we've learned from experience.

Now, let's move on to another point that's related to this. When you talk about Christian beliefs, you claim that some are essential to know, while others aren't; you say that some are hidden, and some are out in the open. With this, you're either mocking us with other people's words that have been forced upon you, or you're attempting a sort of clever rhetorical move on your own. To back up your argument, you quote Paul's words, "Oh, the depth of the riches of the wisdom and knowledge of God!" (Romans 11:33), and also Isaiah's words: "Who has understood the mind of the Lord, or who has been his counselor?" (Isaiah 40:13).

It was easy for you to say those things, knowing that you weren't writing directly to Luther, but for a wider audience. Or perhaps you didn't think about the fact that you were writing against Luther, who I hope you still believe has some knowledge and understanding of the Scriptures. If not, let's see if I can convince you otherwise. If I may take a moment to play the role of a rhetorician or logician, I'd like to make a distinction: God and God's writings are two different things, just as the Creator and the Creator's creations are two different things.

Now, no one doubts that there are many mysteries within God that we don't understand, as He Himself says about the last day, "Of that day no man knows, but the Father" (Matthew 24:36). And again, in Acts 1, "It is not for you to know the times and the seasons." And once more, "I know whom I have chosen" (John 13:18). And Paul says, "The Lord knows those who are His" (2 Timothy 2:19) and similar statements. But there's this rumor spread by disrespectful Sophists (which you seem to be echoing, Erasmus) that some doctrines of Scripture are hidden in darkness, and not all are clearly visible. This is true, but they have never provided a single example, nor can they, to support this wild claim of theirs.

Yet, it's through such scare tactics that Satan has discouraged people from reading the sacred writings and made holy Scripture seem unimportant. This way, he can promote his own harmful heresies, rooted in philosophy, to dominate within the Church.

SECTION 3: CHRISTIAN TRUTH IS REVEALED AND UNDERSTOOD, NOT HIDDEN.

I admit that many parts of the Bible can be difficult to understand. This is not so much because the truths within them are too complex, but because we may not fully grasp the language and grammar. However, I argue that these challenges do not stop us from understanding everything that the Bible teaches. After all, the most important mysteries have been revealed: "Christ, the Son of God, is made man;" "God is at the same time Three and One;" "Christ has suffered for us, and shall reign forever and ever." Aren't these truths well-known and even proclaimed in public? If you remove Christ from the Bible, what is left?

So, everything the Bible teaches is available for us to understand, even if some parts remain difficult due to our lack of understanding of the language. It is foolish and disrespectful to claim that the truths themselves are unclear just because some words are hard to understand. If the words are unclear in one part, they are clear in another. The same truth is both clearly stated in the Bible and hidden within more difficult passages. But does it really matter if one piece of evidence for a truth is hard to understand when there are many other clear pieces of evidence for the same truth? Would you say that a public fountain is hidden just because some people living in a narrow alley can't see it, while everyone in the main square can?

SECTION 4: THE ACCUSATION OF OBSCURITY IN SCRIPTURE IS FALSE.

Your reference to the Corycian cave is not relevant here. The situation with the Scriptures is not as you describe it. The most complex mysteries and those with the greatest significance are no longer hidden but are now out in the open, easily accessible. This is because Christ has opened our understanding so that we can comprehend the Scriptures (Luke 24:45). The Gospel has been preached to every creature (Mark 16:15; Colossians 1:23), and its message has reached all corners of the earth (Psalm 19:4). Everything written in the Scriptures is meant for our learning (Romans 15:4), and since all Scripture is inspired by God, it is useful for teaching (2 Timothy 3:16).

So, I challenge you and all your sophisticated scholars to find a single mystery in the Scriptures that remains locked away. The fact that many truths are still hidden from some people is not due to any obscurity in the Scriptures, but rather to their own blindness or carelessness. They don't make an effort to see the truth, even though it's clearly visible. As Paul says about the Jews, "The veil remains on their hearts" (2 Corinthians 3:15). And again, "If our Gospel is hidden, it is hidden to those who are lost; whose hearts the god of this world has blinded" (2 Corinthians 4:3-4). To blame the Scriptures for this is as foolish as someone complaining about the sun and darkness after covering their own eyes or leaving daylight to hide in a dark room.

So, let's stop these people from wrongly blaming the darkness and dullness of their own minds on the Scriptures of God, which are actually full of light. When you mention Paul saying "how incomprehensible are his judgments," it seems like you think the pronoun "his" refers to the Scripture. But Paul isn't talking about the judgments of Scripture; he's talking about the judgments of God. In the same way, Isaiah 40:13 doesn't ask "who has known the mind of Scripture," but rather, "who has known the mind of the Lord?" Paul does say that Christians can know the mind of the Lord, but only when it comes to "those things which have been freely given to us," as he mentions in the same passage (1 Corinthians 2:10-16).

So, you can see that you haven't really looked closely at the Scripture passages you've mentioned, just like you haven't with most of the others you've used to support the idea of free will. The examples you bring up with suspicion and negativity, like the distinction of persons in the Godhead, the combination of divine and human nature, and the unpardonable sin, aren't really relevant. You claim that their ambiguity hasn't been completely cleared up yet. If you're talking about the questions that scholars have raised about these topics, I have to ask: what has the innocent Scripture done to you that you would blame it for the misuse that some people have subjected it to? The Scripture simply acknowledges the Trinity of persons in God, the humanity of Christ, and the unpardonable sin. There's nothing obscure or ambiguous about that.

The Scripture doesn't tell us how these things exist, as you claim it does, and we don't really need to know. Sophists debate their own fantasies on these topics. Feel free to criticize and condemn them, but don't blame Scripture. If you're talking about the core truth and not just made-up questions, I'll say it again: don't blame Scripture, but rather the Arians and those who are so blind to the Gospel that they can't see the clear evidence supporting the Trinity of Persons in God and the humanity of Christ. This blindness is caused by Satan, who is their god.

In short, there are two types of clarity in Scripture, just as there are two types of obscurity: one is external, found in the preaching of the word; the other is internal, which involves the knowledge that comes from the heart. If you're talking about this internal clarity, no one can understand even a tiny bit of Scripture without the Spirit of God. Everyone has a darkened heart, so even if they can recite and quote every part of Scripture, they don't truly understand or know anything it contains. They don't even believe in God, that they are God's creations, or anything else. As it says in Psalm 14, "The fool has said in his heart, God is nothing." (Psa 14:1.) The Spirit is necessary to understand all of Scripture and any part of it.

But if you're talking about the clarity of the external message, there's nothing left that's obscure or ambiguous. Instead, everything in the Scriptures has been brought into the light and shared with the whole world through the ministry of the word.

SECTION 5: FREE WILL IS AN ESSENTIAL TOPIC

It's even more unacceptable that you consider the question of free will to be unimportant and unnecessary, listing a number of other beliefs that you think are enough to make someone a devout Christian. Honestly, any Jew or non-believer who knows nothing about Christ could easily come up with a similar list of beliefs as yours. You don't mention Christ at all, as if you think Christian faith can exist without Christ, as long as we worship God, who is incredibly merciful, with all our strength. What should I say here, Erasmus? That your whole attitude is like Lucian, and you're full of Epicurean ideas? If you think this question about free will is unnecessary for Christians, then please, step aside, because we believe it's essential.

If you think it's irrelevant, overly inquisitive, or excessive to know whether God knows anything as uncertain; whether our will plays an active role in matters related to eternal salvation or is merely passive while grace works; or whether we simply experience (or "suffer") whatever good or evil we do out of necessity, then what, I ask, is relevant? What is important? What is useful to know? This is just nonsense, Erasmus! It's too much. And it's hard to believe that someone like you, an older man who has lived among Christians and studied the Scriptures for so long, could be ignorant about this. We can't find any reason to excuse or think favorably of you in this matter.

Yet the Catholics forgive these odd things in you and tolerate you because you're writing against Luther. These are people who would attack you viciously if Luther wasn't in the picture and you wrote such things! Plato might be my friend, and Socrates might be my friend, but I must honor the truth above both of them. Even if you only knew a little about the Scriptures and Christianity, an enemy of Christians should at least know what Christians consider necessary and useful, and what they don't. But you're a theologian and a leader of Christians. When you try to define Christianity for them, one would expect you to at least hesitate in your usual skeptical way about what is necessary and useful for them. Instead, you go to the complete opposite extreme, which is unlike your usual character, making a never-before-heard assertion, and now you sit as a judge, declaring things unnecessary that, if they aren't necessary and aren't certainly known, leave nothing behind: no God, no Christ, no Gospel, no faith, and nothing else from Judaism, let alone Christianity.

Immortal God! What an opportunity, or rather, what a wide-open field Erasmus provides for people to act and speak against him! How could you possibly write anything good or right about free will when you show such ignorance of Scripture and piety in your words? But I'll hold back for now and talk to you using your own words (though maybe I'll use mine later).

SECTION 6: ERASMUS' CHRISTIANITY

The version of Christianity you outline includes this principle, among others: that we must strive with all our might; that we must turn to repentance as a remedy and seek God's mercy in every way. Without this mercy, neither human will nor effort can be effective. Also, no one should ever doubt that they can receive forgiveness from God, whose nature is to be most merciful.

In your words, there's no mention of Christ or the Spirit. They're colder than ice, lacking even your usual eloquence. Maybe the fear of priests and kings made it difficult for the poor guy to express himself, so he wouldn't seem like a complete atheist. Still, your words include some claims, like we have strength within ourselves, that striving with all our strength is possible, that God's mercy exists, that there are ways to ask for mercy, and that God is naturally just and merciful.

So, if someone doesn't know what those powers are, what they do, what they allow, what their striving means, and their effectiveness or ineffectiveness, what should they do? What would you teach them? You say it's ungodly, nosy, and unnecessary to want to know if our will is active or passive in matters related to eternal salvation. But here, you say the opposite: that it's a Christian virtue to strive with all our might and that our will isn't effective without God's mercy. In these words, it's clear that you believe our will plays a role in matters related to eternal salvation since you think it strives. On the other hand, you also believe it's passive when you say it's ineffective without God's mercy. However, you don't explain the extent of this activity and passivity.

So, you try to keep us in the dark about the power of our own will and the power of God's mercy, right in the place where you teach us about the combined power of both. Your clever strategy to avoid taking sides and safely navigate between two dangers only ends up spinning you around in confusion. In the midst of this turmoil, you end up contradicting yourself, affirming what you deny and denying what you affirm.

SECTION 7: ERASMUS' THEOLOGY ILLUSTRATED WITH EXAMPLES.

Let me show you your theology through a few examples. Imagine someone trying to write a great poem or speech without considering their own abilities, what they can and cannot do, or what the topic requires. Instead of following Horace's advice to know "what your shoulders are able to bear, and what is too heavy for them," they just dive in, thinking they must give it a try and that it's unnecessary to question whether they have the knowledge, language skills, and talent needed for the task. Or picture someone eager to harvest a bountiful crop from their land but not bothering to carefully examine the soil's nature, as Virgil advises in his Georgics. Instead, they rush ahead, focused only on finishing the job, plowing the shore and scattering seeds wherever there's space, whether it's sand or mud. Finally, imagine someone going to war, hoping for a glorious victory or to serve their country in some way, but not bothering to assess their own capabilities, the resources at their disposal, the skill of their soldiers, or their ability to carry out their plan.

Instead, he completely disregards the historian's advice: "before you act, there is need for deliberation; and when you have deliberated, you must be quick to execute." He charges forward with his eyes closed and ears plugged, shouting only "war," "war," and passionately pursuing his goal. Erasmus, what would you say about such poets, farmers, generals, and politicians? I'll also mention the parable in the Gospel: if someone starts building a tower without first calculating the cost and determining if they can finish it, what does Christ think of that person?

So, you tell us to just work and not to first investigate and assess our abilities, what we can and cannot do, as if this is nosy, unnecessary, and unspiritual. The result is that, in trying to be overly cautious, you discourage recklessness and appear to be level-headed; but in the end, you actually advise the utmost recklessness. Although the Sophists may act impulsively and foolishly by discussing trivial matters, their actions are less harmful than yours, as you teach and instruct people to be mad and reckless. To make matters worse, you convince us that this recklessness is wonderful, Christian piety, moderation, religious seriousness, and sound judgment. In fact, if we don't act this way, then you, who are so opposed to assertions, claim that we are unspiritual, inquisitive, and vain. So, you've skillfully avoided your Scylla while steering clear of your Charybdis.

Your confidence in your own abilities has led you to this point. You believe that your eloquence can influence people's minds so much that they won't realize the monster you're hiding within yourself and the goals you're trying to achieve with your deceptive writings. But remember, "God is not mocked," and it's not wise to challenge Him.

If you had encouraged us to be reckless in creating poetry, farming, waging wars, managing civil affairs, or building houses, it would be unacceptable, especially coming from someone like you. However, you might have received some leniency from Christians who don't prioritize worldly matters. But when you tell Christians to be careless in their eternal salvation and not to be concerned about their natural abilities – what they can and cannot do – that's an unforgivable offense. They won't know what they're doing as long as they're unaware of their capabilities. And if they don't know what they're doing, they can't repent if they make a mistake; and not repenting is an unpardonable sin. That's where your moderate, skeptical theology leads us!

SECTION 8. THE ABSOLUTE NECESSITY OF DISCUSSING FREE WILL FOR TRUE PIETY.

It's not disrespectful, nosy, or unnecessary for a Christian to know whether their will plays a role in their salvation. In fact, it's extremely useful and essential. To be honest, this is the crux of our debate – the main question revolves around it. We're discussing what free will does, what it allows, and how it relates to God's grace.

If we don't understand these things, we won't know anything about Christianity and will be worse than non-believers. If someone doesn't understand this subject, they should admit that they're not a Christian. If someone criticizes or looks down on it, they should know that they're the worst enemy of Christians. Because if I don't know what I can do with my own natural abilities towards God, then it will be unclear to me what God can do within me, even though God "works all in all!"

Furthermore, if I don't know the works and power of God, then I don't know God himself. And if I don't know God, I can't worship, praise, thank, or serve him – since I won't know how much credit I should give to myself and how much to God. So, if we want to live a pious life, we should clearly distinguish between God's power and our own power, and between God's work and our own work.

You see, this question is a crucial part of understanding Christianity! Both our self-knowledge and our knowledge and appreciation of God depend on how we answer it. That's why it's unacceptable for you, Erasmus, to call the knowledge of this truth ungodly, overly curious, and pointless. We owe a lot to you, but we owe everything to piety. In fact, you yourself believe that all good should be attributed to God, and you've expressed this in your description of your own Christian beliefs.

If you claim this, you're definitely saying in the same words that God's mercy does everything, and our will doesn't do anything but is acted upon. Otherwise, everything wouldn't be attributed to God. But then, shortly after, you say that claiming and even knowing this truth is neither religious, pious, nor beneficial. However, a mind that's inconsistent with itself and unsure and inexperienced in matters of piety has no choice but to speak this way.

SECTION 9: ERASMUS HAS LEFT OUT THE QUESTION OF GOD'S FOREKNOWLEDGE.

The other main aspect of Christianity is to know whether God knows anything contingently and whether we do everything necessarily. You also portray this aspect as irreligious, curious, and pointless, just like all other secular people do. In fact, devils and the damned consider it completely hateful and detestable. You're smart to distance yourself from these questions if you're allowed to. But in the meantime, you're not much of a rhetorician or theologian when you assume you can talk and teach about free will without addressing these aspects. I'll be your sharpening stone, and even though I'm not a rhetorician myself, I'll remind a skilled rhetorician of their responsibility.

If Quintilian were to say, intending to write on oratory, "In my opinion, those foolish and useless topics of invention, distribution, elocution, memory, and delivery should be left out; it's enough to know that oratory is the art of speaking well" — wouldn't you laugh at this craftsman? This is exactly what you're doing. When you claim to write about free will, you start by pushing away and dismissing the entire body and all the components of this subject you intend to write about. Because it's impossible to understand what free will is until you know what the human will can do and what God does — whether he knows beforehand or not.

Don't your rhetoric teachers tell you that when discussing a topic, you should first address whether it exists or not, then what it is, its components, its opposites, its connections, and the matter of its similarities? Yet, you strip poor Freewill, as miserable as it is, of all these aspects and only define one question related to it: whether Freewill exists or not. We'll soon see how well you argue this point. I've never seen a more foolish book on Freewill, except for its eloquent writing style. The Sophists, who know nothing about rhetoric, have at least proven to be better logicians than you in this case. In their essays on Freewill, they address all the questions like 'does it exist,' 'what is it,' 'what does it do,' 'how does it work,' and so on. However, they don't even fully address what they set out to discuss.

So, in my treatise, I'll push both you and all the Sophists to define the abilities and actions of Freewill for me. With Christ's help, I'll push you so much that I hope it'll make you regret publishing your Diatribe.

SECTION 10: GOD'S ABSOLUTE FOREKNOWLEDGE COMES FROM ERASMUS' CONFESSION.

It is essential and beneficial for a Christian to understand this: God doesn't foreknow anything by chance. Instead, He foresees, plans, and achieves everything through an unchangeable, eternal, and infallible will. This idea strikes down the concept of free will, reducing it to dust. Those who want to support free will must either deny, hide, or somehow deflect this powerful argument.

Before I present my own reasoning and scriptural evidence, let me first address you, Erasmus, using your own words. Aren't you the one who just claimed that God is by nature just and most merciful? If that's true, doesn't it mean that He is unchangeably just and merciful – that His nature, justice, and mercy never change for all eternity? The same must apply to His knowledge, wisdom, goodness, will, and other divine attributes.

If these statements about God are made with reverence, piety, and usefulness – as you wrote – then why do you contradict yourself by saying that it's disrespectful, nosy, and pointless to assert that God necessarily foreknows everything? Do you think that God either knows what He doesn't want or wants what He doesn't know? If He wants what He knows, His will is eternal and unchangeable because it's part of His nature. If He knows what He wants, His knowledge is eternal and unchangeable because it's part of His nature.

So, it becomes clear that everything we do and everything that happens, even though it may seem to occur with change and chance, actually happens necessarily and unchangeably, as it relates to God's will. This is because God's will is powerful and cannot be stopped. And since God's power is part of his nature, it is also wise, meaning it cannot be misled. Since his will cannot be stopped, the work that he wants to happen cannot be prevented, but must happen exactly when, where, and how he knows and wants it to.

If God's will were like a human's will, where it stops after creating something that stays the same - like when a person builds a house and then their will about it stops (like when they die) - then we could say that some events happen by chance and change. But in reality, it's the opposite: the work itself might stop existing, but the will remains. So, if we want to use words correctly, in Latin, we can say that a work is done by chance, but we can't say that the work itself is chance-based.

The meaning here is that a task has been carried out by a changeable and temporary will, but this is not the case with God. Moreover, a task can't be called a contingent task unless it's done by us accidentally, without any prior thought on our part. It's called this because our will or actions take hold of it as something that comes our way by chance, and we haven't thought or willed anything about it beforehand.

SECTION 11: OBJECTION TO THE TERM 'NECESSITY' ACKNOWLEDGED; THE ABSURDITY OF DISTINGUISHING BETWEEN THE NECESSITY OF A CONSEQUENCE AND THE NECESSITY OF A CONSEQUENT.

I do wish that a different and better word had been used in our discussion than this common one, 'necessity' – which isn't quite right when referring to the will of either God or humans. It has too harsh and unsuitable a meaning for this context. It brings to mind the idea of something like force, and at least the opposite of willingness. However, our question doesn't imply any such thing. Both the will of God and humans do what they do, whether good or bad, without force, through pure pleasure or desire, and with complete freedom. God's will, though, is unchangeable and infallible, and it governs our changeable will – as Boethius says, "and standing fixed, moves all the rest" – and our extremely wicked will can't do anything good on its own. So, let the reader's understanding fill in what the word 'necessity' doesn't convey. Grasp it as what you might prefer to call the unchangeability of God's will and the powerlessness of our evil will – what some have called "a necessity of immutability," although not very grammatically or theologically.

The Sophists, who have struggled with this issue for years, have finally been defeated and forced to accept that all events are necessary. However, they argue that it's due to the necessity of a consequence, not the necessity of a consequent.

So, they have avoided the intensity of this question, but they are only fooling themselves. I will take the effort to show you how pointless their distinction is. By "necessity of a consequence" (to use their own confusing language), they mean that if God wills something, it must happen. However, it's not necessary for the thing itself to exist. Only God exists necessarily; all other things can cease to exist if God wants them to. So, they claim that God's act is necessary if he wills something, but the thing produced isn't necessary. What do they gain from this wordplay?

Well, I guess this: the thing produced isn't necessary, meaning it doesn't have a necessary existence. This is just another way of saying that the thing produced isn't God himself. Yet, the truth remains that every event is necessary if it's a necessary act of God or a necessary consequence. However, it may not necessarily exist once it's created; that is, it may not be God or have a necessary existence. For if I am created out of necessity, it doesn't matter to me that my existence or creation is changeable. Nevertheless, I - this changeable and non-essential thing, who am not the necessary God - am created.

So, their foolishness (that all events are necessary through a necessity of the consequence, but not through a necessity of the consequent) boils down to this: all events are necessary, true, but even though they're necessary, they aren't God himself. Now, why did they need to tell us this, as if there was any risk of us claiming that the things created are God or have a divine and necessary nature?

The unshakable truth is, "All things are brought to pass by the unchangeable will of God" - what they call the "necessity of a consequence." There's no confusion or uncertainty here. In Isaiah, He says, "My counsel shall stand" and my will shall be brought to pass (Isa. 46.10). Is there any student who doesn't understand the meaning of the words 'counsel,' 'will,' 'brought to pass,' and 'stand'?

SECTION 12: THE WIDESPREAD BELIEF IN THIS IDEA.

But why should this knowledge be kept from us Christians, as if it's disrespectful, nosy, and pointless for us to explore and understand it, when even non-believers and ordinary people are constantly talking about it? The famous poet Virgil often mentions fate in his works: "All things exist by a fixed law," "Every man has his day fixed," "If the fates call you," and "If you can somehow break free from the cruel fates." His main goal is to show that fate played a more significant role than human efforts in the fall of Troy and the rise of the Roman Empire. He even makes his immortal gods, including Jupiter and Juno, submit to fate. That's why people imagined the three unchangeable, relentless, and unforgiving Fates, or Parcae.

Wise people realized (and facts and experience confirm) that no one has ever achieved their goals exactly as planned; instead, they've encountered unexpected outcomes. As Virgil's Hector says, "If Troy could have been defended by human strength, it would have been defended by this." That's why everyone commonly says, "God's will be done," "If it pleases God, we will do it," and "That's what God wanted."

So, it seemed good to those above. "So you would have it," says Virgil. This means that, in the minds of ordinary people, the knowledge of God's predestination and foreknowledge is just as inherent as the very idea that there is a God. Even though the wise and blessed Augustine rightly condemns fate, specifically the fate upheld by the Stoics. However, those who claimed to be wise went so far in their arguments that, in the end, their hearts were darkened, and they became foolish (Romans 1:22). They denied or hid those things that the poets, the common people, and their own consciences considered most common, most certain, and most true.

SECTION 13: THE EXTREME RECKLESSNESS AND HARM OF ERASMUS' ALLEGED AND BOASTED MODERATION.

I want to go further and not only declare how true these things are (I will discuss them in more detail later, using the Scriptures), but also how religious, pious, and necessary it is to know them. Because if these things are not known, it is impossible for faith or any worship of God to be maintained. This would be a real and obvious ignorance of God, which cannot coexist with salvation. For if you doubt or despise the knowledge of this truth - that God foreknows and wills all things, not contingently but necessarily and unchangeably - then how can you believe in his promises and trust and rely on them with full assurance? When he promises something, you should be certain that he knows what he promises and is able and willing to fulfill it. Otherwise, you will consider him neither truthful nor faithful - which is unbelief, the highest impiety, and a denial of the most high God.

How can you be confident and secure if you do not know that he certainly, infallibly, unchangeably, and necessarily knows, wills, and will perform what he promises? It is not only essential to be certain that God necessarily and unchangeably wills and will fulfill what he has promised.

But we should actually take pride in this very thing, just like Paul does in Romans 3: "But let God be true and every man a liar." (Rom 3.4) And again, "Not that the word of God has been of no effect." (Rom 9.6) In another place, "The foundation of God stands sure, having this seal: the Lord knows those who are his." (2Tim 2.19) And in Titus 1, "which God, who cannot lie, has promised before the world began." (Tit 1.2) And in Hebrews 11, "He that comes to God must believe that God exists, and that he is a rewarder of those who hope in him." (Heb 11.6)

So then, the Christian faith is completely extinguished, the promises of God and the entire Gospel fall apart, if we are taught and believe that we don't need to know that God's foreknowledge is necessary, and that all actions and events are necessary. For this is the only and greatest possible comfort for Christians in all adversities: to know that God doesn't lie, but makes everything happen without any possibility of change; and that his will can't be resisted, altered, or hindered.

Now, my dear Erasmus, see where your cautious and peace-loving theology takes us! You discourage us from trying – no, you forbid us to try – to understand God's foreknowledge and necessity, and their impact on people and things. You advise us to leave such topics, to avoid and despise them. By doing this, you unintentionally teach us to be ignorant of God (which happens naturally and even grows within us), to disregard faith, to abandon God's promises, and to ignore all the comforts of the Spirit and the assurances of our own conscience. These are commands that even Epicurus himself would hardly impose on us!

You're saying that someone who seeks knowledge about these things is considered irreligious, curious, and vain, while someone who ignores them is seen as religious, pious, and sober. By doing this, you're basically implying that Christians are curious, vain, and irreligious, and that Christianity is unimportant, vain, foolish, and completely impious. So, while you're trying to warn us against being reckless and jumping to extremes, you're actually teaching us to be extremely reckless and impious, which could lead to our downfall.

Do you realize how impious, blasphemous, and sacrilegious this part of your book is? I'm not talking about your intentions, as I've already mentioned. I don't believe you're so far gone that you'd want to teach these things or see others practice them. But I want to show you how strange and nonsensical a person can sound when they defend a bad cause without understanding what they're saying. I also want to show you what happens when we go against divine truth and the divine word, playing a role to please others and ignoring our own conscience, getting involved in situations where we don't belong.

Teaching theology and piety is not a game or a hobby. In this line of work, it's very easy to make the kind of mistake that James talks about in the Bible when he says, "He that offends in one point becomes guilty of all" (James 2:10). This is because when we lose our respect for the Scriptures and think we're only playing around a little, we can quickly become trapped in ungodly beliefs and end up drowning in blasphemy - just like what has happened to you, Erasmus! May the Lord forgive and have mercy on you!

I know that the Sophists have raised countless questions on these topics and mixed in many other useless matters, as you've mentioned. I agree with you on this and have criticized it even more harshly and extensively than you have. However, you are being foolish and reckless by mixing and confusing the pure, sacred truth with the profane and silly questions of ungodly people. They have tainted the gold and changed its beautiful color, as Jeremiah says (Lamentations 5:1). But we shouldn't immediately compare gold to dung and throw it away with the trash, as you have done.

We must retrieve the gold from their grasp and separate the purity of Scripture from their impurities and filth. I have always strived to achieve this, so that the divine word is treated with one kind of respect, while their trivial ideas receive another. We shouldn't be bothered by the fact that these debates have only resulted in a decrease in harmony and love, while we are overly eager to gain wisdom. Our concern isn't about the benefits gained by argumentative Sophists, but rather how we can become good Christians ourselves. Also, don't blame Christian teachings for the wrongdoings of ungodly people.

This point is irrelevant; you could have mentioned it elsewhere and saved your paper.

SECTION 14: ALL SCRIPTURE TRUTH MAY BE PUBLISHED SAFELY.

In your third chapter, you try to make us into these modest and quiet Epicureans by giving another piece of advice, which is no better than the previous two: that some statements are of such a nature that, even if they were true and could be proven, it would still not be wise to share them with everyone. Once again, you confuse and mix things, as you usually do, in order to bring down what is sacred to the level of the ordinary, without acknowledging any difference between them. And again, you show disrespect towards God and His word. As I have said before, what is either clearly stated in Scripture or can be derived from it is not only visible but also beneficial. Therefore, it can be safely shared, learned, and known; in fact, it should be. So, how can you claim that there are things that should not be shared with everyone if you are talking about what is in Scripture? If you are referring to other things, then your argument does not apply to us: everything is out of context, and you have wasted your paper and time on words.

You know that I don't agree with the Sophists on any subject. So, you should have spared me and not thrown their insults in my face. You were supposed to write about me in this book. I know how guilty the Sophists are, and I don't need you to teach me since I've already criticized them a lot. And I want to say this once and for all: every time you mix me up with the Sophists and burden my cause with their crazy statements, you're being unfair to me, and you know it very well.

SECTION 15: THE ARGUMENT 'SOME TRUTHS SHOULD NOT BE PUBLISHED' IS EITHER INCONSISTENT WITH ERASMUS' ACTIONS OR IRRELEVANT.

Now let's examine the reasons behind your advice. Even if it were true that God is present in a beetle's cave or a sewer just as much as in heaven (which is disrespectful to claim, and you blame the Sophists for saying such things) — you still think it would be unreasonable to argue this point in front of a crowd.

First of all, no matter who says it, we're discussing law and rights here, not people's actions — not how we live, but how we should live! Which of us lives and acts correctly in every situation? Laws and rules aren't condemned because of this; instead, we are condemned by them. The truth is, you're bringing up these unrelated points from far away and gathering many things from all around you because the topic of God's foreknowledge confuses you. And since you can't find any arguments to counter it, you try to tire your reader with a bunch of empty words before concluding, "But we'll let this pass and return to our subject."

So, how do you plan to apply this judgment of yours that there are some truths that shouldn't be shared with the public? Is Freewill one of those truths? If so, everything I said earlier about the necessity of understanding Freewill comes back to you. Also, why don't you follow your own advice and not publish your Diatribe?

If you believe you're right in discussing free will, then why do you criticize it? If it's wrong to do so, then why do you even discuss it? If free will isn't one of these subjects, then you're guilty of straying from the main point during the discussion and talking about unrelated topics at length when there's no place for them.

SECTION 16: ERASMUS' THREE EXAMPLES OF TRUTHS 'NOT TO BE PUBLISHED,' CONSIDERED.

You don't handle the example you give very well when you say it's useless to discuss with the general public that 'God is in the cave, or in the sewer.' You're thinking of God too much like a human. I admit that there are some preachers who lack religion and piety and are motivated only by a desire for fame, a craving for novelty, or an inability to stay silent. They babble and joke with extreme carelessness. But these people don't please God or anyone else, even when they're claiming that God is in the highest heavens. On the other hand, when a preacher is serious and pious, and teaches using modest, pure, and accurate words, such a person can share this truth with the public, not only without danger but even with great benefit.

Shouldn't we all teach that the Son of God was in the Virgin's womb and born from her body? And what's the difference between a woman's insides and any other dirty place? Anyone could describe them in a disgusting and offensive way. But we should rightfully condemn such descriptions because there are plenty of clean words to express this idea, which can be spoken about beautifully and gracefully when necessary. Christ's body was human like ours, and what's filthier than that? Should we then avoid saying that God dwelt in him physically, as Paul says in Colossians 2:9?

What could be more disgusting than death or more horrible than hell? Yet the Prophet takes pride in knowing that God is with him in both death and hell (Psalm 23:4). A person with a strong faith doesn't fear the idea of God being in death or hell, both of which are more terrible than a cave or a sewer. In fact, since the Bible tells us that God is everywhere and fills all things, not only do faithful people believe that He is in those places, but they also understand that He must be there by necessity.

So, if I were somehow captured by a tyrant and thrown into a prison or a sewer (which has happened to many saints), would I not be allowed to call upon my God there or believe that He is with me, unless I'm in some fancy temple? If you teach us to think so lightly of God and are so bothered by where His essence resides, you might eventually not even allow us to believe that He is in heaven. After all, not even the highest heavens can contain Him (2 Chronicles 2:6), nor are they worthy of doing so. But the truth is, you attack with so much venom, as you usually do, trying to bring down our cause and make it seem hateful because you see this argument as unbeatable and invincible.

I admit that the second example you bring up, that "there are three Gods," would be a stumbling block if it were actually taught. But it's not true, and the Bible doesn't teach it. Yes, some philosophers might say that, and they've even come up with a new kind of logic for it. But what does that have to do with us?

Regarding your third example of confession and satisfaction, it's amazing how skillfully you manage to find fault. You always seem to just scratch the surface of the topic, careful not to outright condemn our writings or express disgust with the tyranny of the pontiffs, as neither would be safe for you. So, you temporarily set aside conscience and God, since Erasmus has nothing to do with God's will and conscience in these matters.

You attack a mere illusion, accusing the common people of misusing the preaching of free confession and satisfaction because their own evil nature might lead them to indulge in the flesh. You argue that mandatory confession somehow restrains them. What a brilliant and sophisticated speech! Is this teaching theology? Or is it, as Ezekiel says, to bind and kill the souls that God has not bound (Eze 23; 13.19)? With this logic, you truly support the entire tyranny of the Papal laws against us, claiming they are useful and beneficial because they restrain the wickedness of the people! But I don't want to criticize you as this passage deserves. Instead, I'll simply state the matter as it is, concisely.

A good theologian teaches this: ordinary people should be kept in check by the external force of the sword when they behave badly, as Paul teaches (Rom 13.1-4). However, their consciences should not be trapped by false laws, constantly bothering and tormenting them for sins that God does not consider sins. The conscience is only bound by God's commands. Therefore, this oppressive tyranny of the religious leaders should be completely removed. It falsely scares and kills souls internally while causing unnecessary distress to the body. This tyranny forces people to perform outward acts of confession and other burdens, but the mind is not restrained by these things. Instead, it becomes increasingly resentful towards God and other people. It punishes the body outwardly without any real effect, creating mere hypocrites within. The tyrants who create and enforce such laws are nothing but greedy wolves, thieves, and soul robbers. These wolves and robbers, O most excellent counselor of souls, you recommend to us again. In other words, you suggest we accept the cruelest of soul-killers — those who will fill the world with hypocrites, blaspheming God and despising Him in their hearts, just so that people may be somewhat restrained in their outward behavior. It's as if there isn't another way of restraining people that doesn't create hypocrites and can be achieved without destroying anyone's conscience, as I have mentioned.

SECTION 17: ERASMUS DOESN'T UNDERSTAND OR FEEL THE IMMENSE SIGNIFICANCE OF THIS ISSUE. HERE, YOU COME UP WITH A BUNCH OF COMPARISONS, WHICH YOU STRIVE TO EXCEL IN AND BE CONSIDERED SKILLFUL AT.

You're telling us that some diseases, like leprosy, are better to live with than to try and get rid of. You also mention Paul, who talked about the difference between what's allowed and what's wise. According to you, a person can tell the truth to anyone, anytime, and in any way they want, but that doesn't mean it's always the best thing to do.

Wow, you're quite the speaker! But it seems like you don't really understand what you're talking about. In short, you're treating this issue as if it's just a small matter, like arguing over some money or something insignificant. Losing this shouldn't bother anyone so much that they're not willing to give in, do what's needed, or endure whatever comes their way. It also shouldn't cause the world to be thrown into chaos. So, it seems like you value peace and comfort more than faith, conscience, salvation, God's word, Christ's glory, or even God himself.

I want to make it clear to you, and I ask you to remember this deep in your heart: I'm fighting for something serious, necessary, and eternal in this matter. It's so important that I'm willing to risk my life for it, even if it means the whole world ends up in conflict or returns to its original chaos. If you don't understand or feel the same way, then focus on your own concerns and let those who do understand and feel it do what they need to do, as God has given them the ability.

I'm not a fool or a madman, thank God, to have defended this cause for so long, with such determination and consistency (you call it stubbornness) despite numerous close calls, enemies, and traps - in short, amidst the anger and madness of both people and demons - just for money (which I don't have or want), or for fame (which I couldn't get in a world that's so against me), or for the sake of my physical life, which I can't guarantee for even a moment. Do you think you're the only one affected by these conflicts? I'm not made of stone or born from unyielding rocks, just like you.

But since this is the situation, I choose to withstand the challenges of temporary conflicts while defending the word of God with an unbreakable and uncorrupted mind - all the while rejoicing in the feeling and signs of His favor - rather than be shattered by the unbearable torment of eternal conflict as a victim of God's wrath. I hope and pray that your mindset isn't like Epicurus, but your words make it seem like you think the word of God and the afterlife are just myths.

As a respected authority figure, you want to suggest that we should submit ourselves to please religious leaders and rulers, or to maintain your precious peace, even if it means temporarily giving up the use of the word of God - as certain as that word is. By doing so, we would be giving up God, faith, salvation, and everything that makes us Christian. How much better is Christ's advice, to disregard the whole world rather than do this! (John 12:25)

SECTION 18: THE LACK OF WORLD PEACE DOESN'T ARGUE AGAINST A RELIGIOUS BELIEF, BUT RATHER SUPPORTS IT.

You might think this way because you either don't read or don't notice that the word of God often causes turmoil in the world. Christ himself said, "I have not come to send peace, but a sword" (Matthew 10:34) and in Luke, "I have come to send fire on the earth" (Luke 12:49). Paul also mentions this in 2 Corinthians 6:5, "In seditions," etc. The Prophet confirms this in the second Psalm, stating that nations are in turmoil, people grumble, kings rise up, and princes conspire against the Lord and his Christ. It's as if he's saying that everything powerful and important in the world opposes the word of God.

In the Acts of the Apostles, see what happens just from Paul's preaching (not to mention the other Apostles) – how he alone stirs up both Gentiles and Jews, or as his enemies claim, how he disturbs the whole world. The kingdom of Israel is troubled under Elijah's ministry, as King Ahab complains. What chaos there was under the other

Prophets! The Jews were killed by the sword or stoned, Israel was taken captive to Assyria, and Judah was also taken to Babylon. Was this peace? The world and its god cannot and will not tolerate the word of the true God, and the true God will not be silent. When these two gods are at war, what else can there be but turmoil throughout the world?

Wanting to calm these storms is nothing more than wanting to remove the word of God and stop its progress. The word of God comes to change and renew the world every time it appears. Even non-religious writers agree that change cannot happen without commotion, turmoil, and even bloodshed. In today's world, it is important for Christians to remain calm and composed in the face of adversity. As Christ says, "When you hear of wars and rumors of wars, do not be afraid, for these things must first occur, but the end is not just yet." Personally, I would argue that if I don't see these conflicts, then the word of God is not present in the world. However, when I do see them, I feel joy in my heart and dismiss them, knowing that the Pope's kingdom and his followers are about to fall. This is because the word of God, which is now spreading throughout the world, has particularly infiltrated this kingdom.

I see you, my dear Erasmus, expressing your concerns about these conflicts in many of your writings, and mourning the loss of peace and harmony. You try your best to remedy this situation with various methods, and I truly believe you have good intentions. However, this is like trying to cure gout with your bare hands. In this case, as you've said before, you're truly swimming against the current, and it's like trying to put out a fire with straw. Stop complaining and stop trying to play the role of a healer. This chaos is from God, both in its origin and its progression, and it won't stop until all those who oppose the word of God are brought low.

It's unfortunate that I have to remind you of these things, as you are both a great theologian and a scholar. You should be taking on the role of a teacher instead. This is where your saying, "some diseases are borne with less evil, than removed," should be applied (although you've misused it). Let all these conflicts, commotions, troubles, divisions, disagreements, wars, and any other similar events – which shake and clash the entire world for the sake of God's word – be considered as diseases that are better endured than cured.

These temporary things, I say, are less harmful than old habits of evil, which will cause all souls to perish unless they are transformed through the word of God. So, by removing this word of God, you take away eternal blessings - God, Christ, and the Spirit. But how much better it would be to lose the world than to lose the Creator of the world, who can create countless new worlds and is better than an infinite number of worlds! For what comparison is there between temporary and eternal things? It's much better, then, to endure this disease of temporary evils than to have all the souls in the world suffer eternal damnation in exchange for the world's peace and healing - since one soul cannot be saved by giving the entire world as its ransom.

You have many beautiful and excellent sayings. But when it comes to sacred matters, you apply them in a childish and even twisted way. You focus on earthly things and don't consider anything beyond human understanding. Now, the things that God does are not childish, civil, or human; they are divine and surpass all human comprehension. For example, you don't see that these conflicts and divisions are happening in the world due to divine guidance and action, and you're afraid that the sky will fall. But I, on the other hand (thanks be to God!), see the good in these storms. That's because I see other, greater things in the world to come, compared to which, these current troubles seem like the whispers of a gentle breeze or the murmur of a softly flowing stream.

SECTION 19: DOUBTS ABOUT WHETHER THE BELIEF IN FREE CONFESSION IS BASED ON THE BIBLE. IT'S IMPOSSIBLE TO OBEY BOTH THE POPE AND GOD AT THE SAME TIME. PEOPLE SHOULD BE ALLOWED TO MISUSE THIS BELIEF.

However, you either deny or claim not to know that our belief in free confession and making amends is based on the Word of God. This is another complicated issue. We, on the other hand, are confident that it is the Word of God, and it is this Word that upholds our Christian freedom so that we don't get trapped in slavery by human traditions and laws. I have provided plenty of evidence for this elsewhere, and if you want to challenge it, I am ready to defend it in front of you or debate it with you. Many of our books discussing these issues are available to the public.

You argue that the Pope's laws should be tolerated and followed just like God's laws, out of love - if doing so allows both eternal salvation through God's Word and world peace to coexist without conflict. As I've said before, this is impossible. The ruler of this world, Satan, doesn't allow the Pope's and cardinals' laws to coexist with freedom. Instead, he wants to trap and enslave people's consciences through these laws. The true God cannot tolerate this. As a result, there is an unending conflict between God's Word and human traditions, just as there is between God and Satan.

One undermines the work and challenges the beliefs of the other, like two kings destroying each other's kingdoms. "He that is not with me is against me," says Christ (Matthew 12:30). Now, regarding your concern that the masses, who tend to commit crimes, will misuse such freedom - this must be considered among the disturbances we've been discussing as part of the temporary leprosy that must be tolerated; the evil that must be endured. These individuals are not so significant that the word of God should be abandoned to prevent their misuse of it. If not everyone can be saved, at least some are saved for the sake of the word of God - these people will love it more passionately and respect it more deeply.

And what evils, I ask, have wicked people not committed even before this, when there was no word of God? On the contrary, what good did they do? Hasn't the world always been filled with war, deceit, violence, conflict, and all kinds of wickedness, so much so that Micah compares the very best among them to a thorn (Micah 7:4)? What do you think he would call the rest? Now, it's starting to be blamed on the spread of the Gospel that the world is wicked - because through the good Gospel, it becomes more evident how wicked the world was while it lived in its own darkness, without the Gospel. Similarly, since literacy has flourished, uneducated people attribute to literature the fact that their ignorance has become well-known. Such are the thanks we give to the word of life and salvation! We can only imagine, then, the fear that must have arisen among the Jews when the Gospel freed everyone from the law of Moses!

SECTION 20: ERASMUS' ADVICE ABOUT PEOPLE, TIMING, AND LOCATION IS HARMFUL.

This extreme freedom seems to give wicked people a lot of leeway, doesn't it? But that doesn't mean the Gospel was withheld. Wicked people were left to their own devices, and the godly were warned not to use their freedom as an excuse for sinful behavior (Galatians 5:13). Your advice or solution doesn't hold up when you say, "It's okay to share the truth with anyone, at any time, and in any way, but it might not be the best choice." To support this, you incorrectly use Paul's words, "All things are allowed for me, but not all things are beneficial" (1 Corinthians 6:12). Paul isn't talking about doctrine or teaching the truth here, as you suggest. You're twisting his words and pulling them in any direction you want. Instead, he wants the truth to be shared everywhere, at any time, and by any means. He even celebrates when Christ is preached out of jealousy. In fact, he explicitly says in those very words that he's happy if Christ is preached in any way. Paul is discussing the application and use of doctrine – specifically, those who brag about their Christian freedom and "seek their own" interests (Philippians 2:21) without caring about the obstacles and problems they create for weaker believers.

The true doctrine should always be preached openly, consistently, and without distortion or concealment. There is no reason to stumble upon it, as it is the guiding principle of righteousness. Who gave you the authority to restrict Christian teachings to specific places, people, times, and situations when Christ wants it to be shared and to reign freely throughout the world? "For the word of God is not bound," says Paul (2 Timothy 2:9). So, can Erasmus bind it? God has not given us the word to choose particular places, people, and times, as Christ says, "Go into all the world." He doesn't say, 'Go to a certain place, and don't go to another place,' as Erasmus suggests. Furthermore, "Preach the

Gospel to every creature" (Mark 16:15). He doesn't say, 'Preach it to some and not to others.' In short, you advocate for favoritism of people, places, and manners – in other words, time-serving – when it comes to sharing the word of God. However, one of the great aspects of the word is that "there is no favoritism" (as Paul says), and "God does not show favoritism." You can see how recklessly you wage war against the word of God, as if you value your own thoughts and advice far above it.

If we were to ask you now to identify the right times, people, and ways to speak the truth, when would you decide on them? The world would have ended, and time would have stopped before you could settle on a single reliable rule. In the meantime, what happens to the role of a teacher? Where will we find the souls who need to be taught? In fact, how can you establish any reliable rule when you don't know any criteria to evaluate people, times, and ways of speaking? But even if you were certain about them, you would still not know the hearts of people. That is, unless you decide to use this standard for your way of speaking, and for your time and person: "teach the truth, so that the Pope won't be upset, so that Caesar won't be mad, so that the cardinals and princes won't be displeased; and also, make sure there are no riots or disturbances in the world, and that people aren't confused by it and made worse."

You've already seen what kind of advice this is. But you choose to speak like a rhetorician with empty words, just because you feel like you have to say something. Wouldn't it be better for us, as flawed humans, to give God the credit for guiding us on when, how, and to whom we should speak the truth? He knows all hearts and commands that his Gospel, which is essential for everyone, should have no boundaries in time or place and should be preached to all people, everywhere, and at all times. I've already demonstrated that the things written in the Scripture are accessible to everyone and must be shared among the common people, as they are beneficial. This is what you also argued in your Paraclesis when you gave better advice than you do now.

Let's leave it to those who don't want souls to be saved (like the Pope and his followers) to restrict the word of God and prevent people from attaining eternal life and entering the kingdom of heaven. They don't enter themselves, nor do they let others in (Matthew 23:13). Your suggestion, Erasmus, only serves to fuel their destructive madness.

SECTION 21: THE FATHERS SHOULD NOT BE CONSIDERED EQUAL TO CHRIST; THEIR DECISIONS ONLY HAVE AUTHORITY THROUGH THE WORD.

Next, you cautiously suggest that we shouldn't publicly oppose any decisions made in general councils, even if they were wrong, to avoid disrespecting the authority of the Fathers. You say this to please the Pope, who enjoys hearing it more than the Gospel itself. He would be extremely ungrateful if he didn't reward you with a cardinal's hat and income! But what about the souls who have been bound and destroyed by unjust decrees? Does that not concern you?

You seem to always believe, or at least pretend to believe, that human-made laws can be followed without any issues while also adhering to the pure word of God. If that were true, I would easily agree with your statement. So, if you still don't understand, let me tell you again that "human statutes cannot be observed in conjunction with the word of God." This is because human laws bind people's consciences, while the word of God sets them free. These two forces clash like fire and water, unless human laws are followed without binding one's conscience. This idea goes against the Pope's wishes, and it must be this way unless he wants to destroy his own kingdom, which relies on controlling and restricting people's consciences while the Gospel says they should be free.

Therefore, we must disregard the authority of the Church Fathers and discard any harmful decrees, including those not supported by the word of God. Christ's authority is different from that of the Church Fathers. In short, if your statement includes the word of God, then it's a harmful one. If it only refers to other writings, then your lengthy discussion on the idea you're promoting doesn't concern me; my statements are only about the word of God.

SECTION 22: THE HARM OF CERTAIN PARADOXES, SUCH AS "ALL THINGS ARE BY NECESSITY" AND "GOD IS ALL IN ALL."

In the final part of your introduction, you strongly advise against this type of teaching and believe you've almost succeeded in doing so. You ask, what could be more harmful than spreading this paradox: that everything we do is not done by free will, but by mere necessity?

So, what about Augustine's quote that says, "God works both good and evil in us; he rewards his own good works in us, and punishes his own bad works in us"? You seem eager to question this idea. If this statement becomes widely known, what kind of impact will it have on people's beliefs and actions? Will any wicked person change their ways? Who will believe they are loved by God? Who will fight against their own sinful nature?

I'm surprised that, in your passionate argument, you didn't consider the implications for the concept of free will. Now, let me ask you, Erasmus: if you think these ideas are just human inventions, then why are you arguing so fiercely against them? Who are you opposing? Is there anyone today who has criticized human-made doctrines more strongly than Luther? So, your warning doesn't really affect me.

However, if you believe these ideas are actually the word of God, then how can you say that they are unprofitable to discuss? What kind of respect are you showing to the true God by claiming that his word is not worth discussing? Are you suggesting that God should learn from his creation what should and shouldn't be preached? It seems like you're implying that God has been foolish and misguided all this time, and now you, Erasmus, will finally teach him what is best to teach! It's as if God would have remained ignorant if you hadn't pointed out the consequences of his teachings!

So, if God is willing to have such things spoken openly and shared among ordinary people, without worrying about the consequences, who are you to forbid Him?

Paul the Apostle clearly states the same things in his letter to the Romans, not hiding it but openly and publicly, using even stronger words. He says, "Whom he will, he hardens." (Rom 9:18) And again, "God willing to make his wrath known." (Rom 9:22) What is more challenging for people to accept than Christ's words, "Many are called, but few chosen." (Mat 22:14) And again, "I know whom I have chosen." (Joh 13:18) If we follow your advice, these statements are some of the most harmful ones because they can lead ungodly people to despair, hatred of God, and blasphemy.

It seems like you believe that the truth and usefulness of Scripture should be judged by people, and these people are none other than the most ungodly. So, whatever they find acceptable and tolerable is true, divine, and beneficial. And whatever they don't like is immediately useless, false, and harmful. What are you suggesting with this advice, other than making God's words dependent on the will and authority of people, so that they can accept or reject them as they please? On the contrary, Scripture says that everything depends on the will and authority of God. In fact, it says that "all the earth must keep silence before the face of the Lord." (Hab 2:20) With your way of thinking, one might imagine that the living God is just some careless and uninformed speaker, whose words can be interpreted however you want, accepted or rejected based on the reactions they cause in wicked people.

You clearly demonstrate here, my dear Erasmus, how genuine your previous attempts were in convincing us to respect the awe-inspiring majesty of God's judgments. When we were discussing the teachings of Scripture, there was no need to demand reverence for them on the basis that they were hidden and inaccessible, because there are none like that. In very serious words, you warned us about the Corycian caves,144 trying to prevent us from being too curious. This almost scared us away from reading Scripture at all - the very Scripture that Christ, his Apostles, and even your own writing elsewhere, strongly encourage and persuade us to study!

But now, when we have actually reached not only the teachings of Scripture and the Corycian cave, but truly the awe-inspiring mysteries of God's majesty - specifically, why God works in the way that has been mentioned - here, I say, you break through all barriers and charge forward with almost blasphemous words, expressing extreme indignation towards God because you are not allowed to see the purpose and organization of such a judgment of His!

Why don't you also acknowledge the uncertainties and complexities here? Why don't you both hold back yourself and discourage others from trying to uncover the things that God has chosen to keep hidden from us and not revealed in His word? You should have kept silent here, respecting the unrevealed mystery, admiring the secret plans of the Divine Majesty, and exclaiming with Paul, "No, but, O man, who are you to argue with God?" (Rom 9:20)

SECTION 23: RESPONSES TO ERASMUS' CHALLENGING QUESTIONS, LIKE WHO WILL MAKE AN EFFORT TO IMPROVE THEIR LIFE, ETC.? TWO REASONS WHY THESE MATTERS SHOULD BE PREACHED.

You ask, "who will make an effort to improve their life?" I answer, no one; nor will anyone even be capable of doing so. For God doesn't care about those who try to improve their lives without the Spirit, as they are just hypocrites. But the chosen and godly people will be improved by the Holy Spirit; the rest will perish without improvement. For Augustine doesn't say that no one's good deeds will be rewarded, nor that everyone's good deeds will be rewarded; but that some people's good deeds are rewarded. So, there will be some who improve their lives. You ask, 'who will believe that they are loved by God?' I answer, no one will believe that, or be able to believe that; but the chosen ones will believe it. The rest, not believing, will perish, raging and cursing like you do in this instance. So, there will be some who believe.

As for your claim that these teachings open a window to wickedness — what if the problems arising from them are attributed to that disease of tolerable evil, which I've already mentioned? Nevertheless, through these same teachings, a door is also opened for the chosen and godly people to righteousness, entrance to heaven, and access to God.

Now, if we were to follow your advice and avoid these beliefs, keeping the word of God hidden from people so that everyone, deceived by a false sense of security, didn't learn to fear God and be humbled, eventually finding grace and love through healthy fear, then we would have effectively shut down your path to impiety. But instead, we would be opening not just doors, but massive pits and chasms, leading not only to impiety but straight to the depths of hell for ourselves and everyone else. In doing so, we wouldn't enter heaven ourselves, nor would we allow others who were on their way in to enter.

"What's the point or necessity of sharing such things with the world when it seems like so many problems arise from them?"

My response would be that it's enough to say, 'God wants these things to be shared. When it comes to understanding the reasons behind God's will, we have no right to question them; we should simply worship that will, giving glory to God because He, the only just and wise one, never harms anyone and cannot possibly do anything foolish or impulsive—even if it appears very different to us.'

Godly people are satisfied with this answer. However, to be generous with our understanding, let's say that there are two reasons why these truths need to be preached. The first is to humble our pride and gain a thorough understanding of God's grace. The second is the very nature of the Christian faith itself.

Firstly, God has promised His grace to those who are humble - meaning those who recognize their own limitations and despair in their own abilities. A person can't be truly humble until they understand that their salvation is completely out of their own hands and relies solely on God's strength, guidance, desires, will, and actions. As long as someone believes they can contribute even the smallest effort towards their own salvation, they remain self-confident and don't fully despair in themselves. They aren't truly humbled before God, but instead, they keep trying to find ways to achieve salvation on their own.

On the other hand, someone who has no doubt that their salvation depends entirely on God's will is fully aware of their own limitations and despair. This person doesn't try to control their own fate but waits for God to act. They are close to receiving God's grace, which will make them whole. These truths are shared for the benefit of the chosen ones, so they can be humbled, recognize their own insignificance, and be saved.

Others resist this kind of humility and reject the idea of being completely powerless. They want to hold onto some degree of control over their own salvation. These people secretly remain prideful and oppose God's grace. One reason these truths should be preached is to help the godly become humble, understand the promise of grace, call upon the Lord's name, and receive its fulfillment.

The second reason for this preaching is that faith needs to be focused on things that are not obvious or visible. In order for faith to exist, all the things believed in must be hidden. And nothing is more hidden from us than when the opposite of what we believe is presented to us through our senses and experiences. For example, when God gives us life, He does it by first making us experience death; when He justifies us, He does it by making us feel guilty; and when He raises us to heaven, He does it by first making us feel like we're in hell. As the Scripture says, "The Lord kills and makes alive; he brings down to the grave, and brings up." (1 Samuel 2:6) I won't go into detail about this here. Those who have read our books are already familiar with these ideas.

In this way, God hides His eternal mercy and compassion under eternal wrath, and His righteousness under sin. The highest level of faith is to believe that God is merciful even though He saves so few and condemns so many, and to believe that He is just even though He willingly makes us deserving of damnation. According to Erasmus' view, God seems to enjoy the suffering of the unfortunate, and we should hate Him rather than love Him. If I could somehow understand how this God is compassionate and just while also showing such great anger and injustice, there would be no need for faith. But since this cannot be understood, and while these things are preached and shared, there is room for faith to grow - just as faith in life is strengthened in the face of death, while God is in the process of taking our lives away. That's enough for now, as an introduction.

People who argue and defend these paradoxes actually do a better job of protecting against the irreverence of the masses than you do with your advice to stay silent and avoid them - which, in the end, doesn't really help. If you believe or even suspect that these paradoxes might be true (since they're quite significant), it's due to the insatiable curiosity people have for uncovering hidden knowledge. However, when you most want to keep these ideas hidden, your warning against them will only make people even more curious to find out if they're true. Your enthusiasm will undoubtedly ignite their interest. So, it turns out that none of us have contributed as much to spreading these ideas as you have with your passionate and fervent warning against them. If you really wanted to achieve your goal, you would have been wiser to keep quiet about avoiding these paradoxes.

It's all done now. Since you don't completely deny that the statements are true, they can't be hidden from now on. In fact, by suspecting that they're true, you'll make everyone want to look into them. So, either deny that they're true or stay quiet yourself if you want others to be quiet.

SECTION 24: THE PARADOX THAT "ALL HUMAN WORKS ARE NECESSARY" EXPLAINED AND DEFENDED.

Regarding the other paradox, which states that "whatever we do is done by mere necessity, and not by Freewill," let's examine it here so that we can prevent it from being labeled as extremely harmful. What I'm saying right now is this: once it has been demonstrated that our salvation is beyond our own control and wisdom, and relies solely on God's work (which I hope to fully prove later in my main argument), won't it logically follow that everything we do is evil when God is not actively working within us? And won't it become evident that we necessarily do things that don't contribute to our salvation? Because if it's not us, but only God, who works salvation in us, then before He works in us, we do nothing beneficial for our salvation, whether we want to or not.

When I say "necessarily," I don't mean by force — but rather, as it is said, by a necessity of unchangeability, not of compulsion. In other words, when a person lacks the Spirit of God, they don't commit evil against their will, as if it was forced upon them; it's not like someone grabbing them by the throat and twisting them around, just as a thief or highwayman is dragged to the gallows against their will. Instead, they commit evil willingly and with a desire to do so. However, they cannot, by their own power, put aside, restrain, or change their desire or their will to act; they continue to want and enjoy it. And even if they were forced from the outside to do something else, their inner will would still be opposed, and they would be angry with the person who compels or resists them.

Now, he wouldn't be upset if he changed his mind and willingly followed the force acting upon him. This is what I currently call "a necessity of immutability" - meaning the will can't change itself and go in a different direction. Instead, when resisted, the will becomes even more determined, as shown by its indignation. This wouldn't happen if the will were free or had free will. Just think about how stubborn people can be when they're attached to something. If they let go, it's usually because they're forced to or because they see a greater benefit in something else. They never let go willingly; it's always due to some constraint. On the other hand, if they don't care about the thing, they'll let whatever happens, happen.

Similarly, if God works within us and changes our will through the gentle guidance of the Holy Spirit, our will then acts according to its own desires, inclinations, and self-agreement, without being forced. In this state, the will can't be changed or overcome by any opposing forces, not even by the gates of hell. Instead, it continues to desire and love good, just as it previously desired and loved evil. Experience shows how unyielding and steadfast holy people can be, even when they're pushed towards other things by force. In fact, they become even more determined to follow their will, just like how wind fuels a fire rather than extinguishing it! So, in this situation, the will doesn't have the freedom to change direction or desire something else, as free will might suggest, as long as the Spirit and God's grace remain within the person.

In short, if we're under the control of the god of this world and lack the work and Spirit of the true God, we're held captive by him and subject to his will, as Paul says in 2 Timothy 2:26. In this state, we can't desire anything other than what he wants.

For he is the strong man who guards his palace, ensuring that those he possesses are at peace, so they don't cause any trouble or think against him. Otherwise, Satan's kingdom, divided against itself, wouldn't be able to stand. However, Christ confirms that it does stand. We willingly and wholeheartedly follow his will, in accordance with our own will. If our will were forced, it wouldn't be a will at all, since compulsion is more like a lack of will, if I may say so. But if a stronger will overcomes it and takes it as a prize, then we become servants and captives through His spirit (which is actually a royal freedom), willingly doing what He wants.

In this way, the human will is like a packhorse caught between two opposing forces. If God is in control, it wants and goes where God wants, as the Psalmist says, "I have become like a beast of burden, and I am always with you" (Psalm 73:22-23). If Satan is in control, then it wants and goes where Satan wants. The will itself doesn't choose which of the two riders it goes to or seeks as its rider; instead, the riders themselves fight for control and possession of it.

SECTION 25: ERASMUS CONVICTED BY HIS OWN CONCESSION: THE FOLLY AND MADNESS OF MAN'S CLAIMING FREE WILL.

What if I were to show you, using your own words in which you support the idea of Free Will, that there is no such thing as Free Will? In doing so, I would prove that you unintentionally deny the very conclusion you're trying so carefully to establish. Honestly, if I can't do this, I promise to take back everything I've written against you in this book, from start to finish, and support everything your Diatribe either claims or questions about me.

You describe the power of Free Will as something very small and completely ineffective without God's grace. Don't you agree with this? So, I ask and demand: if God's grace is missing or separated from this tiny bit of power, what can it do on its own?

You're saying that it's ineffective and doesn't do any good. So, it won't do what God or his grace would have done (since we're assuming here that God's grace is separate from it), and anything that God's grace doesn't do isn't good. Therefore, free will without God's grace isn't truly free; instead, it's stuck as a prisoner and slave to evil because it can't turn to good on its own. If you accept this, I'll let you make free will's power not just a small something, but as powerful as an angel, or even divine if you want. But if you still say it's ineffective without God's grace, you're taking away all its power. What's the point of having power if it's ineffective? That's not power at all.

So, saying that the will is free and has power, but its power is ineffective, is a contradiction. It's like saying the will is free, but it's not free. It's like saying fire is cold and earth is hot. Even if fire were incredibly hot, if it didn't warm or burn but was cold and made things cold, I wouldn't call it fire, let alone hot—unless you want to think of it as a picture or drawing of fire.

However, if we define Freewill as the power that makes humans suitable to be influenced by the Spirit and filled with God's grace, as beings created for eternal life or eternal death, then we would be speaking correctly. We also acknowledge this power (or suitability) in the will, or as some scholars say, this disposability and passive adaptability, which we all know is not present in trees or animals. As the saying goes, "God has not created heaven for geese and ganders."

So, even by your own admission, it is clear that we do everything out of necessity and not by Freewill, as long as the power of Freewill is nonexistent and cannot do good without God's grace. Unless you want to redefine "efficacy" as "completion," suggesting that Freewill can initiate and desire good deeds but not complete them – which I don't believe. We'll discuss this more later.

Based on what has been said, Freewill is a title that belongs solely to God and cannot be associated with any other being except the Divine Majesty. As the Psalmist sings, the Divine Majesty can and does accomplish all that He desires in heaven and earth (Psalms 135:6). However, if this title is attributed to humans, it would be like attributing divinity to them – a sacrilege that cannot be surpassed.

So, theologians should avoid using the word "Freewill" when talking about human power and reserve it only for God. They should also remove it from everyday conversations, considering it a sacred and respected term for their God. If they must attribute some power to humans, they should use a different term than "Freewill." This is because the general public is easily misled by this term, and they often understand it differently than what theologians intend.

When people hear "Freewill," they usually think of a power that can freely choose between options and isn't controlled by anyone. If they knew that the reality is different – that "Freewill" actually refers to a tiny, ineffective spark that is enslaved by the devil – they might feel deceived and angry. It's even more confusing because theologians themselves haven't agreed on what "Freewill" truly means.

As the wise man says, "he who speaks deceitfully is detestable," especially when it comes to matters of faith and eternal salvation.

We've lost the meaning behind such a magnificent term, or rather, we've never truly had it. The Pelagians believe that we do possess it, just as you are misled by this word. Why do we stubbornly hold onto an empty title, which only mocks and endangers the common people who believe in it?

This is similar to the way kings and princes either keep or claim to have empty titles of kingdoms and countries when they are actually quite poor and far from ruling those lands. However, this foolishness can be tolerated since they don't deceive or mislead anyone; they only feed their own vanity without any real benefit. But in our case, the danger to the soul and the deception are extremely harmful.

Who wouldn't laugh at (or even hate) someone who tries to change the way we use words, going against common usage, and attempts to introduce a way of speaking that calls a beggar rich—not because they have any money, but because some king might give them his? This would be especially ridiculous if they did this seriously, without using any figures of speech like antiphrasis or irony. Similarly, it would be absurd to call someone who is gravely ill perfectly healthy because another healthy person might be able to heal them. Or to call an uneducated person highly knowledgeable because a learned person might teach them. It's just like saying, "Humans have free will," which is true only if God were to give them His. With such a misuse of language, anyone could boast about anything, like claiming to be the ruler of heaven and earth—if only God would grant it to them. However, this isn't the language of theologians, but rather of actors and braggarts.

Our words should be clear, genuine, and sensible, or what Paul refers to as "sound and irreprehensible" (Tit 2.7-8). If we are not willing to completely abandon the term (which would be the safest approach and most in line with piety), we should at least teach people to use it with caution and within certain boundaries. In this way, we can grant free will to humans, but only concerning matters that are less significant than themselves, and not those that are greater.

In other words, let individuals understand that they have the right to use their abilities and possessions as they wish - to act or not act according to their own free will. However, even this right is ultimately under God's control, as He alone can intervene whenever He deems necessary. When it comes to our actions towards God, especially in matters of salvation or damnation, we do not possess free will. Instead, we are either bound by and subject to God's will or Satan's will.

SECTION 26: LUTHER WRAPS UP HIS REVIEW OF ERASMUS' PREFACE BY PRESENTING HIM WITH A DILEMMA AND QUICKLY ADDRESSING SOME OF HIS POINTED REMARKS.

I've discussed the main points from your Preface, which actually cover most of our topic - even more so than the rest of the book. But to sum it up, we can use this simple dilemma: Your Preface either criticizes the words of God or the words of man. If it's about the words of man, then it's irrelevant and I don't need to worry about it. If it's about the words of God, then it's completely disrespectful. So, our main question should be: Are the words we're debating from God or from man? Maybe the Proem and the actual debate will address this.

The things you mention at the end of your Preface don't bother me, like calling my beliefs "fables" and "useless," or saying we should follow Paul's example and preach about Christ's crucifixion. You also mention that wisdom should be taught among mature individuals and that Scripture has different language for different audiences, which makes you think it's up to the teacher's judgment to decide what to teach their neighbor.

All of this is nonsense and shows a lack of understanding. I also preach about Jesus' crucifixion, but "Christ crucified" includes all of these other topics as well. Plus, it brings the very wisdom meant for mature individuals, since there's no other wisdom to teach among Christians than the one hidden in mystery and meant for mature people, not for children of a Jewish and legalistic background who focus on works without faith.

In 1 Corinthians 2, Paul's message is about more than just saying "Christ was crucified." He wants us to understand the deeper meaning behind the preaching of Christ's crucifixion. When it comes to phrases like "God is angry," "has fury," "hates," "grieves," "pities," and "repents," we know that these emotions don't actually apply to God.

You're trying to find a problem where there isn't one. These expressions don't make the Scripture unclear or something that needs to be adjusted for different listeners. Some people just like to create confusion where there is none. These phrases are simply figures of speech that even young students can understand. In our discussion, we're focusing on the actual teachings, not just the figurative language used to express them.

PART TWO
LUTHER'S THOUGHTS ON ERASMUS' INTRODUCTION

SECTION 1. CANONICAL SCRIPTURES SHOULD BE THE MAIN REFERENCE POINT.

Human authority is acknowledged but not highly valued when arguing against Luther. So, when you start your debate, you agree to rely solely on Canonical Scriptures, as Luther doesn't consider himself bound by any other author's authority.

I'm okay with that, and I accept your promise, even though you don't make it because you think other writers don't contribute to the cause, but to save yourself unnecessary effort. You don't fully agree with my boldness, or whatever you want to call the principle I follow in this case.

You're indeed influenced by the long list of highly educated people who have been recognized by the general agreement of many generations. Among them are experts in sacred literature, some of the holiest martyrs, and many known for their miracles. Add to these numerous contemporary theologians, universities, councils, bishops, and pontiffs. In summary, on one side, there's knowledge, talent, quantity, greatness, high status, courage, holiness, miracles, and more. But on my side, there's only Wickliff and one other person, Laurentius Valla, whose importance is nothing compared to the others (although Augustine, whom you ignore, completely agrees with me).

So you're saying that only Luther, a regular guy from the past, and his friends are left - and they don't have much knowledge, talent, or numbers, no greatness, no holiness, and no miracles. They can't even heal a lame horse. They show off their knowledge of the Bible, but both they and their opponents think it's open to interpretation. They also claim to have the Spirit, but they don't show any signs of it. And if you wanted, you could list even more issues. So, all we have on our side is what the wolf said about the eaten nightingale: "You're just a voice and nothing more." "They talk," you say, "and just for that, they expect to be believed."

I admit, Erasmus, that you have good reasons to be bothered by all this. I was so affected by these things for over ten years that I think no one else has ever experienced such inner turmoil. I couldn't believe that my beliefs, which had stood strong for so long and through so many battles, could ever be defeated. Honestly, I swear to God that I would have stuck to my beliefs and still felt the same way as you do now if it weren't for my own conscience and the undeniable facts forcing me to think differently. It's not hard for you to imagine that even though my heart isn't made of stone, it could have melted in the struggle and clash with the waves and tides I brought upon myself by daring to do something that would, as I saw it, make all the authority of those people you mentioned come crashing down on my head like a flood.

This isn't the right place for me to write a history of my life or my work. I didn't start this book to praise myself, but to celebrate God's grace. The kind of person I am, and the spirit and purpose behind my actions, are known to the One who understands that all these things have happened not by my own free will, but by His. The world should have realized this by now.

Your introduction puts me in a difficult position, where it's hard for me to respond without boasting about myself and criticizing many of the Fathers. But I'll keep it brief. When it comes to education, talent, numbers, authority, and everything else, I'm willing to let the matter be judged by you, and I admit that I am the lesser one.

But if I were to question my judge and ask you these three questions - What is the manifestation of the Spirit? What are Miracles? What is Sanctification? - you would be too inexperienced and uninformed (based on what I know about you from your letters and books) to provide me with even a single syllable in response.

So, if I were to ask you which of all these heroes you brag about, you could definitely prove to have been or to be holy, to have had the Spirit, or to have shown real miracles, I believe you would have to work very hard and still not succeed. Much of what you say comes from everyday conversations and public discussions, which lose more credibility and authority than you think when examined by one's conscience. The saying is true, "Many are considered saints on earth, but their souls are in hell."

SECTION 2: THE GREATNESS OF THE FATHERS WAS NOT BECAUSE OF, OR FOR, FREE WILL.

But let's assume, if you want, that all of them were holy, had the Spirit, and performed miracles (even though you don't ask for this). Tell me, was any of them made holy, received the Spirit, or performed miracles in the name of or by the power of Free Will, or to confirm the doctrine of Free Will? You would say, "God forbid! All these things were done in the name of and by the power of Jesus Christ, and to support the teachings of Christ." So why do you use their holiness, their possession of the Spirit, and their miracles to support the doctrine of Free Will, for which they were not given or performed? Their miracles, their possession of the Spirit, and their holiness all belong to us, who preach Jesus Christ against the powers and actions of humans. Now, is it any surprise if those men (holy, spiritual, and miracle-workers as they were) occasionally spoke and acted according to their human nature?

This has happened more than once to the Apostles themselves when they were living under the direct guidance of Christ. You don't deny, but even claim, that free will is not a matter of the Spirit or Christ, but a purely human issue. So, the Spirit that was promised to glorify Christ cannot possibly preach free will. Therefore, if the Fathers have sometimes preached free will, then they have certainly spoken as humans, driven by their own desires, and not by the Spirit of God. Even more so, they haven't performed miracles to support it. So, your claim about the Fathers being sanctified, having the Spirit, and performing miracles is irrelevant – since it's not free will that's proven by this, but the teachings of Jesus Christ, which stand in opposition to the concept of free will.

SECTION 3: LUTHER CHALLENGES ERASMUS TO DEMONSTRATE THE EFFECTS OF FREE WILL IN THE THREE SPECIFIC AREAS HE HAS CHOSEN FROM ERASMUS' LIST.

Now, those of you who support the idea of Free Will, argue that this belief is true and comes from the Spirit of God. I urge you, show us the Spirit, reveal your miracles, and demonstrate your sanctification. Surely, you who claim this should provide these things to us who deny it. The Spirit, sanctification, and miracles should not be demanded from us who reject Free Will, but rather from you who support it. A negative claim doesn't need to prove anything, nor should it be proven itself. It's the affirmative claim that needs to be proven.

You assert the power of Free Will, a human concept. However, no miracle has ever been seen or heard of, performed by God, in support of a human idea, but only for a divine one. We are instructed not to accept any belief that hasn't first been proven by divine evidence (Deuteronomy 18:15-22). Furthermore, the Scripture refers to humans as vanity and lies, essentially stating that all human ideas are vain and false.

So come on, come and prove that your belief in support of human vanity and lies is true. Where is your display of the Spirit? Where is your sanctification? Where are your miracles? I see talents, education, and authority, but God has given these to non-believers as well.

We won't force you to perform great miracles, like healing a lame horse, in case you complain about the materialistic nature of the times.

However, God usually confirms his teachings with miracles, regardless of the materialism of the times. He is not influenced by the merits or demerits of a materialistic age, but by pure compassion and grace, and by a desire to establish souls in solid truth for His glory. You are free to perform a miracle as small as you like. In fact, to provoke your false god to action, I mock you and challenge you to create even a single frog in the name and by the power of Free Will. The wicked non-believer magicians in Egypt were able to create many of these. I won't ask you to create lice, which they also couldn't produce. I'll give you an even easier task: just take a single gnat or louse (since you taunt and mock my God with your joke about healing a lame horse). And if, with the combined force and efforts of both your god and yourselves, you can kill it in the name and by the power of Free Will, then you will be declared victorious. We will admit that you have defended your cause, and we will quickly come and worship this god of yours, the incredible killer of a louse!

I'm not denying that you have the power to move mountains, but there's a difference between claiming that something has been done by the power of Freewill and actually proving it. The same goes for sanctification.

If you can show me just one example from all these years and people you've mentioned, where someone has done even the smallest thing (like picking up a straw), said a single word (like the syllable 'my'), or had a single thought (even the weakest sigh) that came from Freewill and led them to grace, earned them the Spirit, obtained forgiveness for their sins, or had any interaction with God (no matter how small), then you'll have won and we'll admit defeat. But it has to be through the power and in the name of Freewill! There are plenty of examples in Scripture of things done through divine power.

You really should be able to show some evidence of this if you don't want to look like foolish teachers, spreading your beliefs all over the world with such arrogance and authority, without any proof to back it up. It's quite embarrassing when people of "such great importance, living through so many ages, highly educated and holy men, who can even perform miracles" can't provide any results. In that case, we might as well choose the Stoics over you. At least they tried to show some aspects of the wise man they described, even if they never actually saw one. You, on the other hand, have nothing to show for your beliefs, not even a shadow of your doctrine.

So, once again, regarding the Spirit - if you can find a single person among all the supporters of Freewill who has even the slightest strength of mind or good feeling to allow them to disregard a single penny, skip a single roll of the dice, or forgive a single hurtful word or letter (I won't even mention despising wealth, life, and fame) in the name and through the power of Freewill, then go ahead and claim victory, and I'll accept being your captive. You should at least demonstrate this after all your grand, exaggerated claims about Freewill. Otherwise, it will seem like you're just arguing about something trivial, like goat's wool, or like the famous Argian, watching plays in an empty theater.

SECTION 4: IN PRACTICE, THE SAINTS REJECT FREEWILL, EVEN IF THEY DEBATE ABOUT IT.

However, contrary to what you claim, I can easily demonstrate that holy individuals, like the ones you boast about having, often approach God in prayer or supplication with a complete disregard for their own free will. They feel hopeless about their own abilities and ask for nothing but pure grace, which they admit is far beyond what they deserve.

Augustine often showed himself to be such a man, and Bernard did too when, on his deathbed, he said, "I have wasted my time, for I have lived terribly." I don't see any mention of grace in these statements. Instead, they seem to accuse these men of completely rejecting any power that a person might have. Yet, these same holy men sometimes spoke differently about free will in their debates. I notice this happening with everyone: people act and speak one way when they're focused on words and arguments, and another way when they're experiencing and acting on their feelings. In the first case, their language doesn't match their later feelings, and in the second, their feelings contradict their earlier words. But whether they are truly good or bad, people should be judged more by their feelings than their words.

SECTION 5: REGARDLESS OF HOW THEY ARGUE ABOUT IT, LUTHER WANTS A CLEAR DEFINITION OF FREE WILL, INCLUDING ITS PARTS, POWERS, CHARACTERISTICS, AND RELATED FACTORS.

But we're asking for even more. We don't demand miracles, the Spirit, or sanctification. We go back to the main idea itself, asking you to at least show us what action, word, or thought this power of free will initiates or tries to carry out in order to connect with grace. It's not enough to just say, "there is a power," "there is a power," "there is a certain power, I say, in free will;" because what's easier than saying that? This isn't fitting for those highly educated and holy men who have been respected for so many generations. As the German proverb goes, "The baby must be named." You need to define what that power is, what it does, what it permits, and what its related factors are.

For example, speaking as someone who might not fully understand, I would ask, is the purpose of this power to pray, fast, work, control the body, give to charity, or do anything else like that? Or does it even try to do these things? If it is a power, then it must be trying to achieve something. But here, you are quieter than the Seriphian frogs and fishes.

And how can you define it when, according to your own words, you are still unsure about what the power itself is, as you disagree with each other and are inconsistent with yourselves? What will happen to the definition when the thing being defined means one thing in one place and another in another place?

But let's assume that, since Plato's time, there has finally been some sort of agreement among you about the power itself. Let's also define its purpose as praying, fasting, or doing something similar, which might still be hidden in the complexity of Plato's "Ideas." Who will guarantee that this belief is true, that it pleases God, and that we are safe in supporting it? Especially when you admit that it is a human concept, which doesn't have the backing of the Spirit.

For this idea was discussed by philosophers and existed in the world before Christ came and before the Spirit was sent from heaven. This makes it very clear that this belief was not sent from heaven, but had been around for a long time, originating from the earth. So, a lot of evidence is needed to confirm it as certain and true.

Let us be ordinary people and few in number, while you are influential and many; let us be uneducated, and you highly knowledgeable; let us be simple-minded, and you extremely clever; let us be newcomers, and you older than Deucalion; let us be unimportant, and you, people who have been approved by generations; let us, in short, be sinners, worldly, and foolish; and you be individuals who can even scare the devils with your holiness, the Spirit within you, and your miracles. At least give us the same right as Turks and Jews: to ask for a reason for your belief, in accordance with what your great patron St. Peter has commanded you.

We ask this with the utmost humility. We don't demand that you prove your beliefs to us through sanctification, the Spirit, or miracles, as you might expect from others based on your own laws. In fact, we don't even require you to provide any examples of thought, word, or deed in your doctrine; just teach us the basic, bare proposition. At least tell us what you mean by it and what its form is.

If you can't or won't give us an example, let us try to give you one. Follow the example of the Pope and his cardinals, who say, "Do as we say, not as we do." Similarly, if you tell us what actions your doctrine requires from its followers, we will strive to do them, leaving you to your own devices. What! Can't we even get that much from you? The larger your numbers, the older your tradition, and the better you are in every way compared to us, the more shameful it is that you can't prove your doctrine - not even by performing a small miracle like killing a louse, or showing any sign of the Spirit or holiness - to us, who are insignificant in your eyes and merely want to learn and follow your teachings. You can't even provide a single example of your doctrine in action or explain its meaning (something unheard of), so that we might at least try to imitate it. What wonderful teachers of free will you are! What are you now, but a mere voice with no substance? Erasmus, who are those who brag about having the Spirit but show no evidence of it, who only speak and expect to be believed without question?

Aren't these admired individuals of yours the ones who do all this? Even though they're praised to the skies, they don't even respond, yet they make such grand claims and demands. So, we kindly ask you and your group, Erasmus, to at least allow us, who are frightened by the danger our conscience faces, to indulge our fears or at least delay our agreement to a belief that you yourself see as nothing more than an empty phrase and the sound of a few words (specifically, "There is such a thing as Free Will;" "there is such a thing as Free Will"). This is even if you had achieved your ultimate goal and all your arguments had been proven and accepted.

Moreover, even within your own group, it's still uncertain whether this concept exists or not, since they disagree with one another and each person isn't consistent with themselves. It's incredibly unfair – no, it's the most miserable thing imaginable – that the consciences of those whom Christ has redeemed with his own blood should be tormented by the mere illusion of a single, insignificant word, and that word's existence is even in doubt. Yet, if we don't allow ourselves to be troubled in this way, we're accused of unprecedented arrogance for disregarding so many Fathers from so many eras who have supported the idea of Free Will. But the truth is, they haven't provided any clear statements about it, as you can see from what's been discussed. And the belief in Free Will is promoted under the protection of their name, while its defenders can't even show its nature or its title. This is how they've managed to deceive the world with a false word!

SECTION 6: ERASMUS' ADVICE TURNED AGAINST HIMSELF: PRESUMPTION, CRUELTY, AND LACK OF DISCERNMENT ARE CHARGED UPON HIM.

And here, Erasmus, I call upon your own advice, not someone else's, to help me. You, who earlier suggested that we should avoid these types of questions and instead focus on teaching about Christ crucified and the essentials of Christian faith. For quite some time, our discussions have revolved around these topics. Our main goal is to ensure that the simplicity and purity of Christ's teachings prevail, while abandoning and disregarding any doctrines that have been created and introduced by humans.

However, while you give us this advice, you don't follow it yourself. Instead, you do the exact opposite. You write lengthy arguments, praise the decisions of Popes, boast about the authority of people, and use every possible means to drag us into matters that have nothing to do with the holy Scriptures. You want us to engage in unnecessary debates, so that we may corrupt and confuse the simplicity and authenticity of Christian faith with human additions.

So, it's clear that you're not giving us this advice from your heart, and you're not writing anything seriously. Instead, you rely on the fancy and childish aspects of your language, thinking it will let you lead the world wherever you want. But in reality, you're leading it nowhere because you're just saying contradictory things throughout your entire argument. Someone could accurately describe you as Proteus or Vertumnus, or even quote Christ by saying, "Physician, heal yourself!" It's embarrassing for a teacher to be called out for the same flaw they're criticizing in others.

So, until you can prove your point, we'll stick to our opposing view. We're even willing to proudly stand by our position in front of any judge, even if that judge was the group of holy men you claim to have on your side, or even the whole world. We won't accept a belief that is essentially meaningless and can't be clearly defined. Furthermore, we'll accuse you of being incredibly presumptuous or even insane for demanding that we accept this belief without any reason, other than the fact that it pleases your "High Mightinesses" – who are so numer-ous, so great, and so ancient – and that we should acknowledge some-thing that you yourselves admit is nothing.

Is it really appropriate for Christian teachers to deceive the poor and miserable common people in matters of faith, by presenting something insignificant as if it were crucial to their salvation? What happened to the cleverness of the Greeks, who used to come up with lies that at least seemed beautiful? But in this case, they only produce blatant and obvious falsehoods. And what about the Latin diligence, which is not inferior to the Greek, but in this case, both deceives and is deceived by empty words?

This is what happens to careless or manipulative readers of books: they consider all the teachings of the Fathers and Saints, which are the result of their human weaknesses, to be of the highest authority. The fault lies not with the authors, but with the readers. It's as if someone, relying on the holiness and authority of St. Peter, claimed that everything Peter ever said is true, including Matthew 16:22, when he advised Jesus not to suffer due to his human frailty; or when he told Jesus to leave his boat in Luke 5:8; and many other instances where he was corrected by Jesus himself.

SECTION 7: UNFAIR TREATMENT OF THE FATHERS BY FOCUSING ON THEIR NEGATIVE STATEMENTS AND IGNORING THEIR POSITIVE ONES.

People like this are similar to those who mock the Gospel by claiming that not everything in it is true. They latch onto the parts where the Jews say to Jesus, "Aren't we right in saying that you are a Samaritan and have a demon?" (John 8:48) or that "He deserves to die;" or "We found this man causing trouble among our people and telling them not to pay taxes to Caesar."

The advocates of free will often do the same thing (with a different intention, of course, and not on purpose, but due to misunderstanding and ignorance) when they use the statements made by the Church Fathers in support of free will, even though these statements were made when the Fathers were weak in their faith. They then contrast these statements with the stronger, more spiritual statements made by the same Fathers against free will. As a result, they end up giving more weight to the weaker statements because they align with their own beliefs, while disregarding the stronger statements that go against their views.

Why don't we choose to focus on the better, more spiritual statements instead? There are many such statements in the works of the Church Fathers. For example, consider this statement by Jerome:

"Virginity fills heaven, and marriage fills earth." This statement is quite problematic, as it implies that those who marry, including patriarchs, apostles, and ordinary Christians, are only worthy of earth, not heaven. It also suggests that even pagan virgins who don't believe in Christ are deserving of heaven. Yet, people who support free will often collect these and similar statements from the Church Fathers, focusing more on the quantity of statements rather than their quality, in order to gain the support of these authoritative figures.

This is similar to the recent case of Faber of Constance, who published his work "Margaritum" (which would be better called his "Augean stable"), causing disgust and rejection among the pious and learned.

SECTION 8: OBJECTION: GOD SHOULD HAVE PREVENTED THE ERROR OF HIS CHURCH, ANSWERED.

You say, "It is unbelievable that God would have allowed the mistake of his Church for so many ages, and not have revealed to any of his saints what we believe to be the core of evangelical doctrine."

I reply, first, that we do not claim that this error has been permitted by God in his Church, or in any of his saints. For the Church is guided by the Spirit of God; the saints are led by the Spirit of God (Rom 8:14); Christ remains with his Church until the end of the world (Mat 28:20); and the Church of God is the pillar and foundation of the truth (1 Tim 3:15). I say, we know these things. For even our common creed states; "I believe in the holy Catholic Church;" so it is impossible for her to be wrong in even the smallest matter.

Even if we were to accept that some chosen individuals are mistaken throughout their lives, they must still find the right path before they die, because Christ says in John 10:28, "No one shall pluck them out of my hand." However, it's up to you to prove with certainty that those you consider the Church are indeed the Church, or rather, that those who were lost throughout their lives have finally returned to the fold before their death. Just because God may have allowed all those you mention to remain in error (even if they were highly educated and lived in different ages), it doesn't mean that He has allowed His Church to remain in error.

Consider the people of Israel, God's chosen people: among all their kings, who were numerous and ruled for a long time, not a single one is mentioned as being without error. And during the time of the prophet Isaiah, everyone, including the leaders of the people, had turned to idolatry to such an extent that Isaiah thought he was the only one left. Yet, while God was about to destroy kings, princes, priests, prophets, and everyone else who could be considered part of God's people or Church, He saved 7,000 individuals for Himself (1 Kings 19:18). But who saw or knew that these were God's people? So, who can deny that God has even now preserved a Church among ordinary people, hidden under those prominent individuals (since you only mention well-known figures), and has allowed all the others to perish, just as He did in the kingdom of Israel? After all, it is God's unique right and action to ensnare the best of Israel and destroy their strongest (Psalm 78:31), but to keep the remnants and outcasts of Israel alive, as Isaiah says.

What happened when Christ himself was present, and all the Apostles were offended, and he was denied and condemned by the whole people? Only one or two, like Nicodemus and Joseph, and later the thief on the cross, remained loyal to him. But were these few called "the people of God" at that time? There was indeed a group of God's people remaining, but they weren't referred to as such. What was called "the people of God" wasn't actually them. Who knows if this has always been the case for the Church of God throughout history, from the beginning of the world: that some were called God's people and saints, but weren't truly so, while others, remaining as a small group among them, were indeed his people and saints, but weren't recognized as such? This is illustrated by the stories of Cain and Abel, Ishmael and Isaac, and Esau and Jacob.

Take a look at the Arian period. This was a time when barely five Catholic bishops remained in the entire world, and they were forced out of their positions - the Arians ruled everywhere under the public name and filled the roles within the Church. However, even under the control of these heretics, Christ managed to preserve his Church. But it was in such a way that it wasn't considered or seen as the Church at all.

During the Pope's reign, can you point out a single bishop who fulfilled his duties, or a single Council that focused on matters of piety instead of discussing robes, status, revenues, and other worldly trivialities? Surely, no sane person would attribute these things to the Holy Spirit. Yet, these people are considered the Church, even though anyone who lives like them is far from being part of the true Church.

Despite this, Christ managed to preserve his Church under such conditions, but it shouldn't be called the Church. Over the years, how many saints do you think these self-proclaimed inquisitors of heresy have burned and killed? Saints like John Huss and others, who undoubtedly had many holy followers with the same spirit.

Erasmus, why don't you instead marvel at the fact that since the beginning of time, there have always been people among the heathens who possessed greater genius, knowledge, and dedication than those among Christians or God's people? Even Christ himself admitted that the children of this world are wiser than the children of light (Luke 16:8). Can any Christian truly compare to someone like Cicero in terms of genius, knowledge, and diligence, let alone the Greeks?

So, what can we say has been the obstacle preventing any of them from achieving grace? They have undoubtedly used their free will to the fullest extent. And who would dare to say that none of them were passionately committed to discovering the truth? Yet, we must admit that none of them have found it. Would you also argue that it's unbelievable that God would leave so many great individuals on their own throughout history, allowing them to struggle in vain? Surely, if free will had any substance or power, it would have been evident in at least one of these people. But it has accomplished nothing; in fact, its impact has always been the opposite. Thus, free will can be conclusively proven to be non-existent by this single argument: there is no evidence of it from the beginning of the world to the end.

SECTION 9: THE CHURCH IS NOT YET FULLY REVEALED; THE SAINTS ARE HIDDEN.

But let's get back to the main point. Is it really surprising that God allows all the prominent figures of the Church to follow their own paths when He has allowed all nations to do the same, as Paul mentions in Acts 14:16? The Church of God is not as ordinary, Erasmus, as the name by which it is known, "The Church of God." Nor are God's saints encountered as frequently as their title suggests: "The Saints of God." They are precious pearls and noble gems that the Spirit does not throw before swine, but as the Scripture says, keeps hidden so that the wicked cannot see God's glory.

Otherwise, if everyone openly acknowledged these things, how could it be that they are so mistreated and persecuted in the world? As Paul says, "If they had known, they would not have crucified the Lord of glory."

SECTION 10: DISTINCTION BETWEEN JUDGMENT OF FAITH AND JUDGMENT OF CHARITY

I'm not saying this to deny that the people you mentioned were saints or part of God's Church. I say this because it can't be proven (if someone were to argue against it) that these specific individuals were saints; it must be left entirely uncertain. And as a result, an argument based on their sainthood isn't credible enough to confirm any belief. I consider them saints, and I believe they were part of God's Church.

But this is according to the law of love, not the law of faith - that is, through kindness - which assumes the best of everyone and is never suspicious. It believes and presumes the best of our neighbors, calling any baptized person "a saint." And if we are mistaken, there's no harm done, because love is often deceived, being exposed to the actions and manipulations of all people. Love helps everyone, good and evil, faithful and unfaithful, true and false. However, faith only calls someone a saint if they are declared so by divine judgment, as faith cannot be deceived. So while we should all consider each other saints through the law of love, no one should be declared a saint through the law of faith - as if it were a matter of faith that this or that person is a saint. This is how the Pope, that great enemy of God who puts himself in God's place, canonizes his saints, even though he doesn't know if they are truly saints.

As for those saints of yours (or rather, ours), I only say this: since they disagree among themselves, we should follow those who speak the best things - that is, against free will and in favor of grace - and leave those who, due to their human weakness, testify to the flesh rather than the spirit. Also, we should accept and embrace those writers who are inconsistent with themselves when they speak in the spirit, and leave them when they lean towards the flesh. This is the role of a Christian reader, a clean animal that has a divided hoof and chews the cud.

However, our approach has been to delay making judgments and to consume all kinds of information without discrimination. Or even worse, by making misguided judgments, we have rejected the better aspects and accepted the worse aspects of these authors. And after doing so, we have attributed the title and authority of their sainthood to those very parts that are worse – a title they have earned for their better parts and for the Spirit only, but not for their free will or flesh.

SECTION 11: ERASMUS' CONFUSION AND ADVICE IS SOMEWHAT ACKNOWLEDGED BUT NEEDS IMPROVEMENT.

So, what should we do? The Church is a hidden community, and the saints are not yet revealed. What and whom should we believe? Or as you cleverly argue, who will assure us? How will we test their spirit? If you consider education, there are knowledgeable people on both sides. If you consider their lives, there are sinners on both sides. If you consider Scripture, both parties embrace it passionately. The dispute is not so much about Scripture (which is still not entirely clear) but about its interpretation. Furthermore, on both sides, there are people who, if they don't support their cause with numbers, education, or dignity, they certainly don't support it with their scarcity, ignorance, or lowliness. The issue remains uncertain, and the debate is still in the hands of the judge.

It seems that the most prudent course of action would be for us to collectively adopt a skeptical stance, unless we prefer to follow your excellent example: those who claim to be in such a state of doubt that it allows you to declare that you are still seeking and learning the truth, leaning towards the side that supports free will, only until the truth reveals itself.

In response to this, I would say, "What you mention is true, but it's not the entire truth." We won't judge the spirits based on the education, lifestyle, intelligence, number, status, ignorance, simplicity, scarcity, or insignificance of those involved in the debate. I also don't agree with those who claim to have the Spirit as their refuge. This year, I've had a tough battle with fanatics who interpret the Scriptures according to their own spirit, and I'm still fighting it. I've even criticized the Pope himself on this matter. In his realm, it's widely believed and accepted that "the Scriptures are obscure and ambiguous" and that "we must seek the interpreting spirit from the Apostolic See of Rome." This is a dangerous belief, as it has led ungodly people to elevate themselves above the Scriptures and create whatever they want - until eventually, the Scriptures were completely disregarded, and we ended up believing and teaching nothing but the delusions of madmen. In short, this belief is not a human invention but a poisonous idea introduced by the devil himself.

SECTION 12: THERE ARE TWO COURTS FOR THE SPIRITS OF MEN; ONE IS PRIVATE, AND THE OTHER IS PUBLIC.

Now, let's talk about how we should judge the spirits of people. There are two types of judgment: private and public. The private judgment is an internal process where a person who has been enlightened by the Holy Spirit or has received a special gift from God judges and discerns the beliefs and thoughts of others for their own personal salvation. This judgment is done with great certainty.

The Apostle talks about this judgment in 1 Corinthians 2:15: "He that is spiritual judges all things, and is judged by no man." This judgment relates to faith, and it's essential for every individual Christian. I've referred to it as 'the internal clarity of Holy Scripture.' Perhaps this is what those who responded to you meant when they said that 'everything must be determined by the judgment of the Spirit.' However, this judgment is only beneficial to ourselves and not to others. It's not the focus of our discussion here, and I'm sure no one doubts that this judgment is exactly what I've described it as.

So, there's another judgment that is external, and with it, we can judge the spirits and beliefs of everyone - not just for ourselves but for others and their salvation as well. This judgment is the most certain. It's the judgment of the public ministry, an external role that relies on the word. This responsibility mainly falls on the leaders of the people and those who preach the word. We use this judgment to strengthen the weak and refute those who argue against us. Earlier, I referred to this as "the external clearness of Holy Scripture." Our statement is: "Let all the spirits be tested in the presence of the Church, at the judgment of Scripture." It should be a fundamental principle, strongly upheld among Christians, that the Holy Scriptures are a spiritual light, much brighter than the sun, particularly in matters related to salvation or necessity.

SECTION 13: CLEARNESS OF SCRIPTURE PROVEN BY TESTIMONIES FROM THE OLD TESTAMENT

However, due to the harmful belief spread by the Sophists that "The Scriptures are obscure and ambiguous," I must first prove this very basic principle, which will be used to prove all the others and may seem absurd and impossible to philosophers.

Firstly, Moses states in Deuteronomy 17:8 that if any difficult issue arises, they must go to the place God has chosen for His name and consult the Priests, who must judge it according to the Lord's law. "According to the law of the Lord," he says. But how can they judge, unless the Lord's law, which the people must accept, is extremely clear? Otherwise, it would be enough to say, 'They shall judge according to their own spirit.' No, the truth is that in every civil government, all the cases of all the subjects are resolved by the laws. But how could they be resolved, unless the laws were very certain and acted like shining lights among the people? For if the laws were ambiguous and uncertain, not only would it be impossible for any cases to be decided, but there could be no definite standard of behavior.

Laws are created for this very purpose: to regulate the behavior of the people according to a specific model and to define the principles by which cases are to be determined. That which is to be the standard and measure of other things should be measured by the surest and clearest of all things, and that is the law. Now, this clarity and certainty in their laws are both necessary and also freely given to the whole world as a divine gift. If this is the case in secular governments (which deal with temporal matters), then how is it possible that God would not have granted laws and rules of even greater clarity and certainty to His Christian people (His chosen ones) – laws and rules by which to guide their own hearts and lives individually, and to resolve all their cases since He wants His children to disregard temporal matters?

So, "if God clothes the grass, which is here today and gone tomorrow, how much more will He clothe us?" Let's continue to counter this harmful idea from the Sophists with Scripture. Psalm 19:8 says, "The commandment of the Lord is pure, enlightening the eyes." I assume that something that enlightens the eyes is neither obscure nor ambiguous. Similarly, Psalm 119:130 says, "The unfolding of your words gives light; it imparts understanding to the simple." Here, the words of God are described as 'a door,' 'something wide open' - exposed for everyone to see and providing enlightenment even to the inexperienced.

Isaiah 8:20 directs all questions "to the law and to the testimony," warning that we will be denied the light of the morning if we don't follow this guidance. In Malachi 2:7, we are instructed to seek the law from the mouth of the Priest, as he is the messenger of the Lord of Hosts. A messenger or ambassador of the Lord would be quite ineffective if he speaks ambiguously and unclearly, leaving both himself and the people confused about the message.

Throughout the Old Testament, and particularly in Psalm 119, Scripture is frequently praised for being a certain and clear light in and of itself. So, the clarity of the scripture is celebrated like this: "Your word is a lamp to my feet, and a light to my paths," (v. 105). It doesn't just say, 'only your Spirit is a lamp to my feet,' but it also assigns its role to the Spirit, saying, "your good Spirit shall guide me in the right direction." That's why it's called both a 'way' and 'a path,' probably because of its incredible certainty.

SECTION 14: THE CLARITY OF SCRIPTURE IS PROVEN BY TESTIMONIES FROM THE NEW TESTAMENT.

Now let's look at the New Testament. Paul says in Romans 1:2 that the Gospel was promised by the law and the Prophets in the Holy Scriptures. And in Romans 3:21, he says that the righteousness of faith was witnessed by the law and the Prophets. But what kind of witnessing would this be if it was unclear? No, Paul not only refers to the Gospel as 'the word of light' and 'the gospel of clarity' in all his letters, but he does so deliberately and with many words in 2 Corinthians 3 and 4. There, he confidently discusses the clarity of both Moses and Christ.

Peter also says in 2 Peter 1:19, "We have a very sure word of prophecy; to which you do well to pay attention, as to a light that shines in a dark place." Here, Peter considers the word of God as a clear lamp, and everything else as darkness. So, why would we consider it obscure and dark? Christ often calls himself "the light of the world" and John the Baptist "a burning and shining light" — not because of their holy lives, but because of the word. Similarly, Paul calls the Philippians "bright lights of the world" and says it's "because you hold fast to the word of life." Without the word, life is uncertain and unclear.

So, what are the Apostles doing when they use the Scriptures to support their teachings? Are they trying to make things more confusing for us by adding more uncertainty? Or are they trying to confirm something more familiar with something less familiar? What is Jesus doing in John 5:39 when he tells the Jews to study the Scriptures because they testify about him? Is he trying to make them doubt their faith in him? And what about those people in Acts 18:2 who, after hearing Paul, read the Scriptures day and night to see if what he said was true? Don't all these examples show that the Apostles, as well as Jesus himself, refer to the Scriptures as the clearest evidence for the truth of their teachings? So why do we portray them as unclear?

I'd like to know if these words from the Scripture are unclear or ambiguous: "God created the heavens and the earth;" and "the word became flesh;" and all those statements that the whole world has accepted as essential beliefs. And where did they get these beliefs from, if not from the Scriptures? And what about those who continue to preach today? Are they interpreting and explaining the Scriptures?

If the Scripture they claim is unclear, then who can assure us that even this claim is certain? Do we need another new explanation? And who will provide that? At this rate, we'll have an endless chain of explanations. In short, if Scripture is unclear or doubtful, why did God bother to reveal it to us from heaven? Aren't we already unclear and ambiguous enough without having our confusion and uncertainty increased by heavenly revelations? What will happen to the Apostle's statement, "All Scripture, given by inspiration from God, is useful for teaching, for correcting, and for convincing?" (2 Tim 3:16) No, it's completely useless, Paul! And what you attribute to Scripture must be sought from the Church Fathers, who have been accepted for many generations, and from the Roman see! Therefore, you must take back your statement to Titus, that "a bishop must be strong in sound doctrine, so he can encourage others and refute those who oppose the truth, and silence foolish talkers and deceivers." How can he be strong if you give him unclear Scriptures - that is, weak weapons and a flimsy sword? Christ must also take back his own words, who falsely promises us, "I will give you a mouth and wisdom, which all your adversaries will not be able to resist." How can they not resist if we fight against them with unclear and uncertain weapons? Why do you, Erasmus, prescribe a form of Christianity to us if the Scriptures are unclear to you?

But I think I've been tiresome, even to those who aren't easily bothered, by taking so long to address a proposition that is quite obvious. But it was necessary to counter that bold and disrespectful claim, "The Scriptures are obscure," so that you, my dear Erasmus, could also see what you're saying when you deny that the Scripture is entirely clear. You must agree with me that all the saints you mention are much less clear. For who will assure us of their clarity if you claim the Scriptures are obscure? So, those who deny that the Scriptures are extremely clear and evident leave us with nothing but darkness.

SECTION 15: THE CONCLUSION - IF THE DOCTRINE OF FREE WILL IS OBSCURE, IT'S NOT IN SCRIPTURE.

But you might say, "This doesn't concern me; I don't claim that the Scriptures are obscure on all subjects (for who would be crazy enough to say that?); but only on this and similar topics." My response is that I'm not arguing against you alone, but against all who share your opinion. And specifically against you, I assert that I won't allow any part of Scripture to be called obscure. The quote I used from Peter still applies here, that "the word of God is a lamp shining for us in a dark place." Now, if there's a part of this lamp that doesn't shine, it becomes part of the darkness rather than the lamp itself. Christ hasn't enlightened us only to intentionally leave some part of his word dark while commanding us to pay attention to it. It would be pointless for him to command us to pay attention if it doesn't shine.

So, if the doctrine of Free Will is obscure or ambiguous, it doesn't belong to Christians and the Scriptures, and should be completely abandoned and considered among those fables that Paul criticizes Christians for arguing about.

If this belief belongs to Christians and the Scriptures, then it should be clear, open, and evident, just like all the other aspects of the faith, which are very clear. All the beliefs that Christians accept should not only be certain to themselves, but also defended against the attacks of others with such clear and obvious Scriptures that they prevent anyone from having the power to argue against them. As Christ says in his promise, "I will give you a mouth and wisdom, which all your adversaries shall not be able to resist." If our argument in support of this belief is so weak that our opponents can resist it, then what Christ says is false: that no adversary can resist our argument. So either we will encounter no opponents while defending the belief in free will (which would be the case if it doesn't belong to us); or if it does belong to us, then we will have opponents, but they will be unable to resist us.

SECTION 16: MEANING AND EXAMPLES OF THE PROMISE, 'ALL YOUR ADVERSARIES SHALL NOT BE ABLE TO RESIST.'

However, this inability of the adversaries to resist (since we're discussing it here) doesn't mean they are forced to abandon their own mindset or be persuaded to either confess or remain silent. Who would force someone unwilling to believe, admit their mistake, or stay quiet? Augustine asks, "What is more talkative than vanity?" But their mouths are shut so tightly that they have nothing to say in response. Even if they do say a lot, common sense tells us that they're not really saying anything meaningful. This is best demonstrated through examples.

When Christ silenced the Sadducees by quoting Scripture (Matthew 22:23-32) and proving the resurrection of the dead using Moses' words (Exodus 3:6), "I am the God of Abraham," "He is not the God of the dead, but of the living" – they couldn't argue or respond. But did they change their opinion? And how many times did he prove the Pharisees wrong using clear Scriptures and arguments, so that the people saw them as defeated and even they themselves knew it? Yet, his opponents persisted.

In Acts 7, Stephen spoke so powerfully, as Luke describes, that "they were not able to resist the wisdom and the Spirit which spoke in him." But what did they do? Did they give in? Not at all. Ashamed of being defeated and unable to fight back, they became furious. Closing their eyes and ears, they brought false witnesses against him (Acts 6:10-14). Look at how he stands before the council and proves his adversaries wrong!

In this passage, the author discusses the various blessings that God had given to the people since their beginning. They also argue that God never specifically commanded the construction of a Temple in his name. This point was a significant matter of debate, as the author was accused of making such a claim. Eventually, they acknowledge that a Temple was indeed built in God's honor during the time of Solomon.

However, he weakens the impact of his concession by adding, "Nevertheless, the Most High does not live in temples made by human hands." To support this, he quotes the final chapter of the Prophet Isaiah, "What kind of house will you build for me?" (Isa 66:1). So, tell me, what could they argue against such clear Scripture? Yet, they were not swayed by it and remained firm in their own beliefs. This leads him to criticize them as well: "You who are uncircumcised in heart and ears, you always resist the Holy Spirit." 'They resist,' he says – even though, in reality, they were unable to resist.

Now let's consider the people of our time, like when John Huss debates against the Pope, using Matthew 16:18 and so on. "The gates of hell will not overcome my Church." (Are these words unclear or ambiguous?)

However, the Pope and his supporters are indeed overcome by the gates of hell, as they are widely known for their blatant impiety and wickedness throughout the world. (Is this still unclear?) Therefore, the Pope and his followers are not the Church that Christ refers to. So, what could they say against him, or how could they stand up to the mouth that Christ had given him? Yet, they did oppose him and continued to do so until they burned him. They were far from changing their minds.

Christ doesn't hide this fact when he says, "the adversaries shall not be able to resist." He calls them adversaries, which means they will resist. If they didn't resist, they wouldn't be adversaries but friends. And yet, they won't be able to resist. What does this mean, if not to say that even though they resist, they won't be able to succeed in their resistance?

SECTION 17: WE MUST ACCEPT THIS KIND OF VICTORY. OUR OPPONENT WILL NOT ADMIT DEFEAT.

If we can effectively refute the concept of free will in a way that our adversaries cannot argue against - even if they maintain their own beliefs and stubbornly resist - then we have done enough. I have experienced time and time again that no one wants to be defeated. As Quintilian said, "there is no one who would not rather seem to know, than to be a learner." We often hear people say things like, "I want to learn; I'm open to being taught; and when taught better things, I want to follow them. I'm human; I can make mistakes." The truth is, people use these phrases because they provide a cover of humility, allowing them to confidently say, "I'm not convinced; I don't understand him; he's twisting the Scriptures; he's stubborn" - all while knowing that no one would suspect such humble individuals of being stubborn in their resistance to the truth or of attacking the truth once they recognize it.

So then, it shouldn't be blamed on their stubbornness that they maintain their old mindset; instead, it should be attributed to the unclear and vague arguments they face. This was also the behavior of the Greek philosophers, so that none of them would seem to give in to another, even if clearly defeated, they started to question fundamental principles, as Aristotle mentioned.

In the meantime, we kindly convince ourselves and others that there are many good people in the world who would be willing to accept the truth if they only had a teacher who could explain things clearly to them. And we shouldn't assume that so many educated people, throughout so many generations, have been mistaken or that they haven't fully understood the truth. It's as if we don't know that the world is Satan's kingdom, where, in addition to the blindness that comes naturally with our human nature, malicious spirits have control over us, causing us to become even more blind – no longer held back by mere human ignorance, but by a darkness imposed on us by demons.

SECTION 18. WHY GREAT GENIUSES HAVE BEEN BLIND ABOUT FREE WILL: NAMELY, TO EXPOSE FREE WILL. BUT IT'S NO SURPRISE THAT THE NATURAL PERSON IS BLIND TO THE THINGS OF GOD.

"If the Scriptures are so clear, then why have highly intelligent people been blind to this topic for so many generations?"

I answer, they have been blind in order to praise and glorify Free Will. This way, the highly praised power that allows humans to focus on matters related to their eternal salvation – a power that neither sees what it sees nor hears what it hears (let alone understands or seeks these things) – can be revealed for what it truly is.

This relates to what Christ and his Evangelists often quote from Isaiah, "Hearing, you shall hear and shall not understand; and seeing, you shall see and shall not perceive" (Isaiah 6:9). What does this mean if not that free will, or the human heart, is so controlled by Satan that unless it is miraculously lifted up by the Spirit of God, it cannot see or hear those things that are so obvious and clear, even when they are right in front of our eyes and ears? This is the unfortunate and blind state of the human race.

Even the Evangelists themselves refer to this passage in Scripture, expressing their amazement that the Jews were not convinced by the works and words of Christ, which were undeniably powerful and persuasive. This truly implies that when left to our own devices, we as humans, even when seeing, do not truly see; and when hearing, we do not truly hear. How astonishing is that? As John says, "The light shines in darkness, and the darkness does not comprehend it" (John 1:5).

Can you believe this? Has anyone ever heard of such a thing? The light shines in the darkness, but the darkness remains and isn't transformed into light.

It's not surprising that highly intelligent people have been blind to divine matters for so many ages. In human affairs, it would be surprising. But in divine matters, it's more surprising if one or two people aren't blind. It's not surprising at all if everyone is blind without exception. After all, without the Spirit, the entire human race is nothing but the kingdom of the devil, as I've said before. It's a chaotic mess of darkness. That's why Paul refers to the devils as "the rulers of this darkness" and says in 1 Corinthians 2:8, "None of the princes of this world knew the wisdom of God!" What do you think he thought of everyone else when he claimed that the world's leaders were slaves to darkness? By "princes," he means the most important and influential people in the world, those whom you would call highly intelligent.

Why were all the Arians blind? Weren't there intelligent people among them? Why is Christ "foolishness" to the Gentiles? Aren't there intelligent people among the Gentiles? Why is he "a stumbling block" to the Jews? Haven't there been intelligent people among the Jews? "God knows the thoughts of the wise," says Paul, "for they are vain."

He wouldn't say "of men," as the Psalm itself states (Psa 94:11), but he specifically mentions 'the first and best among men,' so we can evaluate the rest of them based on these. I might discuss this topic more extensively later. For now, let's just establish that 'the Scriptures are very clear,' and that 'our beliefs can be defended so well by these that our opponents won't be able to resist.' Beliefs that can't be defended this way belong to others and not to Christians.

Now, if there are people who don't see this clarity and are blind or stumble in this bright light, then these individuals, assuming they are ungodly, demonstrate the immense majesty and power of Satan in humanity – so much so that they can't hear or understand even the clearest words of God. It's like someone being deceived by a magic trick into thinking the sun is a piece of unlit coal or that a stone is gold!

Assuming they are godly people, let's consider them among the elect who are led astray for a while, so that God's power may be demonstrated in us. Without this power, we can't see or do anything at all. It's not a weak intellect (as you complain) that prevents the words of God from being understood. In fact, nothing is more suited to understanding God's words than a weak intellect. This is because Christ came and sent his word for the weak and to the weak (Luke 5:31). What gets in the way is Satan's mischief, who sits and rules in our weakness, opposing the word of God. If it weren't for Satan's influence, the entire world of people would be converted by just one word of God, once heard; there would be no need for more.

SECTION 19: ERASMUS IS SHOWN TO ADMIT THAT SCRIPTURE IS CLEAR.

And why am I arguing for so long? Why don't we just end this debate with this introduction and judge you based on your own words, according to what Christ said, "By your words you shall be justified, and by your words you shall be condemned" (Matthew 12:37)? You claim that Scripture is not clear on this topic. And then, as if the judge's decision is on hold, you argue both sides of the question, presenting all the arguments for and against free will. This is all you're trying to achieve with your entire effort. That's why you chose to call this a "Diatribe" rather than an "Apophasis" or anything else: because you write with the intention of bringing all the evidence together without actually asserting anything.

If Scripture is not clear, then why are those whom you admire - that is, such a long line of highly educated people, whom the agreement of so many generations has approved even up to today - not only blind on this subject, but also reckless and foolish enough to define and assert free will from Scripture as if it were clear and straightforward?

You mentioned that most of these men are not only known for their exceptional understanding of the sacred writings but also for their pious lives. Some of them have even defended the doctrine of Christ through their writings and ultimately gave their lives for it. If you truly believe this, then you must also acknowledge that these advocates of free will are incredibly skilled in interpreting the Scriptures and have even shed their blood as a testament to Christ's teachings. If this is the case, they must have considered the Scripture to be clear. Otherwise, how could they be said to have such a remarkable understanding of the sacred writings? Moreover, it would be quite reckless and thoughtless of them to give their lives for something uncertain and obscure. This would not be the act of Christ's martyrs, but of devils.

Now, I ask you to consider and reflect on whether you think more weight should be given to the previous judgments of so many learned, orthodox, holy, and martyred individuals, as well as numerous theologians, universities, councils, bishops, and popes from both ancient and modern times—who have all believed the Scriptures to be clear and have confirmed their opinion through both their writings and their blood—than to your own singular judgment as a private individual, who denies the clarity of the Scriptures. This is especially important to consider if you have never shed a tear or sighed for the doctrine of Christ.

If you truly believe that these men were thinking correctly, then why not follow their example? If not, then why brag with such arrogance and a mouthful of words, as if you're trying to overpower me with a storm and flood of words? However, this actually backfires on you even more, while I remain safe and secure. Because at the same time, you attribute great foolishness and recklessness to so many great individuals when you write that they were highly skilled in the Scriptures, yet they expressed through their writing, life, and death, a belief that you still claim to be unclear and ambiguous. What is this, if not to make them extremely ignorant in knowledge and incredibly foolish in their claims? As someone who privately disdains them, I would never have given them such praise as you do, their public admirer.

SECTION 20: ERASMUS FACES A DILEMMA.

So here, I've got you in a tricky situation, or as they say, a "horned syllogism." One of these two statements you've made must be false: either "these men were worthy of admiration for their knowledge of the sacred writings, life, and martyrdom," or "the Scripture is not clear."

But since you insist on this point, that the Scripture is not clear (which is what you're trying to argue throughout your whole book), it seems that when you called them experts in Scripture and martyrs for Christ, you did it either as a joke or to flatter them. It definitely wasn't done seriously, but just to confuse the common people and to cause trouble for Luther by making his cause seem hateful and contemptible through empty words. However, I say that both of these claims are false. I assert, first, that the Scriptures are very clear; secondly, that those people, as far as they support the idea of free will, are very ignorant of the Scriptures; and thirdly, that they didn't make this claim with their lives or their deaths, but only with their writing - and they did that without really thinking about it.

So, I'll conclude this small debate like this. According to your own testimony, "Since the Scripture is unclear, nothing certain has been or can be determined about free will." "No evidence supporting free will has been shown by the lives of all people since the beginning of the world." This is what I argued earlier. Now, it's not part of Christian teaching to promote something that isn't supported by a single word in Scripture or demonstrated by a single fact from Scripture; instead, it belongs to the 'true stories' of Lucian. The only difference is that Lucian, who jokes about ridiculous subjects and does so knowingly, doesn't deceive or harm anyone.

However, our opponents seem to be going crazy on such a serious topic, one that even relates to eternal salvation, leading to the destruction of countless souls.

SECTION 21: LUTHER BELIEVES HE HAS ALREADY WON, BUT WILL CONTINUE.

In this way, I could have already resolved the entire debate about free will, especially since even my adversaries' testimony supports my position and contradicts their own. After all, there's no stronger evidence against someone than their own testimony against themselves. But, since Paul tells us to silence those who speak nonsense, let's get to the heart of the matter and address it in the order that Diatribe presents it. So, first, I'll refute the arguments made in favor of free will; second, I'll defend our own arguments that have been challenged; and finally, I'll stand up for God's grace in a direct confrontation with free will.

PART THREE
LUTHER REFUTES ERASMUS' ARGUMENTS IN FAVOR OF FREE WILL

SECTION 1: EXAMINING ERASMUS' DEFINITION OF FREE WILL

First, as I am obliged to do, I will start with your definition of free will, which goes like this:

"Furthermore, by Free Will, I mean the power of the human will, by which a person can choose to pursue things that lead to eternal salvation or turn away from them."

You wisely provide a simple definition here without elaborating on any parts of it, as others usually do. Perhaps you're worried about encountering more problems than one! So, I am forced to analyze the different aspects of it myself. Upon close examination, the concept being defined seems broader than the definition itself. Therefore, it could be considered an incomplete definition, as it does not fully encompass the concept being defined, according to the Sophists.

As I have mentioned before, free will belongs only to God. You might be able to attribute the concept of will to humans, but attributing free will to them in divine matters is going too far. This is because the term "free will" is generally understood as the ability to do whatever one pleases without being restricted by any laws or commands, especially when it comes to our relationship with God. You wouldn't call a slave free if they act under the command of their master. So, it's even less appropriate to call a person or an angel free when they live under complete subjection to God (not to mention sin and death), and can't even exist for a moment on their own strength.

Right away, at the very beginning of our discussion, we have a disagreement between the definition of the term and the definition of the thing itself. The word means one thing, but the thing itself is understood to be something else. It would be more accurate to call it a changeable will or a mutable will. This is how Augustine (and later, the Sophists) downplays the importance and virtue of the term "free," adding this negative aspect to it: they talk about the changeability of the free will. We should speak in this way to avoid misleading people with grand, empty, and showy words. Augustine also believes that we should use simple and straightforward language, following a set rule. In teaching, we need clear and precise speech, not exaggerated words and persuasive rhetoric.

SECTION 2: DEFINITION CONTINUED.

But, so that I don't seem to be arguing just for the sake of a word, I'll accept for now this misuse of terms, as significant and dangerous as it is, and allow "free" will to mean the same as "changeable" will. I'll also let Erasmus define "free will" as "a power of the human will," as if angels don't have it, since he only focuses on human free will in this work. Otherwise, the definition would be too narrow for the thing being defined.

I'll quickly go over the parts of the definition that are crucial to the topic. Some of these are quite clear, while others seem to avoid clarity, as if they're afraid of being exposed. However, a definition should be the simplest and most certain thing in the world; to define something vaguely is just like not defining it at all. The clear parts are: (1) a power of the human will; (2) by which a person is able; (3) to achieve eternal salvation. But those other phrases, 'to apply oneself;' and again, 'those things which lead;' and again, 'to turn oneself away;' — these are the words of someone who's trying to hide their true intentions. What are we supposed to understand by 'to apply oneself'? And 'to turn oneself away'? What do the words 'which lead to eternal salvation' really mean? Where are they trying to hide?

I can see that I'm dealing with a real master of confusion, like Scotus or Heraclitus, who makes me work twice as hard. First, I have to search for my opponent and try to find them in the dark, full of traps and with a racing heart (it's a bold and risky task); and if I don't find them, then I have to fight with imaginary enemies and waste my energy in the dark, all for nothing.

Secondly, if I manage to bring him into the light, then eventually, once I'm exhausted from the chase, I have to face him in a fair fight. By "a power of the human will," I assume it means an ability, skill, readiness, or suitability to make decisions, to accept or reject, to choose or despise, to approve or disapprove, and to carry out any other actions related to the human will. But I don't understand what this power "applying itself" and "turning itself away" means if it's not the actual act of deciding and rejecting, choosing and despising, approving and disapproving – in short, if it's not "the will performing its very function." So, we must imagine this power as something that comes between the will itself and its actions: a power that enables the will to carry out the acts of deciding and rejecting, and that brings forth these very acts. It's impossible to think of anything else in this context. If I'm wrong, blame the author who defines it, not me who's trying to understand his meaning. As the legal experts say, if someone speaks unclearly when they could speak more plainly, their words should be interpreted against them. And by the way, I wish I didn't have to deal with these modern thinkers and their complexities: we should be satisfied with speaking plainly so that we can teach and understand.

I guess the things that lead to eternal salvation are the words and works of God. These are presented to our free will, so we can either choose to follow them or turn away from them. By the words of God, I mean both the Law and the Gospel: the Law requires works, while the Gospel calls for faith. There's nothing else that leads to God's grace or eternal salvation, except for God's word and work - since grace, or the Spirit, is the very life we're led to by God's word and work.

SECTION 3: CONTINUING THE DEFINITION

Eternal life, or eternal salvation, is something that's beyond human understanding. As Paul quotes from Isaiah in 1 Corinthians 2:9, "No eye has seen, no ear has heard, and no human heart has imagined the things God has prepared for those who love him." This is also one of the main beliefs in our faith. When we confess our faith, we say, "and the life everlasting." And Paul explains in 1 Corinthians 2:10 how much free will can do when it comes to this belief: "God has revealed these things to us by his Spirit." It's like he's saying, 'If the Spirit hadn't shown us these things, no one would know or think about them; free will is far from being able to desire or strive for them.'

Think about your own experiences. What have the most brilliant minds among non-believers thought about life after death and the resurrection?

Isn't it true that the more brilliant people were, the more they found the idea of resurrection and eternal life ridiculous? You can't say that those philosophers and other Greeks, the ones who called Paul a babbler and accused him of introducing new gods when he taught these things in Athens, weren't intelligent. In Acts 26:4, Porcius Festus even calls Paul a madman for preaching eternal life. What does Pliny say about these things in his seventh book? What about Lucian, who was known for his wit? Were these men not smart?

No, even today, it's true for most people that the more intelligent and educated they are, the more they laugh at this idea and consider it a fable. They do this openly. As for their inner thoughts, unless someone is touched by the Holy Spirit, no one truly knows, believes in, or desires eternal salvation, even if they often talk or write about it. I wish that both you and I, my dear Erasmus, were free from this same mindset, as it's so rare to find someone who genuinely believes in this concept. Have I captured the essence of your definition?

SECTION 4: INFERENCES FROM ERASMUS' DEFINITION

So, according to Erasmus, free will is a power of the will that can, on its own, choose to accept or reject the word and work of God. Through this word and work, it is guided towards things that go beyond its understanding and thoughts.

But if we have the ability to choose and to reject, then we also have the ability to love and to hate. If we can love and hate, then we can, to some extent, follow the Law and believe in the Gospel. Because if you choose or reject something, it's impossible not to be able to do something towards it with that choice, even if you can't finish it due to someone else's interference. Now, since death, the cross, and all the world's evils are considered part of God's work leading to salvation, our free will must be able to choose even death and our own destruction. In fact, we can choose everything as long as we can choose God's word and work. For what else is there, above, below, within, or outside of God's word and work, except for God himself? And what's left for grace and the Holy Spirit? This clearly gives divine power to free will – since choosing the Law and the Gospel, rejecting sin, and embracing death are exclusive properties of divine virtue, as Paul teaches in several places.

Thus, it seems that no one since the time of the Pelagians has written more accurately about free will than Erasmus. As I mentioned before, free will is a term unique to God, and it represents divine perfection. However, until now, no one has attributed this divine power to free will, except for the Pelagians. Erasmus goes even further than the Pelagians by attributing divinity to half of free will. The Pelagians divide free will into two parts: the ability to discern and the ability to choose. They claim that one part belongs to the understanding and the other to the will, just like the Sophists do.

But Erasmus, only mentioning the power of choosing and not the power of discerning, seems to praise a kind of limited and incomplete free will. What do you think he would have done if he had to describe the entire concept of free will?

Yet, he even goes beyond the ancient philosophers. They haven't yet decided 'whether any substance can put itself into motion.' The Platonists and the Peripatetics have different opinions on this matter throughout their entire philosophies. But according to Erasmus, free will not only moves itself, but it also applies itself, by its own power, to things that are eternal and beyond its understanding. As a completely new and unique definer of free will, he surpasses ancient philosophers, Pelagians, Sophists, and everyone else! And that's not all: he even contradicts himself more than he does with others. He previously said that 'the human will is completely ineffective without grace.' Was he joking? But now, when he seriously defines it, he claims that the human will has the power to effectively apply itself to matters related to eternal salvation - that is, to things far beyond its capabilities. In this case, Erasmus even outdoes himself.

SECTION 5. ERASMUS' DEFINITION.

Do you see, my dear Erasmus (I assume unintentionally), how your definition reveals that you either don't understand these concepts at all or that you write about them carelessly and dismissively, without proving or supporting your claims?

As I've mentioned before, you seem to argue less and claim more for free will than any other advocate, because you don't fully describe free will, yet you attribute everything to it. The Sophists, or at least their founder Peter Lombard, have a more acceptable view when they say that free will is the ability to first distinguish good from evil, and then choose good or evil, depending on whether grace is present or absent. They completely agree with Augustine that free will, on its own, can only fall and has no power except to sin. That's why Augustine suggests it should be called "bond will" instead of "free will" in his second book against Julian.

However, you portray free will as having equal power on both sides, meaning it can, by its own strength and without grace, choose to do good or turn away from it. You don't realize how much power you're giving to free will by saying "it can apply itself!" In doing so, you're excluding the Holy Spirit and all its power as unnecessary. Your definition is therefore condemnable, even by the Sophists' standards. If they weren't so blinded by envy against me, they would criticize your book instead of mine. But since you're attacking me, everything you say is considered holy and catholic, even though you contradict both yourself and them. Such is the patience of the saints.

I'm not saying I agree with the Sophists' view on free will, but I think it's more tolerable than Erasmus' perspective because they come closer to the truth. However, they don't go as far as I do in saying that free will is basically non-existent. Even though they claim (especially the Master of the Sentences) that free will has no power on its own without grace, they still disagree with Erasmus. In fact, they seem to be arguing with themselves too, focusing more on debating words than seeking the truth, which is typical of Sophists.

Imagine if I were having a casual conversation with a reasonable Sophist about this topic, and I asked for their honest opinion on this idea:

'If someone told you that something is free when it can only lean towards one side (the bad side) by its own power, and it has the ability to lean towards the other side (the good side) but only with the help of something else, wouldn't you find that amusing?'

Based on this idea, I could argue that a stone or a tree trunk has free will because it can lean both up and down. However, it can only lean down by its own power, and it needs help from something else to lean up. So, as I've mentioned before, by twisting the meanings of words and language, we could end up saying things like 'no man is all men' or 'nothing is everything,' by referring to the thing itself in one case and to something else that might be related to it in another.

In this way, after countless debates, they argue that free will is only free by chance - meaning it can be made free by something else. However, the real question is about the freedom of the will in and of itself, and in its essence. If this question is answered, then all that remains for free will is an empty name, whether they like it or not.

The Sophists also make a mistake by attributing to free will the ability to distinguish between good and evil. They downplay the importance of regeneration and the renewal brought by the Holy Spirit, treating external support as a mere accessory to free will. I'll discuss this more later. But for now, let's move on from your definition and examine the arguments that are meant to support this hollow concept.

SECTION 6: ECCLESIASTICUS 15:15-18

The first argument comes from Wisdom 15:15-18: "The Lord created humans from the beginning and left them to their own devices. He gave them his commands and instructions. If you choose to follow his commandments and demonstrate your faithfulness, they will protect you. He has placed both fire and water before you; reach out and choose whichever you want. Before each person lies life and death, good and evil, and they will receive whichever they choose."

Even though I could justifiably dismiss this book, I'll accept it for now, so I don't waste my time getting caught up in a debate about the books included in the Hebrew canon (which you mock and criticize quite a bit) — comparing Solomon's Proverbs and the Love-song (as you sarcastically call it) with the two books of Esdras, Judith, the stories of Susannah and the Dragon, and Esther. However, they have included Esther in their canon, even though, in my opinion, it deserves to be left out more than the others. But I'll respond briefly using your own words: "the Scripture is unclear and vague in this passage." So, it doesn't prove anything for sure. And since we're arguing against it, I challenge you to find a passage that clearly explains what Freewill is and what it can do. Maybe you'll do this on the Greek calends. However, to avoid this task, you spend a lot of words beating around the bush and listing so many opinions on Freewill that you almost make Pelagius sound like a true believer.

Once again, you come up with four types of grace so that you can attribute some level of faith and charity even to non-Christian philosophers. You also create a threefold law of nature, works, and faith. This is a new idea that allows you to argue that the teachings of non-Christian philosophers align closely with the teachings of the Gospel. Furthermore, you refer to the verse in Psalm 4:6, "The light of your countenance has been marked upon us, Lord." This suggests that the knowledge of God's very presence (i.e., an act of faith) is available to those with blinded reason.

Now, any Christian who considers all these points might feel compelled to question whether you are joking around with Christian beliefs and practices. It's hard for me to believe that someone as knowledgeable as you, who has thoroughly examined our texts and remembered them so well, could be so mistaken. However, I'll hold back for now and wait for a more appropriate time to discuss this further. But please, Erasmus, don't keep taunting us with your "Who sees me?" questions. It's not safe to constantly play word games with everyone when it comes to such important matters.

SECTION 7: DIFFERENT VIEWS ON FREEWILL

You seem to create three different views on Freewill from just one. You consider it a harsh view that a person cannot will anything good without special grace - that they cannot start, continue, or complete anything good. However, you also find this view highly acceptable. It appeals to you because it allows people to have desire and effort, but doesn't give them any credit for their own abilities. The belief that Freewill can only lead to sin and that only grace can bring about goodness in us seems even harsher to you. But the harshest view of all is the one that claims Freewill is just an empty concept, and that God is responsible for both good and evil in us. It is against these last two views that you claim to be writing.

SECTION 8: ERASMUS' INCONSISTENCY WITH HIS DEFINITION

Do you even know what you're saying, Erasmus? You present these three views as if they belong to three separate groups of people. You don't realize that they're actually the same idea expressed in different ways, with some variations, by us - the same people who belong to one group. But let me point out your carelessness or lack of understanding and expose it.

I want to ask you, how does the definition of Freewill that you provided earlier align with this first view of yours, which you say is highly acceptable?

You mentioned earlier that Free Will is the power of the human will, allowing a person to choose good. But now you're saying and agreeing that a person can't choose good without grace. Your definition supports what your example contradicts, creating a contradiction in your concept of Free Will. So, you're both approving and disapproving our stance at the same time. In fact, you're contradicting yourself within the same argument. Don't you think it's good to choose things related to eternal salvation? That's what your definition of Free Will says, but if there's so much good in Free Will, then there's no need for grace to help us choose good. So, the Free Will you're defining is different from the Free Will you're defending, and it seems like you have two different versions of Free Will that contradict each other.

SECTION 9: THE ACCEPTABLE VIEWPOINT EXAMINED.

Now, let's set aside the Free Will from your definition and focus on the other version presented in your opinion. You agree that a person can't choose good without special grace. We're not discussing what God's grace can do right now, but what humans can do without grace. So, you're admitting that Free Will can't choose good. This is the same as saying it can't choose things related to eternal salvation, as you mentioned in your definition. In fact, you said earlier that the human will is so corrupted that it lost its freedom, is forced to serve sin, and can't improve itself. If I'm not mistaken, you claim that the Pelagians held this view. At this point, I don't think there's any way for you to escape this contradiction.

He is trapped and controlled by open words; in other words, the will, having lost its freedom, is forced into and held tightly in the service of sin. Oh, what a wonderful concept of free will, which, after losing its freedom, is declared by Erasmus himself to be a servant of sin! When Luther said this, it was considered the most absurd thing ever heard, and nothing more harmful could be published than this paradox. Diatribes must be written against him!

But maybe no one will believe me that Erasmus actually said these things. Just read this passage from Diatribe, and it will amaze you. I'm not too surprised. A person who doesn't take this topic seriously and isn't emotionally invested in the cause they're arguing for, but is instead detached from it and bored or repulsed by it, can't help but say ridiculous, inconsistent, and contradictory things here and there while making their case. They're like a drunk or sleeping person who mumbles "yes" and "no" as they hear different sounds. That's why rhetoricians demand that an advocate has passion, and theology needs even more emotion from its champion, making them alert, perceptive, focused, reflective, and determined.

SECTION 10: THE ACCEPTABLE OPINION FURTHER CONSIDERED.

If free will, without grace and having lost its freedom, is forced to serve sin and cannot desire good, then I'd like to know what kind of desire and effort this first and approvable opinion leaves for a person? It can't be a good desire or good effort because they can't desire good, as the opinion states and as you've agreed. Therefore, only evil desire and evil effort remain, which, now that freedom is lost, are forced to serve sin. And what does it mean when they say, "This opinion leaves desire and effort, but it doesn't leave that which can be attributed to a person's own abilities?"

Who can understand this? If desire and effort are left to free will, then why shouldn't they be attributed to it? If they aren't attributed to free will, then how can they be left to it? Are these desires and efforts, which exist before grace, left to the grace that is yet to come and not to free will? This means that they are both left and not left to free will at the same time. If these aren't contradictions or even absurdities, I don't know what is.

SECTION 11: FREE WILL IS NOT "A NEUTRAL POWER OF THE WILL."

Maybe Diatribe is imagining that there's something between being able to will good and not being able to will good, which is just the power of willing, separate from any consideration of good or evil. In this way, we can avoid the pitfalls through a kind of logical cleverness. We claim that in a person's will, there's a certain power of willing that can't incline toward good without grace, but also doesn't directly will only evil without grace. It's a pure and simple power of willing that can be turned upward toward good by grace and downward toward evil by sin. But then, what happens to the statement that 'having lost its freedom, it is forced to serve sin?' Where is the 'desire and effort' that is left? Where is the power to apply oneself to things related to eternal salvation? That power to apply oneself to salvation can't be just an abstract power of willing unless salvation itself is considered nothing.

Moreover, desire and effort can't be just a power of willing, since desire must lean and strive toward something and can't be directed toward nothing or remain inactive. In short, no matter where Diatribe tries to go, she can't escape contradictions and conflicting statements. Even free will itself isn't as trapped as Diatribe, who tries to defend it. She gets so tangled up in her attempts to give freedom to the will that she ends up bound with unbreakable chains, along with her freed servant.

On the other hand, the idea that humans have a middle ground of simply willing things is just a made-up concept in logic, and those who claim it exists can't prove it. This idea comes from not understanding things and focusing too much on words, as if the will must be a real thing just because we talk about it. There are many such false ideas created by Sophists. The truth is more like what Christ says: "He who is not with me is against me." He doesn't say, 'He who is not with me, nor against me, but in the middle.' Because if God is within us, then Satan is not, and we only have the will to do good. If God is not present, then Satan is, and our will is only directed towards evil. Neither God nor Satan allows us to have a neutral will – as you correctly pointed out, having lost our freedom, we are forced to serve sin, meaning we desire and commit sinful acts.

It's clear that Diatribe has been backed into a corner without realizing it, as the powerful truth has made their argument look foolish. They've unintentionally supported our point and argued against themselves. This is what happens when "free will" tries to do something good – by opposing evil, it actually ends up doing more harm and working against good. So, Diatribe's argument is as effective as "free will" itself. In fact, the entire Diatribe is just a great example of "free will" in action, as it tries to defend its position but ends up condemning itself and looking foolish.

SECTION 12: NOW LET'S COMPARE THE FIRST OPINION WITH THE OTHER TWO.

The first opinion, when considered on its own, denies that humans can will anything good, yet it still claims that some form of desire exists within us, even if it's not our own. Let's see how this opinion stacks up against the other two.

The second view is more severe, stating that free will only has the power to commit sin. This is actually Augustine's opinion, which he expresses in many places, particularly in his treatise on the Letter and Spirit (I believe it's in the fourth or fifth chapter). He uses these exact words:

"The third view is the harshest of all, claiming that free will is just an empty term, and that everything we do is inevitably under the control of sin." Diatribe argues against these last two opinions. Now, I admit that I might not be fluent enough in German or Latin to clearly explain the subject matter. However, I swear to God that I intended to convey the same meaning in these last two opinions as I did in the first one. I also believe that Augustine meant the same thing, and I understand his words to support the first opinion.

In my opinion, the three views presented by Diatribe actually represent the same idea that I have put forward. Once it's agreed that free will, having lost its freedom, is forced to serve sin and has no power to desire anything good, I can only understand these statements to mean that free will is just an empty phrase, since the essence behind the term has been lost. My understanding of grammar tells me that lost freedom is not freedom at all, and to call something "freedom" when it has no freedom is just giving it an empty label. If I'm wrong here, I invite anyone who can to correct me. If my words are unclear or confusing, I ask anyone who can to clarify and support them. I can't call lost health "health," and if I were to attribute such a quality to a sick person, what have I given them but a meaningless label?

Enough with such absurd statements! How can we tolerate this misuse of language where we claim that humans have free will, yet simultaneously say that they've lost their freedom, are forced into sin, and can't desire anything good? These phrases contradict common sense and completely undermine the purpose of communication. Diatribe is the one to blame here, not us. She carelessly throws out her own words as if she's asleep, not paying attention to what others are saying. She doesn't think about the implications and impact of declaring that humans have lost their freedom, are forced to serve sin, and can't do any good. If she were more alert and attentive, she'd realize that these three opinions, which she distinguishes and opposes, actually mean the same thing. A person who has lost their freedom, is forced to serve sin, and can't desire good – what can we conclude about them other than they only commit sin and desire evil? Even the Sophists would agree with this conclusion through their sophisticated arguments. So, Diatribe is quite misguided in supporting the first opinion while rejecting the other two, which are essentially the same thing. Moreover, she contradicts herself and supports my views in the same argument.

SECTION 13: ECCLESIASTICUS 15:14-18 REVISITED AND EXPLAINED.

Now, let's get back to the passage in Ecclesiasticus and compare the first opinion, which you claim is acceptable, to it, just as we did with the other two opinions. The first opinion states that 'free will cannot desire good.' The passage from Ecclesiasticus is cited to prove that 'free will is nothing and can do nothing.' So, the opinion that's supposed to be supported by Ecclesiasticus actually says one thing, while the passage is used to confirm something else. It's like someone trying to prove that Christ is the Messiah by quoting a passage that shows

Pontius Pilate was the Governor of Syria, or something else entirely unrelated.

Your argument for free will here is not very convincing, not to mention what I've already addressed. There's nothing clearly and certainly stated or proven about what free will is and what it can do. But let's take a closer look at this whole passage.

First, it says, "God created man in the beginning." Here, it talks about the creation of man, but it doesn't mention anything about free will or precepts. Then it continues, "and left him in the hand of his own counsel." What do we have here? Is free will established here? There's still no mention of the precepts needed for free will, and we don't read anything about this in the story of man's creation. So, if the phrase "in the hand of his counsel" means anything, it must be more related to what we read in the first and second chapters of Genesis: "Man was made the ruler of the created things, so he could have free control over them," as Moses says, "Let us create man, and let him rule over the fish of the sea," and so on. Nothing else can be proven from these words. In that state, man had the power to interact with the creatures according to his own will since they were made to be under his control. And this is referred to as man's counsel, as opposed to God's counsel. But after stating that man was made the ruler and left in the hand of his own counsel, it continues: "He added his own commands and precepts."

What did he add them to? Well, to the counsel and will of man, and in addition to the establishment of man's rule over the other creatures.

Through these rules, God removed human control over a part of His creation (for example, the tree of knowledge of good and evil) and preferred that it should not be free. After mentioning the addition of rules, the focus shifts to human will towards God and divine matters.

"If you are willing to follow the commandments, they will protect you," and so on. From this point, 'if you are willing,' the issue of free will begins. We can learn from the Preacher that humans are caught between two realms. In one realm, people are guided by their own will and advice, without any rules or commands from God. This applies to their interactions with lesser creatures. Here, humans have power and control, having been left to their own devices. It's not that God doesn't work with them in this realm, but rather that He allows them to freely use the creatures according to their own will, without limiting them through laws or commands. To make a comparison, you could say, 'The Gospel has left us to our own devices to rule over the creatures and use them as we wish; but Moses and the Pope have not allowed us this freedom, instead restricting us with laws and subjecting us to their wills.'

In the other realm, humans are not left to their own devices but are guided and led by the will and advice of God. So, while in their own realm they are guided by their own will without the rules of another, in God's realm they are guided by the rules of another, without their own will. This is what the Preacher confirms when he says, "He added rules and commands. If you will," and so on.

SECTION 14: ECCLESIASTICUS DOESN'T NECESSARILY SUPPORT THE IDEA OF FREE WILL.

If my interpretation of this passage from Ecclesiasticus is correct, then it actually argues against free will, since it emphasizes that humans are subject to God's will and not their own. However, if my interpretation isn't entirely clear, I've at least shown that this passage can't be used to support the idea of free will, as it can be interpreted in a completely different way.

For example, as I mentioned earlier, our interpretation is not only reasonable but also consistent with the overall message of the Bible. On the other hand, the interpretation supporting free will contradicts the rest of the Bible and is based solely on this one passage. Therefore, we confidently maintain our understanding of the passage, which denies free will, until those who argue for free will can provide a more convincing and consistent interpretation.

So when the Preacher says, "If you are willing to keep the commandments, and to maintain acceptable faith, they shall preserve you" — I don't see how this proves the existence of free will. The verb is in the conditional mood ('If you will'); which doesn't make a definite statement. Here are some examples: 'If the devil is God, he is worthy to be worshipped,' 'If a donkey flies, it has wings,' 'If the will is free, grace is nothing.' If the Preacher wanted to assert the freedom of the will, he should have said, 'Man can keep the commandments of God;' or, 'Man has the power to keep the commandments.'

SECTION 15: WHAT IS MEANT BY "IF YOU WILL," ETC.

But Diatribe argues that by saying, "If you will keep," the Preacher suggests that there is a will in humans to both keep and not keep the commandments. Diatribe asks, 'What's the point in saying to someone who has no will, 'If you will'? Wouldn't it be ridiculous to say to a blind person, 'If you will see, you will find a treasure?' Or, to a deaf person, 'If you will hear, I will tell you a nice story?' This would only be mocking their misfortune.

I respond that these are the arguments of human reason, which tends to spout a lot of such "wise" sayings. Now I have to argue not only with the Preacher but also with human reason about a conclusion. That lady interprets the Scriptures of God based on her own assumptions and logic, pulling them in any direction she wants. I will gladly and confidently take on this task because I know that she only talks nonsense, especially when she tries to show her wisdom on sacred matters.

Now, if I were to ask how it's proven or how it follows that humans have free will - as often as it's said, "If you will," "if you will do," "if you will hear" - Diatribe would say it's because the nature of words and the way people speak seem to require it. So, she measures God's words and actions based on human experiences and customs. What could be more misguided than this, when one is earthly and the other is heavenly? In doing so, she reveals her foolishness, assuming that God only thinks and acts like humans.

But what if I were to argue that even among humans, the nature of words and the way we speak doesn't always make those who can't comply with a demand seem ridiculous when they hear phrases like "If you will," "if you will do," or "if you will hear"? How often do parents playfully challenge their children by asking them to come or do something, just to show how incapable they are and to encourage them to ask for help? How often does a wise doctor tell their stubborn patient to do or avoid things that are impossible or harmful, just to help them realize their illness or weakness through self-examination, which couldn't be achieved any other way? And how common are words of insult and provocation, used to show friends or enemies what they can and can't do?

I bring up these examples to demonstrate to human reason how foolish Diatribe is in applying her conclusions to the Scriptures, and how blind she is not to see that these conclusions don't always hold true, even in human words and actions.

However, if she occasionally sees these predictions come true, she hastily jumps to conclusions and claims that they generally occur in all human and divine forms of speech. In this way, she turns a specific instance into a universal rule, as is typical of her wisdom.

SECTION 16: THE PURPOSE OF SUCH FORMS OF ADDRESS.

Now, God interacts with us like a father does with his children, demonstrating our powerlessness, which we are unaware of, or like a trustworthy doctor who reveals our illness to us. Alternatively, he challenges us as his adversaries who arrogantly oppose his advice, presenting laws to us (the most persuasive method) by saying, "do, hear, keep," or "if you hear, if you are willing, if you do." Can we then conclude that we have free will, or else God is mocking us? Isn't the more accurate conclusion that God is testing us to see if we are friends or foes? If we are his friends, he can guide us to recognize our powerlessness through the law; but if we are prideful enemies, then he can rightfully and deservedly mock and ridicule us. This is why God provides laws, as Paul teaches. Human nature is so blind that it doesn't recognize its own abilities or, more accurately, its own sickness. Moreover, it is so arrogant that it believes it knows and can do everything.

Now, God has no better way to address this pride and ignorance than by presenting his law, which I will discuss more in the appropriate place. For now, let's just take a small taste of this topic to refute this foolish, worldly wisdom: "If you will - therefore the will is free." Diatribe assumes that humans are healthy and complete, just as they appear to others in everyday human interactions. So, she argues that people would be mocked by phrases like "if you will," "if you will do," and "if you will hear," unless their will is free. However, Scripture tells us that humans are corrupt and enslaved, not only that, but also proud and dismissive of God, and unaware of their own corruption and captivity. So, Scripture uses these phrases to try to wake people up and make them realize, through their own experiences, how incapable they are of doing these things.

SECTION 17: DIATRIBE'S INSINCERITY IN HER ARGUMENT

Now, I'll take the offensive in this debate and ask, "If you truly believe, Madam Reason, that these conclusions are valid ('if you will - therefore you can will freely'), then why don't you follow them? You say in your approved opinion that Free Will cannot desire anything good. So, how can you then argue from this passage ('If you are willing to keep') that humans can both will freely and not will freely at the same time? Can sweet and bitter water flow from the same fountain (James 3:11)? Aren't you, in fact, mocking people even more by saying they can keep what they can't even want or desire? So, it seems that you don't actually believe this conclusion, 'If you will - therefore you can will freely,' even though you argue for it so passionately. Or perhaps, deep down, you don't really agree with the opinion that 'humans cannot desire good.' Reason is so entangled in its own conclusions and clever words that it doesn't even know what it's saying or what it's talking about.

Of course, unless the only way to defend Freewill is by using arguments that contradict and destroy each other (which is quite fitting for Freewill) - just like the Midianites who ended up killing each other while fighting against Gideon and God's people.

But let me discuss this further with you, wise Diatribe. The Preacher doesn't say, "If you have a desire or effort to keep, which isn't due to your own abilities;" - as you might interpret from his words. Instead, he says, "If you will keep the commandments, they will preserve you." Now, if we were to draw conclusions like you tend to do in your wisdom, we would conclude, "Therefore, humans can keep the commandments." And so, we would not only leave a little bit of desire or effort in humans, but we would attribute to them the full power and ability to keep the commandments. Otherwise, the Preacher would be mocking human misery by telling them to keep what he knows they cannot keep. It wouldn't be enough for humans to have just the desire and effort. Even then, the Preacher wouldn't avoid the suspicion of mockery: he must imply that humans have the ability to keep the commandments.

But let's say this desire and effort of Freewill is something. What would we say to those Pelagians who, based on this passage, used to deny grace altogether and attributed everything to Freewill? No doubt, the Pelagians would have won if Diatribe's conclusion is accepted. Because the Preacher's words imply keeping the commandments, not just desiring or trying. Now, if you deny the Pelagians the conclusion of keeping, they will, in turn, more rightfully deny you the conclusion of trying. And if you take away complete Freewill from them, they will take away that little bit of it that you say remains - not allowing you to claim for a small part what you have denied to the whole.

So, whatever arguments you make against the Pelagians, who attribute complete free will to this passage, will be even more powerful when used against the tiny bit of desire that you consider to be free will. The Pelagians will also agree with us that if their view cannot be proven from this passage, then no other view can be proven from it either. For if we have to rely on inferences, then the Preacher's words actually support the Pelagians the most, as he specifically mentions complete obedience: "If you will keep the commandments." In fact, he also talks about faith: "If you will keep acceptable faith." So, by the same logic, we should have the power to maintain faith as well. However, this faith is a unique and rare gift from God, as Paul says.

In short, since there are so many different opinions supporting free will, and each one claims this passage from Ecclesiasticus as evidence, yet these opinions are diverse and contradictory - it must mean that they consider the Preacher's words to be inconsistent and conflicting with each other.

So, they can't prove anything from him. However, if we accept that argument, it only supports the Pelagians and goes against everyone else. This means it also goes against Diatribe, who is basically shooting herself in the foot here.

SECTION 18: CONCLUDES THAT ECCLESIASTICUS DOESN'T PROVE ANYTHING FOR FREEWILL, WHETHER IT'S TALKING ABOUT ADAM OR PEOPLE IN GENERAL.

But I want to reiterate my initial point: this passage from Ecclesiasticus doesn't support any of those who argue for Freewill; in fact, it opposes them all. That's because the idea that 'if you want to, then you can' just doesn't hold up. The real meaning behind passages like this is that they serve as a warning to people about their own limitations, which they might not realize or accept due to their ignorance and pride.

Now, I'm not just talking about the first man here, but any and every person. Although it doesn't really matter whether you interpret it as referring to the first man or anyone else. Even though the first man wasn't powerless because he had grace, God still clearly showed him through this command how powerless he would be without grace.

Now, if that man, who had the Spirit, was unable to choose good - that is, to choose obedience - when his will was still new and good was newly presented to him, because the Spirit didn't provide it, then what could we, who don't have the Spirit, do to achieve the good that we've lost? Therefore, it was demonstrated in that first man, through a terrible example meant to crush our pride, what our free will can accomplish when left on its own - even when continuously encouraged and increased by the Spirit of God. The first man couldn't attain a greater amount of the Spirit, of which he possessed the initial portion, but instead fell from having that initial portion. So how could we, in our fallen state, have the power to regain that initial portion that's been taken from us? This is especially true since Satan now rules over us with full power - the same Satan who brought down the first man with just a temptation, before he even ruled over him.

It would be impossible to argue more strongly against free will than by discussing this passage from Ecclesiasticus in relation to Adam's fall. However, I don't have space for such an in-depth discussion here, and perhaps the topic will come up elsewhere. For now, it's enough to show that the Preacher doesn't support free will in this passage (which its proponents consider to be their main evidence), and that phrases like "if you will," "if you will listen," and "if you will do" don't indicate what a person can do, but rather what they should do.

SECTION 19: GENESIS 4:7 RECONSIDERED

Another passage that the Diatribe brings up is from Genesis chapter 4, where the Lord says to Cain, "Sin's desire is for you, but you must rule over it." The Diatribe argues that this shows that the urges of the mind towards evil can be overcome and don't necessarily lead to sinning.

The statement that "the urges of the mind towards evil can be overcome" is unclear, but the general understanding and consequences of it, as well as the facts, lead us to interpret it like this: 'It is the ability of free will to conquer its own evil urges, and those urges don't force us to sin.' But why is it not mentioned here that this is not attributed to free will? What need do we have for the Spirit, Christ, or God if free will can overcome the urges of the mind towards evil? Also, what happened to the widely accepted idea that free will can't even desire good?

Here, however, victory over evil is attributed to a substance that doesn't want or desire good. The Diatribe's carelessness is extreme in this case. Let me explain the truth of the matter in a few words. As I've said before, expressions like these show people not what they can do, but what they should do. So, Cain is told that he should rule over sin and keep its desires under his control. But he couldn't do this, since he was already under Satan's control.

It's well-known that Hebrews often use the future tense to give commands, as in Exodus 20: "You shall not have any other gods," "You shall not kill," "You shall not commit adultery," and countless other examples. On the other hand, if we take these words literally, they would be promises from God, who cannot lie. In that case, no one would sin, and there would be no need for these commands.

In fact, the translator could have better conveyed the meaning here by saying, "Let sin's desire be subject to you, and you rule over it." Similarly, it should have been said to the woman, "Be subject to your husband, and let him rule over you." The fact that it wasn't said as a promise to Cain is clear because the opposite happened, and Cain did the opposite of what was commanded.

SECTION 20: DEUTERONOMY 30:19 CONSIDERED.

Your third passage is from Moses, where he says, "I have set before you the way of life and death; choose the good path," and so on. Diatribe asks, "What could be more clear? He gives people the freedom to choose."

My response is, how can you not see the obvious? I ask you, where does this freedom of choice come from? Just because Moses says "choose"? So, as soon as Moses says "choose," people automatically make the right choice? Once again, this would mean that the Spirit isn't necessary. And since you keep repeating the same arguments, let me also be allowed to say the same thing many times over. If we have free choice in our souls, then why has your agreeable opinion stated that free will cannot desire good? Can it choose without wanting to, or against its will? But let's hear your analogy.

It would be absurd to tell someone standing at a crossroads, "you see two paths; go down whichever you like," when only one is actually open. This is similar to what I mentioned earlier about the arguments of worldly reasoning. It believes that people are deceived by an impossible command, while we argue that they are encouraged and motivated by it to recognize their own powerlessness. So, we are indeed at this kind of crossroads, but only one path is available to us, or rather, no path is available. However, the law shows us how impossible it is for us to choose the path leading to good unless God grants us His Holy Spirit. The other path is wide and easy to follow if God allows us to walk down it. Therefore, without mockery and with all seriousness, we should tell someone standing at the crossroads, "choose either of the two paths as you please," if they either want to seem strong in their own eyes (despite being weak), or if they claim that neither path is closed off to them.

The words of the law are spoken not to confirm the power of the will, but to enlighten blind reasoning so that it may realize how insignificant its light is, and how insignificant the power of the will is.

"By the law is the knowledge of sin," says Paul. He doesn't claim that the law abolishes or avoids sin. The main purpose and power of the law is to provide knowledge, specifically about sin, not to display or grant any power. This knowledge isn't power itself, nor does it give power. Instead, it teaches and reveals that there is no power in that area, and it shows the extent of our weakness in that area. The knowledge of sin is essentially the knowledge of our weaknesses and wickedness. Paul doesn't say that the law brings knowledge of virtue or good; according to him, the law's only function is to make sin known.

This passage is where I got my answer that the words of the law teach and instruct people about what they should do, not what they can do. In other words, the law helps us understand our sins and not to assume that we have any power. So, whenever you bring up the words of the law, I'll respond with Paul's saying: "By the law is the knowledge of sin," not power in the will. Now, gather your larger Concordances and compile all the imperative verbs into one chaotic pile (as long as they're not words of promise, but words of demand and law), and I'll quickly show you that these always indicate not what people do or can do, but what they should do.

Grammar experts and even kids on the streets know that imperative verbs express what should be done, while indicative verbs declare what is done or can be done. So, why do you theologians, acting like you're in a second childhood, take a single imperative verb and foolishly assume it means an indicative verb? It's as if you think that as soon as something is commanded, it automatically becomes done or at least doable.

But we all know that many things can happen between the time something is ordered and when it actually takes place, even if it seems quite doable. There's a big difference between imperative and indicative verbs in everyday situations. And when the things being commanded are far more difficult or even impossible to achieve, you still try to turn imperatives into indicatives. You assume that as soon as the command is given, we can "do, keep, and choose" by our own power.

SECTION 21: PASSAGES FROM DEUT. 30, ETC. CONSIDERED.

In the fourth place, you bring up many similar verbs related to choosing, refusing, and keeping, such as "if you will keep," "if you will turn aside," "if you will choose," etc. from the third and thirtieth chapters of Deuteronomy. You argue that "All these expressions would be inappropriate if a person's will were not free to do good."

I respond, my dear Diatribe, you are quite unreasonable in using these verbs to support the idea of free will! You claimed to only prove desire and effort in free will, yet you didn't provide any passage that demonstrates such effort. Instead, you presented a series of passages that, if your conclusion were valid, would attribute 'a whole' to free will. So, let's distinguish between the words taken from Scripture and the conclusion that Diatribe has attached to them.

The words used are imperative and simply express what should be done. Moses doesn't say that you have the strength or power to choose, but only says 'choose, keep, do.' He gives commands to do, but he doesn't describe a person's ability to do them. However, the uneducated Diatribe adds the conclusion that humans can therefore do these things; otherwise, the commands would be pointless. To which I reply, 'Dear Diatribe, you're making a poor argument, and you haven't proven your conclusion. It's because you're blind and lazy that you believe this conclusion follows and has been proven.'

These commands, however, are not given without reason or in vain. Instead, they serve as lessons for a vain and proud person to learn about their own inability when they try to do what is commanded. So, your analogy doesn't make sense when you say:

'Otherwise, it would be like telling a person who is tied up and can only stretch out their arm to the left, "Look! You have a cup of excellent wine on your right and a cup of poison on your left: reach out your hand to whichever side you want."'

I get the feeling that you really enjoy using these similes. But you don't seem to realize that if your similes are accurate, they actually prove much more than you intended to prove. In fact, they prove something you deny and want to disprove: that free will can do everything. Throughout your entire argument, you seem to forget that you said 'free will can do nothing without grace,' and instead, you end up proving that 'free will can do everything without grace.' This is what you ultimately do with your consequences and similes. You make it seem like free will, on its own, can do the things that are said and commanded, or else these commands are pointless, ridiculous, and ill-timed. However, these are just old arguments from the Pelagians, which even the Sophists have rejected, and you yourself have condemned. In the meantime, your forgetfulness and poor memory show that you are completely unaware of the issue at hand and don't really care about it. What could be more embarrassing for a rhetorician than to constantly argue and prove things that are irrelevant to the main point, and even argue against their own position?

SECTION 22: HIS SCRIPTURES PROVE NOTHING; HIS ADDITIONS TO SCRIPTURE ARE TOO MUCH.

So, I'll say it again: the Scripture passages you've brought up are imperative words, meaning they don't prove or determine anything about human power. They simply prescribe certain actions to be taken or avoided. Your consequences (or additions) and similes, on the other hand, end up proving this (if they prove anything at all): that free will can do everything without grace.

This proposition, however, is not one that you have tried to prove, but have even denied. So, proofs of this kind are actually the strongest disproofs. Let me test now if I can wake Diatribe from her slumber. Imagine I argued like this: When Moses says, "choose life, and keep the commandment," unless a person can choose life and keep the commandment, it's absurd for Moses to demand this from people. With this argument, would I have proven that Free Will can't do anything good, or that it has tried but not on its own power? No, I would have proven through a bold comparison that either a person can choose life and keep the commandment (as they are told to do), or else Moses is a ridiculous teacher. But who would dare to call Moses a ridiculous teacher? Therefore, it follows that people can do what is commanded of them.

This is the way Diatribe consistently argues against her own thesis. She is supposed to maintain a position that shows a certain power of effort in Free Will. However, she is far from proving it and barely mentions it throughout her arguments. In fact, she ends up proving the opposite, making herself the ridiculous speaker and arguer everywhere.

Regarding the idea of it being ridiculous, it's similar to the example you gave - it's like asking a person whose right arm is tied up to stretch out their right hand when they can only stretch out their left. Now, would it be ridiculous if a person whose hands were both tied up were to arrogantly claim or ignorantly assume that they could do whatever they wanted on both sides of them? Asking such a person to stretch out their hand in any direction isn't meant to mock their captive state, but rather to expose their false belief in their own freedom and power, or to make them aware of their ignorance about their captivity and misery.

The Diatribe keeps presenting us with a fictional person who can either do as they're told or at least knows that they can't. But such a person doesn't exist. And if there were such a person, then it would indeed be true that either impossible tasks are absurdly demanded of them, or the Spirit of Christ is given in vain.

However, the Scripture describes a person who is not only bound, miserable, captive, sick, and dead, but also plagued by blindness (due to the influence of Satan, their ruler). This person believes they are free, happy, unshackled, capable, healthy, and alive. Satan knows that if people were aware of their own misery, he wouldn't be able to keep anyone under his control. That's because God would undoubtedly have compassion and help them as soon as they recognized their misery and cried out for assistance. God is praised throughout the Scripture for being close to those with a contrite heart. In Isaiah 61:1-3 and Luke 4:18, Christ even declares that He was sent into the world by God to preach the Gospel to the poor and heal the broken-hearted.

So, Satan's goal is to prevent people from realizing their own misery and to make them believe they have the ability to do everything that is commanded. On the other hand, Moses, the lawgiver, has the opposite goal: he wants to reveal people's misery through the law, so that they can recognize their own shortcomings, be prepared for grace, and be sent to Christ for salvation. The law's purpose, then, is not ridiculous, but extremely serious and necessary.

Those who understand these concepts can easily see that Diatribe's entire line of argument is flawed. She simply gathers a bunch of imperative verbs from the Scriptures, without understanding their meaning or purpose. Then, she adds her own assumptions and worldly comparisons, creating a confusing mess that ultimately supports her own argument and works against her.

So, it won't be necessary to continue going through her various proofs, since dismissing one of them dismisses them all, as they all rely on the same principle. However, I'll still mention some of them, just to show how her own arguments can be used against her.

SECTION 23: ISAIAH 1:19; 30:21; 45:20; 52:1-2, AND SOME OTHER PASSAGES CONSIDERED; THEY PROVE TOO MUCH; NO DISTINCTION BETWEEN LAW AND GOSPEL, ETC.

In Isaiah 1:19, we read, "If you are willing and obedient, you will eat the good of the land." Diatribe thinks it would have made more sense to say, 'If I am willing;' 'If I am unwilling;' assuming that our will is not free.

The response to this is clear from what has already been said. But what sense would it make to say, 'If I will, you shall eat of the good of the land?' Does Diatribe, in her great wisdom, think that we could enjoy the good of the land against God's will, or that it's something new and unusual for us to receive good only if He wills it?

Similarly, in Isaiah 30, we read, "If you seek, seek; turn, and come." Diatribe asks, 'What's the point of encouraging those who have no control over themselves? Isn't it like telling someone in chains to move in a certain direction?'

Instead, ask yourself, what's the point of quoting passages that don't prove anything on their own, but only by adding a consequence - that is, by twisting their meaning - do they give credit to the idea of free will? The goal was to prove that we have some sort of effort or ability, but that wasn't attributed to free will.

I would say the same about the testimony in Isaiah 45:20, "Assemble yourselves, and come; turn to me, and you shall be saved." And also in Isaiah 52:1-2, "Arise, arise, shake yourself from the dust, loose the chains from off your neck." Additionally, in Jeremiah 15:19, "If you will turn, I will turn you; and if you will separate the precious from the vile, you shall be as my mouth." But Malachi makes an even more evident mention of the effort of free will, and the grace that is prepared for those who make the effort. He says, "Turn to me, says the Lord of Hosts, and I will turn to you, says the Lord."

In these passages, our Diatribe doesn't reveal any difference at all between the words of the law and the words of the gospel. It's so blind and ignorant that it can't see which is the law and which is the gospel. Out of the entire book of Isaiah, it doesn't bring a single law word, except for that first one, 'If you have been willing.' All the other passages are made up of gospel words, which call the contrite and afflicted to take comfort from the offers of grace.

But Diatribe interprets these words as if they were about the law. And I ask, what good will someone do in theology or in the Scriptures if they haven't even gotten to the point of knowing what the Law and the Gospel are? Or if they do know, they don't care to observe the difference? Such a person must mix up everything - heaven and hell, life and death - and they won't make any effort to learn anything about Christ. Later, I'll give Diatribe a more thorough reminder on this subject.

Now, let's look at those words from Jeremiah and Malachi: "If you will turn," "I will turn you," and, "Turn to me, and I will turn to you." Does it follow that just because it says "Turn," you can actually turn? Does it follow that because it says, "Love the Lord your God with all your heart," you can actually love Him with all your heart? What's the conclusion from arguments like these, if not that free will doesn't need God's grace because it can do everything by its own power?

It makes much more sense to take the words just as they are: "If you have turned, I will also turn you," meaning "If you stop sinning, I will stop punishing." And if you lead a good life when you're converted, I will also do good for you and turn your captivity and your troubles.

However, these words do not imply that a person can turn to God by their own power, nor do they claim this. They simply state, "If you are converted," reminding people of what they should be. Once someone understands and sees this, they would seek the power they lack from a source where they could obtain it. That is, if Diatribe's Leviathan (her attachment and consequence, I mean) didn't interfere, saying, "It would be pointless to say, 'Turn,' unless a person could turn by their own power." The meaning and proof of this statement have been thoroughly discussed.

It's a result of confusion or sluggishness to think that free will is confirmed by phrases like "Turn," "If you will turn," and similar expressions, without realizing that the same logic would also apply to the statement, "You shall love the Lord your God with all your heart." The requirement in one case is equal to the command in the other. The love of God and all His commandments is no less necessary than our own conversion since loving God is our true transformation.

And yet, no one argues for free will based on the commandment of love. Instead, people argue for it from phrases like "If you are willing," "If you will hear," "Turn," and similar expressions. If free will isn't proven by the command to "Love the Lord your God with all your heart," then it certainly isn't proven by these other phrases, which either demand less or are less forceful than the command to love God.

So, whatever response is given to the command "Love God" that prevents us from concluding free will exists, the same response should be given to all other expressions of command or demand, also preventing the same conclusion. In other words, the command to love shows us what we should do, but it doesn't show the power of human will – what we can or cannot do. The same is true for all other expressions of demand.

It's clear that even the scholars, except for the Scotists and the Moderns, claim that humans cannot love God with their whole heart. From this, it follows that we can't fulfill any of the other commandments either since they all depend on this one, as Christ confirms in Matthew 22:40. Thus, it remains a valid conclusion, even based on the testimony of the scholastic doctors, that the words of the law don't prove the power of free will. Instead, they show what we should do and what we can't do.

SECTION 24: MALACHI 3:7 MORE SPECIFICALLY CONSIDERED.

However, our Diatribe goes even further into absurdity, not only inferring an indicative meaning from Zechariah's statement "Turn to me," but also claiming that it proves a power of effort in free will and grace prepared for those who make the effort.

Finally, she remembers her goal here. Using a new interpretation of grammar, she believes that "to turn" means the same as "to endeavor." So, the meaning is, "Turn to me," which means, "try to turn, and I will turn to you," or in other words, I will "try to turn" to you. In the end, she even attributes effort to God, perhaps intending to prepare grace for His efforts as well. If "to turn" signifies effort in one place, why not in all?

Furthermore, in that passage from Jeremiah, "If you separate the precious from the vile," she claims that not only is "endeavor" proven, but also "free choice" - something she previously taught us was lost and turned into a necessity for serving sin. So, you can see that Diatribe truly has a free will in her interpretations of Scripture, making words with the same form prove effort in one place and free choice in another, as she pleases.

But let's leave those empty arguments behind. The word "turn" has two main uses in Scripture: a legal one and an evangelical one. In its legal use, it demands and commands - requiring not just effort, but a complete change in one's life. Jeremiah often uses it this way, saying, "Turn every one from his evil way," and "Turn to the Lord," where it clearly involves obeying all the commandments. When used in an evangelical sense, it's a word of divine promise and comfort. In this case, nothing is demanded from us, but God's grace is offered to us. Examples of this usage can be found in Psalm 126: "When the Lord turns again the captivity of Zion," and Psalm 116, "Turn again, then, to your rest, O my soul!"

And so, Zechariah manages to include both types of preaching (law and grace) in a very concise summary. It's all about the law, and the essence of the law, when he says, "Return to me." It's about grace when he says, "I will return to you." Therefore, Freewill is proven by the saying, "Love the Lord" - or by any other specific law statement - to the same extent and no further than it is proven by this summary law phrase, "Turn." It is the responsibility of a wise reader of Scripture to recognize which words are related to the law and which are related to grace, so as not to mix them all up, like the misguided Sophists and this tiresome Diatribe.

SECTION 25: EZEKIEL 18:23 CONSIDERED

Now, let's look at how the author interprets that famous passage in Ezekiel 18, "As I live, says the Lord, I would not have the death of a sinner, but rather that he be converted and live." The author points out that this chapter repeatedly mentions phrases like "shall turn away," "has done," and "has wrought" in relation to both good and evil actions. Then, they ask, "Where then are those who deny that humans have any agency?"

What a great point they make! The author intended to prove that people have the desire and effort to make choices, but instead, they end up proving that free will is responsible for all actions, both good and evil. So, where does that leave those who argue for the necessity of grace and the Holy Spirit? The author's clever reasoning goes like this:

"Ezekiel says, If the wicked person turns away from their wickedness and does what is just and right, they shall live. Therefore, the wicked person can and will do so."

Ezekiel is suggesting what should be done, but the author interprets this as what is already being done or has been done. This introduces a new way of understanding language, where owing something is the same as having it, enacting a law is the same as performing it, and demanding something is the same as paying for it.

Next, the author focuses on the comforting words of the Gospel, "I would not have the death of a sinner," and gives it this interpretation: Does the holy Lord lament the death of his people, which he himself causes? If he doesn't want the death of a sinner, then it must be our own will that causes us to perish. But how can you blame someone who has no power to do anything, either good or evil?

Pelagius also argued that Free Will has not only the desire and effort, but also the complete power to fulfill and do everything. These consequences prove this power if they prove anything, as I mentioned earlier. And so, they argue just as strongly, if not more so, against Diatribe herself (who denies this power in Free Will and wants to prove effort only) as against us who deny Free Will altogether. But without focusing on her ignorance, I will explain the matter as it truly is.

SECTION 26: THE TRUE MEANING OF EZEKIEL 18:23 EXPLAINED.

Ezekiel 18:23 is a message of hope and comfort for poor, miserable sinners, saying, "I do not want the death of a sinner, but rather that they should turn from their ways and live." Similarly, Psalm 30:5 says, "For his anger lasts only a moment, but his favor lasts a lifetime." And Psalm 109:21 expresses, "How great is your mercy, Lord!" Also, Jeremiah 3:12 states, "Because I am merciful." And Jesus says in Matthew 11:28, "Come to me, all you who are weary and burdened, and I will give you rest." In Exodus 20:6, it says, "I show love to thousands who love me." In fact, more than half of the Scripture is filled with promises of grace, offering mercy, life, peace, and salvation to people.

What do these words of promise mean other than "I do not want the death of a sinner?" Isn't it the same thing to say, "I am merciful," as to say, "I am not angry," "I do not want to punish," "I do not want you to die," "I want to forgive you," "I want to spare you?" If these divine promises were not in the Scripture to lift up those whose consciences have been wounded by the sense of sin and fear of death and judgment, where would there be room for forgiveness or hope?

What sinner wouldn't lose hope? But just as Freewill isn't proven by other words of sympathy, promise, or comfort, it's not proven by this either: "I would not have the death of a sinner."

However, our Diatribe mixes up the difference between law words and words of promise, interpreting this passage from Ezekiel as a law word. It explains it like this: 'I would not have the death of a sinner; meaning, I don't want them to commit a deadly sin or become a sinner deserving death. Instead, I want them to turn away from their sin, if they've committed any, and live.' If it didn't explain it this way, then it wouldn't support their argument. But this interpretation completely undermines and takes away the powerful message of Ezekiel: 'I would not have the death of a sinner.' If we insist on reading and understanding the Scriptures like this, through our own ignorance, then it's no surprise they seem unclear and confusing.

Ezekiel doesn't say, 'I don't want a person to sin,' but rather 'I don't want the death of a sinner.' This clearly suggests that he's talking about the punishment for sin, which the sinner is experiencing because of their sin: that is, the fear of death. Indeed, he lifts up and comforts the sinner, who is now in a state of suffering and despair, so that he doesn't extinguish the smoldering wick or break the bruised reed. Instead, he wants to inspire hope for forgiveness and salvation, so that the sinner may turn around (meaning, be saved from the punishment of death) and live; in other words, be happy and at peace with a clear conscience.

We must also take note of this: the law's voice is only heard by those who don't recognize or admit their sins (as Paul says in Romans 3:20, "Through the law we become conscious of our sin"). Similarly, the message of grace is only for those who, aware of their sins, feel overwhelmed and close to despair. So, in all legal language, you see sin being exposed by showing us what we should do. On the other hand, in all words of promise, you see the misery that sinners experience (those who need to be lifted up from their despair) being hinted at. For example, the phrase "I don't want the death of a sinner" specifically mentions death and the sinner - the very problem that is felt, as well as the person who feels it. But in this phrase, "Love God with all your heart," what is highlighted is the good we owe, not the evil we feel, so that we can realize how incapable we are of doing that good.

SECTION 27: EZEKIEL 18:23 DISPROVES FREE WILL RATHER THAN SUPPORTING IT.

So, nothing could have been more poorly chosen to support Free Will than this passage from Ezekiel, which actually strongly argues against it. This passage implies how Free Will is impacted and what it can do when sin has been revealed and when it's time to turn to God. It suggests that Free Will could only fall into an even worse state, adding despair and stubbornness to its other sins unless God immediately comes to its aid and revives and lifts it up through His promise of grace. The fact that God is so eager to promise grace to restore and raise up the sinner is a powerful and reliable indication that Free Will, on its own, can only go from bad to worse - and as the Scripture says, "to the deepest hell."

Do you really think that God would carelessly make promises just for the sake of talking, when they aren't even necessary for our salvation? As you can see, not only do all the words of the law go against the idea of free will, but even all the words of promise completely refute it. In other words, the entire Scripture is at odds with the concept of free will. So, when you hear the saying, "I would not have the death of a sinner," you should understand that its main purpose is to preach and offer divine mercy throughout the world. This mercy is gladly accepted by those who have been deeply affected and tormented by their sins. They can do this because the law has already done its job in them, teaching them about their sins. On the other hand, those who haven't yet experienced the law's impact and don't recognize their sins or feel the weight of their actions, they simply ignore the mercy offered in that saying.

SECTION 28: TO WHAT EXTENT CAN GOD BE SAID TO LAMENT THE DEATH HE CAUSES?

As for why some people are affected by the law and others aren't, leading some to accept the offered grace while others reject it, that's a separate question and not addressed by Ezekiel in this passage. He talks about God's proclaimed and offered mercy, not His hidden and mysterious will, which determines who and what kind of people He wants to be able to receive and actually partake in His proclaimed and offered mercy. This will of God is not something we should investigate, but rather, we should respectfully admire it. It is a highly revered secret of God's majesty, which He keeps hidden in His own heart, and it is much more off-limits to us than the Corycian caves are to the countless masses.

When Diatribe sarcastically asks if "the holy Lord bewails that death of his people, which he produces in them himself?— a suggestion too absurd to be entertained," I respond (as I have already done) that we must discuss God or God's will in one way when it comes to what is proclaimed, revealed, offered, and worshipped; and in another way when it comes to what is unproclaimed, unrevealed, unoffered, and unworshipped.

As far as God hides himself and chooses not to be known by us, we have nothing to do with him. This is the true meaning of the saying, "What is above us, is nothing to us." And just to be clear, this idea comes from Paul, who wrote to the Thessalonians about Antichrist (2 Thessalonians 2:4), saying that "he would exalt himself above all that is proclaimed by God, and that is worshipped." This clearly suggests that a person could be exalted above God, as far as he is proclaimed and worshipped - meaning, above the word and worship through which God is made known to us and interacts with us. However, if we consider God not as an object of worship and as he is proclaimed, but as he is in his own nature and majesty, then nothing can be exalted above him, and everything is under his powerful control.

So, we should leave God to himself when it comes to his own nature and majesty. In this aspect, we can't interact with him, and he doesn't want us to. But as far as he is represented by his word and shown to us through it - the word through which he has offered himself to us, which is his glory and beauty, and which the Psalmist praises him for being clothed in - that's how we can connect with him. In this context, we say that the holy God doesn't lament the death of his people that he himself causes; instead, he grieves the death he finds in his people and works to remove. This is what the God we know through his word is focused on: taking away sin and death so that we can be saved. For "He has sent his word and healed them."

However, the God who is concealed within the majesty of His own nature neither mourns nor removes death; instead, He orchestrates life and death, as well as everything else in all things. For when acting in this role, He does not limit Himself by His word, but has retained complete freedom in exercising His authority over everything.

But Diatribe deceives herself due to her lack of knowledge, not distinguishing between the revealed God and the hidden God; that is, between the word of God and God Himself. God does many things that He has not revealed to us in His word.

In this long note, the author discusses the idea of "the great chain of being," which is a hierarchical structure of all life and matter, with God at the top and inanimate objects at the bottom. This concept was prevalent in the Middle Ages and Renaissance, and it influenced many aspects of life, including God also wants many things that He hasn't explicitly revealed to us through His word. For example, He doesn't want the death of a sinner, according to His word, but He might want it according to His mysterious and inscrutable will. Our job is to focus on His word and not try to understand His inscrutable will. After all, who could possibly comprehend and follow such a mysterious and inaccessible will? It's enough for us to know that there is a certain inscrutable will in God.

What that will desires, why it desires it, and to what extent it desires it, are questions that we shouldn't try to investigate, seek knowledge about, or even approach. In these matters, we should simply adore and fear God. So, it's correct to say, "If God doesn't want death, then it's our own fault that we perish." This is true if you're talking about the God that is revealed to us. He wants everyone to be saved (1 Timothy 2:4) and comes with His word of salvation to all people. The problem lies in our own will, which doesn't accept Him, as He says in Matthew 23:37, "How often would I have gathered your children, and you would not?"

But why doesn't God remove or change this fault in our will for everyone, since humans don't have the power to do so? And why does He blame us for this fault when we can't be without it? These are questions that we shouldn't ask, and even if we did, we would never get an answer. The best response is what Paul says in Romans 9:20: "Who are you that replies against God?" Let's leave this passage from Ezekiel and move on to the rest.

SECTION 29: EXHORTATIONS, PROMISES, ETC. OF SCRIPTURE ARE NOT USELESS.

Diatribe argues that if no one has the power to follow what is commanded, then all the exhortations, promises, threats, expostulations, upbraidings, beseechings, blessings, and curses found in Scripture, along with the numerous precepts, must be meaningless.

Diatribe constantly forgets the actual question at hand and ends up proving something different from what she intended to prove. She doesn't even realize that everything she says actually goes against her own argument rather than ours. From all these passages, she tries to prove that there's a freedom and power to follow all the commandments, based on the quotes she provides. But all she really wanted to prove was that 'free will can't do any good without grace, and that there's some effort involved, which shouldn't be attributed to one's own abilities.' I don't see any evidence of such effort in the passages she quotes. All I see is a demand for actions that should be carried out. I've mentioned this too many times already, but I have to repeat it because Diatribe keeps making the same mistake, distracting her readers with a pointless abundance of words.

SECTION 30: DEUTERONOMY 30:11-14 CONSIDERED

One of the last passages Diatribe brings up from the Old Testament is from Moses in Deuteronomy 30:11-14: "This commandment, which I command you today, is not too difficult for you or beyond your reach, nor is it up in heaven, so that you might ask, 'Who can go up to heaven and bring it down for us, so we can hear and obey it?' But the word is very near to you, in your mouth and in your heart, so that you can do it."

Diatribe argues that this passage declares not only do we have the power to do what is commanded, but that it's also easy or at least not difficult to do so. Thank you for sharing your immense knowledge! So, if Moses clearly states that we not only have the ability but also the ease to follow all the commandments, then why bother with all this effort? Why haven't we just used this passage to defend free will without any opposition? What need do we have for Christ or the Spirit anymore? We've finally found a passage that silences every argument and clearly states that not only is our will free, but following all the commandments is easy!

How foolish Christ must have been to buy us that unnecessary Spirit with his own spilled blood, just to make it easier for us to follow the commandments. It seems like we already have that ability naturally! No, Diatribe should take back her own words, where she said that free will can't desire anything good without grace, and instead say that free will is so powerful that it can not only want good but also easily follow all the commandments.

Oh, look at what happens when someone doesn't truly care about the argument they're making! See how impossible it is for them not to reveal their true intentions! Do we even need to refute Diatribe anymore? Who can do it better than she does herself? This is truly a creature that eats its own stomach. The saying "a liar should have a good memory" really holds true here!

I've already discussed this passage in my commentary on Deuteronomy, so I'll keep it brief here. We'll leave Paul out of this conversation, as he strongly addresses this passage in Romans 10. You'll notice that nothing is explicitly stated here, nor is there any mention of how easy or difficult it is, or the ability or inability of free will or humans to follow or not follow the commandment. Instead, it's just that those who twist the Scriptures with their own interpretations and ideas end up making them unclear and open to various interpretations.

But now, if you can't see, at least listen to what's being said here, or feel the letters with your hand. Moses says, "it is not above you, nor placed far away, nor seated in heaven, nor beyond the sea." What does he mean by "above you," "far away," "seated in heaven," or "across the sea"? Are they trying to make our grammar and even the most basic words unclear to us, just to support their claim that the Scriptures are obscure?

According to my understanding, these phrases don't refer to the quality or quantity of human strength, but rather to the distance of a place. When Moses says "above you," he's not talking about a certain power of the will, but a place that is above us. Similarly, the phrases "far away," "across the sea," and "in heaven" don't describe any power within us, but a place that is removed from us – upwards, to the right, to the left, backwards, or forwards.

Some people might laugh at my simple way of explaining things, as if I'm feeding chewed-up food to these sophisticated individuals who should already know their ABCs and teaching them how to combine syllables into words. But what can I do when I see people searching for darkness in the midst of such clear light, and deliberately wanting to be blind? After adding up so many ages, geniuses, saints, martyrs, and doctors, and after praising this passage from Moses with such great authority – even though they don't bother to examine the individual syllables or take a moment to think about the passage they're boasting about.

So tell us, Diatribe, how is it possible that one unknown person can see what so many famous figures and nobles from various eras have missed? Surely, this passage shows that they have often been blind, as even a small child could have judged them.

So, what is Moses trying to say with these clear and straightforward words, if not that he has perfectly fulfilled his role as a faithful lawgiver? He has made sure that there is no reason for people not to know and have access to all of God's commands. There is no excuse for them to claim that they didn't know or didn't have the commandments or needed to look for them elsewhere. The result is that if they don't follow the commandments, the fault lies neither with the law nor the lawgiver, but with themselves – because they have the law, and the lawgiver has taught them. So, there is no excuse of ignorance left for them, only accusations of negligence and disobedience. Moses is saying,

'It's not necessary to get laws from heaven or from distant lands or far away places; you can't claim that you haven't heard them or that you don't have them. You have them close to you; they are what you have heard from God's command through my words. You have understood them with your heart and have received them as read and explained by the Levites who are always among you. This very word and book of mine bear witness. All that's left is for you to follow them.'

What is being attributed to Free Will here, other than the requirement to follow the laws it has? The excuse of ignorance and lack of laws is removed.

SECTION 31: SOME OLD TESTAMENT EXAMPLES SUPPORTING FREE WILL

These are almost all the passages that Diatribe cites from the Old Testament to support Free Will. By addressing them, we leave no remaining passages unaddressed, whether Diatribe brings more or plans to bring more. All she can bring are a bunch of imperative, conjunctive, or optative verbs, which don't signify what we can do or are doing (as I've responded to Diatribe repeatedly), but rather what we should do and what is expected of us. This is so that our own inability becomes clear to us, and we gain the knowledge of sin.

If these texts really prove anything, by adding consequences and similes that come from human reasoning, they actually show that Free Will has not just effort or a tiny bit of desire, but a full power and the greatest freedom to do everything without God's grace and without the help of His Holy Spirit. So, nothing is further from what has been proven by this whole discussion - which has been repeated over and over - than the idea that was supposed to be proven. That is, the acceptable belief that Free Will is so weak that it can't want anything good without grace, that it's forced to serve sin, and that it has effort that shouldn't be credited to its own abilities. Honestly, this is a strange thing that can't do anything by itself but still has the power to try with its own abilities. This is a clear contradiction.

SECTION 32: NEW TESTAMENT SCRIPTURES FOR FREE WILL CONSIDERED, STARTING WITH MATTHEW 23:37-39.

Now we move on to the New Testament, where many imperative verbs are once again used to support the unfortunate idea of Free Will. Also, the helpers of human reasoning, like consequences and similes, are brought in. This is like a picture or a dream where you see the Lord of the Flies with his weak weapons, like straw spears and hay shields, ready to fight against a real and well-prepared army of human warriors.

The Diatribe's human dreams wage a war against the divine testimonies. First, it brings up the text from Matthew 23:37, "O Jerusalem, Jerusalem, how often I would have gathered your children together, and you would not?" The Diatribe argues that if everything is done by necessity, Jerusalem could have justly asked the Lord why He bothered with pointless tears. If He didn't want them to listen to the Prophets, why send them? Why blame them for what was done by His own will, which is their necessity? That's the Diatribe's argument.

Now, let's assume for a moment that the Diatribe's argument is valid and true. What does it prove? Does it support the idea that free will cannot choose good? On the contrary, it seems to prove that there is a free will, a complete one, capable of doing everything the Prophets have spoken about! But the Diatribe didn't set out to prove this kind of will in humans. So, let the Diatribe answer this: If free will cannot choose good, why is it blamed for not listening to the Prophets, who teach good? Why couldn't they listen to the Prophets using their own strength? Why does Christ weep "vain tears" as if they could have chosen what He knew they couldn't choose? Let the Diatribe defend Christ from the accusation of madness in support of its own opinion, and then our opinion will be free from this so-called Achilles of the flies.

This passage from Matthew either proves that there is complete free will, or it goes against Diatribe's own arguments, as well as ours, by using her own weapons against her. As I've said before, we shouldn't debate about God's secret will when it comes to His divine nature.

People tend to be reckless and constantly focus on unnecessary topics, so we should steer them away from trying to understand the mysteries of God's majesty, which are impossible to comprehend. After all, God lives in a light that no one can approach, as Paul says in 1 Timothy 6:16. Instead, let's focus on the incarnate God, or as Paul puts it, Jesus the crucified. In Him, we can find all the treasures of wisdom and knowledge, even if they are hidden. He will teach us what we need to know and what we don't need to know.

So, it is the incarnate God who speaks in this passage: "I would, and you would not." The incarnate God, Jesus, came into the world for a specific purpose: to be willing, to speak, to act, to suffer, and to offer everything necessary for salvation to all people.

Even though he encounters many who, due to the hidden will of His majesty, either reject or are hardened against him, he is still willing to speak, work, and offer himself to them. This is exactly what John says: "The light shines in darkness, and the darkness does not comprehend it." And again, "He came to his own, and his own did not receive him." (John 1:5, 11) So, it is the act of this God-made-flesh to weep, wail, and groan over the destruction of the wicked, while the will of Majesty intentionally leaves and condemns some to perish. We shouldn't question why he does this, but rather, we should respect God, who is both capable and willing to do such things.

No one, I assume, will argue that the will expressed in "how often I would" was shown to the Jews even before God became human. They are accused of killing the Prophets who lived before Christ (Matthew 23:31), and by doing so, they resisted his will. Christians know that everything done by the Prophets was done in the name of the Christ who was to come, the one who was promised to become God incarnate. So, whatever has been offered to humanity by the ministers of the word since the beginning of time can rightly be called the will of Christ.

SECTION 33: THE REALITY OF GOD'S SECRET WILL IS MAINTAINED.

But reason, which is quick to detect and challenge, might say, "What a convenient escape you've found! So, whenever you're cornered by the strength of your opponent's arguments, you just retreat to this fearsome will of sovereignty, and you force your adversary into silence when they become too bothersome - just like how astrologers dodge questions about the movements of the entire sky by inventing epicycles."

I reply, this is not my own idea, but a guidance supported by the divine Scriptures. Paul says in Romans 9:19, "Why does God complain then? Who resists his will? O man, who are you that argues with God? Does the potter not have the power?" and so on. Before him, Isaiah said in 58:2, "For they seek me daily, and desire to know my ways, as a nation which has done righteousness. They ask of me the ordinances of justice, and desire to draw near to God." In these words, I believe, it is clearly shown to us that it is not appropriate for humans to question the will of sovereignty.

Moreover, this is the kind of question that often leads misguided people to challenge that powerful will; so it is particularly fitting to encourage them to be silent and respectful when discussing it. In other questions, where the topics addressed are those that allow for an explanation and which we are commanded to explain, I do not take this approach.

Now, if someone refuses to listen to my advice and insists on examining the intentions of that will, I'll let them continue and battle with God, just like the giants did in the past. I'll wait to see what kind of victories they achieve. In the meantime, I'm confident that they won't take anything away from our cause, nor add anything to their own. It remains clear that either they must prove that free will can do everything, or the Scriptures they quote must contradict their own stance. Whichever outcome occurs, they end up defeated, while I stand victorious.

SECTION 34: MATTHEW 19:17 AND SIMILAR PASSAGES CONSIDERED.

Your second text is Matthew 19:17, "If you want to enter life, keep the commandments." Diatribe asks, 'How can this be said to someone whose will is not free?' I respond, does this statement from Christ prove that the will is free?

So, you wanted to prove that Freewill can't will anything good and will inevitably serve sin if grace isn't present. Then, how can you claim that it's completely free? The same can be said for phrases like "If you will be perfect," "if any man will come after me," "whoever would save his soul," "if you love me," and "if you abide in me." Let's gather all the "if" conjunctions and imperative verbs, as I mentioned before, to help Diatribe at least with the number of quotes. Diatribe claims that all these commands are pointless if we don't attribute anything to human will. But the "if" conjunction doesn't really fit with the idea of necessity, does it?

My response is that if these commands are meaningless, it's your fault for making them so, or rather, for making them nonexistent. You create this nonexistence by claiming that nothing is attributed to human will when you say that Freewill can't will any good. And now, you're saying that it can will all good - unless the same words can be both hot and cold at the same time. The way you use them, they both assert and deny everything. Honestly, I'm not sure why an author would want to repeat the same thing so many times, constantly forgetting their main argument - unless, perhaps, they were trying to win by making their book so long that it overwhelms their opponent or makes it too tedious and burdensome to read.

So, I would ask, how does it necessarily mean that will and power must be present in our minds whenever we hear phrases like "if you will," "if a person wants," or "if you're willing"? Don't we often use such expressions to indicate inability or impossibility, rather than the opposite? For example, in these cases: "If you want to be as good a singer as Virgil, my Maevius, you need to sing different songs;" "If you want to outdo Cicero, my Scotus, you must trade your clever tricks for the most exceptional eloquence;" "If you want to be compared to

David, you must create Psalms like his." It's clear that these conditional statements point to things that are impossible for us to achieve on our own, while with divine power, all things are possible for us.

This is also the case with the Scriptures: such words reveal what can be accomplished in us through God's power and what we cannot do by ourselves. Moreover, if these statements were made about actions that are absolutely impossible, like those that even God would never do through us, then they would be rightly considered pointless or ridiculous. However, the truth is that these expressions are used not only to highlight the powerlessness of Free Will, which prevents us from achieving any of these things, but also to hint that all such things will eventually be done, even if they are done by another's power (like God's). And this is only if we accept that in such words, there is some indication that the things to be done are possible. It's as if someone interpreted the words this way: "If you are willing to keep the commandments," meaning, "If at some point you have the will to keep the commandments (although you would have the will not by yourself, but by God who gives it to whomever He chooses), then they will protect you."

In simpler terms, these verbs, especially the conjunctive verbs, seem to be used this way because of God's predestination, which we don't know, and to involve it. It's as if they're saying, "If you want to," "If you're willing," meaning, "If you are seen by God as worthy of wanting to keep the commandments, then you'll be saved." This idea contains two aspects: first, that we can't do anything on our own, and second, that whatever we do, God works in us. I would explain it like this to those who aren't satisfied with just saying that our inability is expressed by these words, but who also believe that they show a certain power and ability to do what is commanded. So, it would be true that we could do none of the things commanded, and at the same time, we could do all of them - if we attribute our inability to our own powers and the ability to God's grace.

SECTION 35. ERASMUS' OBJECTION THAT PRECEPTS ARE GIVEN, AND MERIT IS ASCRIBED TO FREE WILL, CONSIDERED. ERASMUS INCONSISTENT WITH HIMSELF.

Thirdly, Diatribe raises this concern: "With so many mentions of good and bad works, and rewards, I don't see how there can be room for just necessity. Neither nature nor necessity has merit."

I'm not sure how the concept of mere necessity fits in, except that the 'approvable opinion' claims that Free Will can't do anything good on its own. However, in this discussion, Free Will seems to have progressed to the point where it not only has desire and effort (though not through its own strength), but also does good and even earns eternal life. This is because in Matthew 5:12, Christ says, "Rejoice and be exceedingly glad, for your reward is abundant in the heavens." The reward here is understood by Diatribe as Free Will's reward, which seems to leave no room for Christ and the Spirit. After all, why would we need them if we can achieve good works and merits through Free Will alone?

I bring this up to show how even highly intelligent people can be blind to things that may seem obvious to others with less education or sophistication. This also highlights the weakness of relying on human authority in matters of faith, where divine authority should be the primary source.

SECTION 36: NEW TESTAMENT TEACHINGS ARE INTENDED FOR THE BELIEVERS, NOT FOR THOSE WHO ADHERE TO THE CONCEPT OF FREE WILL

Now, let's briefly discuss two topics: the New Testament's precepts and the concept of merit. I've talked about these at length elsewhere, so I'll keep it short. The New Testament mainly consists of promises and exhortations, while the Old Testament is primarily focused on laws and warnings.

In the New Testament, the Gospel is preached, which is simply a message offering the Spirit and grace for the forgiveness of sins that Christ's crucifixion has provided for us. All of this is given freely, only because God the Father shows mercy to us, even though we are unworthy and deserve damnation. Then, there are exhortations to encourage those who are already justified and have received mercy to actively produce the fruits of righteousness and the Spirit, to show love through good deeds, and to bear the cross and all other worldly tribulations with courage. This is the essence of the entire New Testament.

Diatribe clearly demonstrates her ignorance on this subject, as she cannot distinguish between the Old and New Testaments. She sees almost nothing in either, except for laws and rules for people to follow to be good. She doesn't understand the concepts of new birth, renewal, regeneration, and the work of the Spirit. It's astonishing that someone who has studied the Scriptures so much could be so completely unaware of their meaning.

So, the saying, "Rejoice and be exceedingly glad, for great is your reward in heaven," doesn't really align with the concept of free will, as it's like comparing light to darkness. Christ isn't encouraging free will here, but rather urging his Apostles to endure the tribulations of the world. They were not only already partakers of grace and righteous people, but they were also established in the ministry of the word, which is the highest level of grace. Our discussion is about free will, specifically when it exists without grace. Free will is taught by laws and threats (that is, the Old Testament) to recognize its own limitations, so that it may seek the promises offered in the New Testament.

SECTION 37: MERIT AND REWARD CAN COEXIST WITH NECESSITY.

Regarding merit and proposed rewards, isn't this just like a promise? This doesn't prove that we have any power - all it says is that if someone does a certain thing, they will receive a reward. But our question isn't about the reward or what kind of reward will be given to someone; it's about whether we can do those things for which a reward is given. This is what needs to be proven.

Aren't these conclusions ridiculous? If a prize is offered to all who participate in a race, does that mean everyone can run and win it? If

Caesar defeats the Turk, he will rule over the kingdom of Syria; does that mean Caesar can and will defeat the Turk? If free will triumphs over sin, it will be considered holy; does that mean free will is already holy?

I won't say any more about these extremely foolish and obviously absurd arguments, except that it's fitting for free will to be defended by such twisted reasoning.

Let me address this point: "necessity has neither merit nor reward." If we're talking about a necessity that forces someone, then it's true. But if we're talking about a necessity that can't be changed, then it's false. Who would give a reward or credit to someone who does something unwillingly? However, for those who willingly do good or evil, even if they can't change their will on their own, reward or punishment naturally and necessarily follows, as it is written, "You will render to every man according to his works." It's just like if you're underwater, you'll drown; if you swim out, you'll save your life.

In short, when it comes to merit or reward, we need to consider either the worthiness or the consequences of our actions. If we focus on worthiness, there's no such thing as merit or reward. Because if freewill can't will anything good on its own and only wills good through grace, isn't it clear that the will to do good, along with its merit or reward, comes from grace alone? Remember, we're discussing freewill apart from grace and trying to understand the power each has. Here, Diatribe contradicts itself by arguing for freewill based on merit. It ends up in the same position as me, who it opposes, fighting against itself as much as against me, claiming that there is merit, reward, and liberty. Diatribe says that freewill can't will anything good and has set out to prove the kind of freewill that does will good.

If we focus on the consequences of actions, there's nothing good or bad that doesn't have its reward. We make mistakes because we bring up pointless discussions and questions about the worth of actions - which don't have any - when we should only be talking about their consequences.

Hell and God's judgment inevitably await the wicked, even though they don't want or think about such consequences for their sins. In fact, they strongly hate and curse it, as Peter says. Similarly, the kingdom awaits the godly, even though they don't seek or think about it themselves. It is a gift prepared for them by their Father, not only before they existed, but even before the world was created.

If the godly were doing good just to obtain the kingdom, they would never achieve it. Instead, they would be part of the wicked group who selfishly "seek their own," even in God. But God's children do good out of a genuine desire to please; they don't seek any reward, but simply aim to glorify God and follow His will. They are willing to do good even if, hypothetically, there were no kingdom or hellfire. I believe this is evident from Jesus' words in Matthew 25:34: "Come, you who are blessed by my Father, inherit the kingdom prepared for you from the foundation of the world."

How do people earn what is already theirs, and was prepared for them before they were born? It would be more accurate to say that the kingdom of God earns us as its inhabitants, rather than us earning it. This means placing merit where they place reward, and reward where they place merit. The kingdom doesn't need to be prepared; it has already been prepared. The children of the kingdom need to be prepared for it, not to prepare the kingdom itself. In other words, the kingdom earns its children; the children don't earn the kingdom. Similarly, hell earns its inhabitants and prepares them, rather than them preparing it, as Christ says, "Depart you cursed into everlasting fire, which has been prepared for the devil and his angels."

SECTION 38: WHY THERE ARE PROMISES AND THREATS IN SCRIPTURE.

So, what do those statements mean that promise the kingdom and threaten hell? What does the word 'reward' mean, being repeated so often throughout the Scriptures? "Your work has a reward," 1 Corinthians 3:14 says. "I am your exceeding great reward," Genesis 15:1. Again, "Who renders to every man according to his works," Psalm

62:12. And Paul in Romans 2:7 says, "To those who by the patience of good works seek for eternal life," and many similar sayings.

The answer is that all these sayings prove nothing but a consequence of reward, and by no means a worthiness of merit. Those who truly do good, do it not out of a servile and mercenary mindset to gain eternal life, but they still seek eternal life. This means they are on the path that will lead them to and obtain eternal life.

So, in order to seek eternal life, we must put in great effort and work hard, because it usually comes as a result of living a good life. The Scriptures tell us that these things will happen and are the consequences of either a good or bad life, so that people can be educated, warned, encouraged, or frightened. Just as the law helps us understand sin and our own weaknesses, it doesn't mean we have any power over them. Similarly, the promises and threats in the Scriptures teach us what comes from our sin and weaknesses, but they don't attribute any worthiness to our own efforts.

In the same way that the law serves as guidance and enlightenment, teaching us what we should and shouldn't do, the words of reward in the Scriptures serve as motivation and warning, encouraging and comforting the faithful. This helps them to continue doing good and enduring hardships, so they don't become discouraged or lose hope. It's like when Paul encouraged his followers in Corinth, saying, "Be strong and courageous," and "know that your hard work is not in vain when it's done for the Lord."

God reassures Abraham by saying, "I am your exceeding great reward." It's like encouraging someone by telling them that their actions definitely please God. This is a common form of comfort found in Scripture. It's a significant consolation for someone to know they please God, even if nothing else comes from it - which is impossible, though.

SECTION 39: REASON QUESTIONS THE ACCOUNT, BUT THE ANSWER IS "SUCH IS THE WILL OF GOD."

All discussions about hope and expectation should be based on the certainty that the things hoped for will indeed happen. However, godly people don't hope just because of the things themselves or seek such benefits for their own sake. Similarly, ungodly people are frightened and discouraged by words of warning that announce an upcoming judgment, so they may stop and refrain from doing evil, not become arrogant, and not feel secure and reckless in their sins.

Now, if reason were to question why God uses words to create these impressions when they don't produce any effect and when the will can't change on its own, we might ask: Why doesn't God just do what he wants without mentioning it in words? After all, he can do everything without words, and the will doesn't have more power or accomplish more by hearing the word if the Spirit isn't there to move the soul within. The will wouldn't have less power or accomplish less if the word were silent, as long as the Spirit is present, since everything depends on the power and work of the Holy Spirit.

The answer is that God has decided to give the Spirit through the word, not without it, making us his partners in sharing the message externally while he alone breathes life into it internally, wherever he chooses. He could certainly achieve this without using words, but it's his preference to do so.

Who are we to question why God wants something? It's enough for us to know that God wants it, and we should respect, love, and adore His will, keeping our curious minds in check. Even in Matthew 11, Jesus doesn't give any other reason for the Gospel being hidden from the wise and revealed to the innocent, other than it pleased the Father. God could nourish us without bread, and in fact, He has given us the ability to be nourished without it, as He says in Matthew 4:4, "Man does not live on bread alone, but on every word that comes from the mouth of God." Yet, He chose to nourish us internally with His word through the use of bread, which we receive from the outside world.

Therefore, it remains true that merit is not proven by reward, at least not in the Scriptures. And again, free will is not proven by merit, especially not the kind of free will that Diatribe tries to argue for: one that cannot will anything good on its own.

So, if you were to accept the idea of merit and include those common comparisons and logical outcomes - like commandments being pointless, rewards being promised for no reason, and threats being made without purpose, unless there's free will - then these arguments, if they prove anything, show that free will can do everything on its own. Because if it can't, then those logical outcomes still stand: it's pointless to command, promise, or threaten. In this way, Diatribe keeps contradicting itself while trying to argue against me. The truth is that God alone creates both merit and reward within us through his Spirit, and he announces and declares these things to the whole world through his external word. This is so that his power and glory, as well as our weakness and disgrace, can be proclaimed even among the ungodly, unbelievers, and ignorant - even though only the godly truly understand and faithfully keep this word in their hearts; the rest just ignore it.

SECTION 40: APOLOGY FOR NOT ADDRESSING ALL THE SUPPOSED TEXTS INDIVIDUALLY - RIDICULOUS OBJECTION FROM MATTHEW 7:16.

Now, it would be too tedious to go through all the imperative verbs that Diatribe lists from the New Testament, always adding its own conclusions and claiming that all these expressions are pointless, excessive, meaningless, absurd, laughable, and worth nothing unless there's free will. I've already said more than enough about how these expressions don't prove anything. If they do prove something, it's that free will is entirely capable.

This just completely undermines Diatribe's argument, which set out to prove a limited free will that can't do anything good and is enslaved to sin, but ends up proving a free will that can do everything - constantly forgetting its own position. So, it's just nitpicking when Diatribe argues like this:

"You will know them by their fruits," says the Lord, referring to works as fruits. He calls these works ours, but they wouldn't be ours if everything happened out of necessity.

What! Aren't those possessions most rightly called ours, which it is true, we have not made ourselves, but which we have received from others? Why shouldn't those works be called ours, which God has given to us through the Spirit? Shouldn't we call Christ ours, because we haven't made him, but only received him? On the other hand, if we say that we make all those things which are called ours, then we must have made our own eyes, hands, and feet for ourselves – unless we're not allowed to call them ours! Indeed, what do we have that we haven't received, as Paul says in 1 Corinthians 4:7? Should we say, then, that these possessions are either not ours or they have been made by ourselves? But let's assume that these fruits are called ours because we have produced them – what then happens to grace and the Spirit? For he doesn't say, "by their fruits, which are in some very small degree and portion theirs, you shall know them." These, rather, are the ridiculous, superfluous, vain, meaningless sayings – indeed, a bunch of foolish and offensive arguments – by which the sacred words of God are polluted and profaned.

SECTION 41. LUKE 23:34 IS AGAINST, NOT FOR FREEWILL.

In the same way, that saying of Christ on the cross is mocked: "Father, forgive them; for they know not what they do."

Here, when you expect a sentence that links "Freewill" to the evidence just mentioned, the author once again focuses on the consequences. She says, 'How much more fair would it have been for him to excuse them by saying that they were those who didn't have free will and couldn't do anything different, even if they wanted to!' However, this argument doesn't prove the type of free will in question, which is the ability to choose only good. Instead, it supports the idea of a free will that can do anything, which no one argues for and everyone denies, except for the Pelagians.

Now, when Christ explicitly says that they don't know what they're doing, doesn't he also imply that they can't choose good? Because, how can you choose something you don't know? There can't be any desire for something unknown. What stronger argument against free will can there be than the fact that it's so powerless that it not only can't choose good, but it doesn't even know how much evil it's doing or even what 'good' means? Is there any ambiguity in the words, 'They don't know what they're doing'? What's left in the Scripture that might not prove free will, according to the author's suggestion, when this clear statement from Christ says the opposite?

Someone could just as easily claim that free will is proven by phrases like, "The earth was empty and void," or "God rested on the seventh day," and similar statements. Then, the Scriptures would indeed be ambiguous and obscure! These statements would mean everything and nothing at the same time. But such a bold manipulation of God's word shows a mindset that has little respect for both God and people - and it deserves no patience at all.

SECTION 42: JOHN 1:12 IS ALL ABOUT GRACE.

So, let's look at the quote from John 1:12: "To them he gave power to become the sons of God." The argument here is, 'How can people be given the power to become God's children if there's no freedom in our will?'

This passage actually goes against the idea of free will, as does much of the Gospel of John. Yet, it's being used to support it. Please notice that John isn't talking about any human action, big or small. Instead, he's discussing the transformation of the old person, who is a child of the devil, into a new person, who is a child of God. This person doesn't do anything but is entirely changed. John talks about becoming: "to be made the sons of God." This happens through a power freely given to us by God, not through the natural power of free will.

However, the argument made here is that free will has the power to make us children of God. Otherwise, John's statement would be pointless and absurd. But who has ever praised free will so highly that it can make us God's children, especially when it's a free will that can't choose anything good? This is the kind of free will that the argument is trying to prove. But let's set that aside, along with the other repeated claims that, if proven, only show what the argument denies: that free will can do everything.

What John really means is this: when Christ came into the world, he gave all people a tremendous power through the Gospel (which offers grace, not demands work) – the power to become children of God if they choose to believe!

But this "being willing" and "believing in his name" is something that Free Will has never known or even considered before. It's even further from being something that Free Will can achieve on its own. After all, how could reason ever imagine that faith in Jesus, who is both the Son of God and of man, is necessary when it doesn't yet understand or believe that there is a person who is both God and man at the same time - even if the whole creation were to proclaim it loudly? In fact, reason is even more offended by such preaching, as Paul points out in 1 Corinthians 1:18, 23. That's how far reason is from being either willing or able to believe.

John, therefore, proclaims the riches of God's kingdom, which are offered to the world through the Gospel, not by the virtues of Free Will. This also suggests how few people actually receive these riches because, in truth, Free Will resists this offer. Under Satan's control, Free Will's only power is to reject the offer of grace and the Spirit who would fulfill the law. Her desire and effort to fulfill the law are so incredible! But later on, I'll show in more detail how this passage from John is a powerful argument against the idea of free will. In the mean-time, I can't help but feel annoyed that the Diatribe uses such clear and strong passages against free will to support their own view. They seem to be so clueless that they can't tell the difference between words about the law and words of promise. First, they foolishly try to prove free will using passages about the law, and then they take it to the extreme by trying to confirm it with words of promise. This absurdity can be easily explained when you consider how unwilling and dismissive the Diatribe is when discussing this topic. They don't really care if grace stands or falls, or if free will is proven right or wrong, as long as they can show themselves as humble servants of a group of tyrants by spouting a bunch of pointless words to make our cause look bad.

SECTION 43: OBJECTIONS FROM PAUL QUICKLY ADDRESSED.

Now let's move on to Paul, who is actually a strong opponent of free will, but the Diatribe still tries to use his words in Romans 2:4 to support their view: "Or do you show contempt for the riches of his kindness, forbearance and patience, not realizing that God's kindness is intended to lead you to repentance?" How can someone be blamed for disregarding the commandment if their will isn't free? How can God call us to repent when he's the one causing us not to repent? And how can it be fair for someone to be condemned when the judge is the one forcing them to commit the crime?

I respond, let Diatribe deal with these questions, because they don't concern me. She has already shared her acceptable opinion that Free Will cannot desire good, which inevitably forces us into sin's service. Indeed, how can she be blamed for disregarding the commandment if she cannot desire good and has no freedom, but is unavoidably enslaved to sin?

How is it that God calls us to repent when He is the cause of our unrepentance, by either abandoning us or not providing us with grace when we cannot desire good on our own? How can damnation be fair when the judge, by withholding his help, ensures that the wicked person continues in their evil ways, as they can do nothing else by their own power?

All these statements backfire on Diatribe, or if they prove anything, they prove (as I have said) that Free Will can do everything, which contradicts her own words and everyone else's. These logical consequences bother Diatribe throughout all her Scripture references. Isn't it truly absurd and pointless to attack and demand so forcefully when there is no one present who can meet the requirement? All the while, the Apostle's goal is to guide ungodly and arrogant people to self-awareness and recognition of their own powerlessness through these warnings, so that by humbling them with the knowledge of sin, he can prepare them for grace.

SECTION 44: WYCLIFFE'S CONFESSION IS ACKNOWLEDGED.

Why do I need to go through all the texts from Paul's writings one by one, when Diatribe simply gathers a bunch of imperative or conjunctive verbs, or those expressions that Paul used to encourage Christians towards the fruits of faith? This is because Diatribe adds its own conclusions, imagining a Free Will with such great power that it can do everything Paul prescribes without the need for grace. However, Christians are not guided by Free Will, but by the Spirit of God (Romans 8:14). To be led is not to lead ourselves, but to be moved along, just like a saw or an axe is moved by the carpenter.

And here, just in case anyone doubts that Luther said such "absurd" things, Diatribe quotes Wickliff's words, which I openly admit, fully supporting his Article 16 as I do: that 'all things are done by necessity;' meaning, by the unchangeable will of God; 'and our will, although not forced to do evil, is unable to do any good by its own power.'

He was wrongly judged by the Council of Constance (or more accurately, through conspiracy and rebellion). In fact, even Diatribe supports him along with me, claiming that "Freewill can will nothing good by its own powers" and that it inevitably serves sin - although, while presenting her argument, she ends up proving the exact opposite.

PART FOUR
LUTHER ARGUES IN FAVOR OF CERTAIN TESTIMONIES AGAINST FREE WILL

SECTION 1: ERASMUS ONLY HAS TWO TEXTS TO REFUTE.

Let's consider what has been said in response to Diatribe's first part, where she tries to prove the existence of free will. Now, let's look at her second part, where she attempts to disprove the evidence on our side of the argument - the evidence that denies the existence of free will. You'll see how weak human arguments are when compared to God's powerful truths.

First, Diatribe lists countless Bible passages that support free will, as if they were a terrifying army. She does this to encourage those who defend free will, like confessors, martyrs, and other holy men and women, and to scare those who deny its existence. Then, she claims that the opposing side has only a few weak arguments. She highlights two main Bible passages that argue against free will. It seems like she's eager to defeat these arguments easily. One of these passages is from Exodus 9:12, "The Lord hardened Pharaoh's heart." The other is from Malachi 1:2-3, "Jacob I have loved, but Esau I have hated."

It's strange how Diatribe thinks that Paul's discussion on these topics was so unpleasant and unproductive when he explained them in detail to the Romans. In short, if the Holy Ghost wasn't a bit skilled in rhetoric, Paul might have felt overwhelmed by the strong arguments against free will and given up on his cause before the debate even began. But soon, I'll join in and support these two Scriptures, showing my own arguments as well. However, when one person can defeat ten thousand opponents, as in Joshua 23:10, there's no need for additional forces. If one Scripture passage has already defeated the concept of free will, then countless other arguments won't help it.

SECTION 2: TRIES TO AVOID THE CLEAR MEANING OF CERTAIN TEXTS BY INTERPRETING STRAIGHTFORWARD LANGUAGE AS FIGURATIVE EXPRESSIONS.

Previously, when arguing for free will, Diatribe sidestepped the impact of all the command and conditional words in the law by using examples, drawing conclusions, and adding her own invented comparisons.

So now, as she sets out to argue against us, she manipulates and twists all the words of divine promise and affirmation in any way she wants, by finding a hidden meaning in them. This makes it difficult to pin down her argument, just like the elusive Proteus. She even has the audacity to demand this from us, claiming that we too tend to escape from our opponents when under pressure by finding hidden meanings in words.

For example, when the phrase says, "Stretch out your hand to whichever you will," she interprets it as "grace will stretch out your hand to whichever she wills." Or when it says, "Make yourself a new heart," she claims it means "grace will make you a new heart," and so on. It seems quite unfair then, if Luther can impose such a twisted and forced interpretation, but we are not even allowed to follow the interpretations of the most respected scholars. So you see, our disagreement here is not about the text as it is written, nor is it about drawing conclusions and making comparisons like before – but rather about hidden meanings and interpretations.

"Oh, when will the day come," some people ask, "when we finally get a clear and straightforward text about free will, without having to rely on interpretations and figures of speech? Doesn't the Bible have any such texts? Will the issue of free will always remain unresolved, with no definitive answer provided by any clear text, but instead swayed back and forth like a reed in the wind, because all we have are various interpretations and figures of speech put forth by people arguing with each other?"

SECTION 3: WHEN TO ACCEPT FIGURES OF SPEECH AND INTERPRETATIONS

We should decide that neither interpretations nor figures of speech should be accepted in any part of the Bible, unless a clear context and some absurdity in the plain meaning, which goes against one of our core beliefs, force us to adopt such an interpretation or conclusion. Instead, we should always stick to the simple, pure, and natural meaning of words, as guided by both the rules of grammar and the everyday use of language as God created it in humans.

For if anyone can just come up with their own interpretations and figures of speech for the Bible, what will the Bible become but a reed shaken by the wind, or a constantly changing entity? In that case, it would indeed be true that nothing certain can be said or proven about any aspect of our faith, since any point could be dismissed with some clever figure of speech. So, let's avoid using figures of speech as much as possible, like a dangerous poison, unless the Bible itself forces us to accept them.

Look at what has happened to the great Origen, the master of interpreting the Scriptures! He has given a perfect opportunity for Porphyry to criticize him. Even Jerome thinks it's not worth defending Origen. What about the Arians, who use their own interpretation to claim that Christ is only a God in name? And what about these new prophets in our time, who try to find hidden meanings in Christ's words, "This is my body" - one of them in the pronoun "this," another in the verb "is," and a third in the noun "body?"

Based on my observations, I've noticed that all the heresies and errors that have arisen from false interpretations of Scripture haven't come from understanding words in their simple, everyday sense. Instead, they come from ignoring this simple usage and focusing on more complex figures of speech or inferences that are the product of one's own imagination.

SECTION 4: LUTHER DENIES USING FIGURES OF SPEECH IN HIS INTERPRETATION OF "STRETCH OUT" AND "MAKE YOURSELF."

For example, I don't recall ever using such a forceful interpretation of the words "Stretch out your hand to whichever you will," as to say, "Grace will stretch out your hand to whichever she wills." Or, "Make yourself a new heart," meaning, "Grace will make you a new heart," and similar interpretations. However, Diatribe falsely accuses me in a published work of having said such things. In reality, Diatribe is so confused and misled by their own figures of speech and inferences that they don't even know what they're saying about anyone.

What I really meant was, when the words "stretch out your hand," etc., are taken simply, according to their actual meaning, without considering any hidden meanings or interpretations, they only ask us to stretch out our hand. This implies what we should do based on the nature of the imperative verb - as explained by grammarians and used in everyday language.

However, Diatribe ignores this simple use of the verb and forcefully brings in her own interpretations and hidden meanings. She interprets it like this: "Stretch out your hand" means you can stretch out your hand using your own power; "Make a new heart" means you can create a new heart for yourself; "Believe in Christ" means you can believe in Christ on your own. In her view, it doesn't matter if words are spoken as commands or statements; if not, she's ready to portray Scripture as ridiculous and pointless. Yet, these interpretations, which no scholar can tolerate, are not considered forced or far-fetched when used by theologians. Instead, they are welcomed as the teachings of the most respected doctors who have been accepted for centuries!

But it's very easy for Diatribe to allow hidden meanings and adopt them in this text. It doesn't matter to her whether what is said is certain or uncertain. In fact, her main goal is to make everything uncertain, advising that all teachings on free will should be left alone rather than investigated.

So, she could have just dismissed the sayings that made her uncomfortable in any way she wanted. But for me, who is genuinely seeking the undeniable truth to guide people's conscience, I need to approach this differently. It's not enough for you to tell me that there might be a hidden meaning here. The real question is whether there should be and must be a hidden meaning in this context. If you haven't proven that there must be a hidden meaning here, then you haven't accomplished anything.

Here's what the word of God says: "I will harden Pharaoh's heart!" If you tell me it should be understood as 'I will allow it to be hardened,' then all I hear is that it could be interpreted that way. I understand that this kind of interpretation is common in everyday conversation, like when someone says, 'I ruined you because I didn't correct you right away when you were going off track.' But that's not the point here.

The question isn't whether this kind of interpretation is commonly used. It's not about whether someone might apply it to this particular passage in Paul's writings. The real question is whether it's safe and accurate to use this interpretation in this context, and whether Paul intended to use it that way. We're not looking at how a reader might interpret it, but how Paul, the author, meant it.

So, what would you say to someone whose conscience questions you like this? 'Look, God, the author of the book, says, "I will harden Pharaoh's heart." The meaning of the word 'harden' is clear and well-known. But a human reader tells me, 'to harden, in this context, means to provide an opportunity for hardening because the sinner isn't corrected right away.'

With what authority, purpose, or necessity is the natural meaning of the word twisted for me? What if my interpretation is wrong? Where is the proof that this distortion of the word should happen here? It's dangerous and even disrespectful to twist God's word without necessity and authority. Will you then teach this struggling soul by saying, "Origen thought so?" Or like this: "Stop looking into such matters, as they are pointless and empty." The response would be, "Moses and Paul should have been warned before they wrote; or rather, God himself. Why do they confuse us with pointless and empty sayings?"

SECTION 5: DIATRIBE MUST PROVE THROUGH SCRIPTURE OR MIRACLE THAT THE PASSAGE IN QUESTION IS METAPHORICAL.

This poor excuse of using metaphors doesn't help Diatribe at all. Instead, we must firmly hold onto our argument until it is proven beyond doubt that there is a metaphor in this specific passage, either through clear scriptural evidence or undeniable miracles. We won't believe it just because they think so, even if it's supported by the efforts of all ages. But I'll go even further and argue that there can be no metaphor here, and that God's statement must be understood simply, according to the literal meaning of the words. It's not up to us to create and change words for God as we wish. What would be left of all Scripture if we just followed Anaxagoras' philosophy, "Make whatever you want out of anything"?

Imagine if I were to say, "God created the heavens and the earth," meaning 'He organized them, but didn't make them from nothing.' Or, "He created the heavens and the earth," meaning the angels and the devils, or the righteous and the wicked. Based on this principle, anyone can just open the Bible and suddenly become a theologian.

So let's establish a solid principle: if Diatribe can't prove that there's a hidden meaning in the passages we're discussing, then she has to accept our interpretation. The words must be taken at face value, even if she could prove that hidden meanings are frequently used elsewhere in the Bible or in everyday conversation. If we agree on this principle, then all the evidence we presented, which Diatribe tried to refute, has been successfully defended. Her attempts at refutation have accomplished nothing and hold no weight.

When Diatribe interprets Moses' statement, "I will harden Pharaoh's heart," to mean 'My patience with sinners leads some to repentance, but it will make Pharaoh more stubborn in his wickedness' — that's a nice interpretation, but there's no evidence to support it. We're not satisfied with just taking her word for it; we need proof.

So she believes that Paul's statement, "He has mercy on whom he will have mercy, and whom he will, he hardens," means that God hardens when he doesn't immediately punish a sinner, and he shows mercy when he uses afflictions to quickly call us to repentance. But is there any proof for this interpretation?

Similarly, there's the quote from Isaiah, "You have made us stray from your ways; you have hardened our hearts from fearing you." What if Jerome, following Origen, interpreted it like this: 'A person is said to lead astray when they don't immediately correct someone's mistake.' Can we be sure that Jerome and Origen are interpreting this passage correctly? And even if they are, we agreed to base our argument on the authority of Scripture alone, not on the opinions of human teachers. So why is Diatribe bringing up Origen and Jerome, especially when they are among the least reliable interpreters of Scripture?

In short, such a loose interpretation leads to a confusing mix-up of meanings. For example, when God says, "I will harden Pharaoh's heart," you switch the focus and interpret it as, 'Pharaoh hardens himself because of my leniency.' 'God hardens our hearts' becomes 'we harden our own hearts because God delays our punishment.' "You, O Lord, have made us stray" turns into 'we made ourselves stray because you didn't punish us.' As a result, 'God having mercy' no longer means giving grace, showing compassion, forgiving sins, justifying, or saving from evil. Instead, it means 'God inflicting evil and punishing us.'

In the end, you'll see from these examples that God had compassion on the children of Israel when he took them to Assyria and Babylon. It was there that he punished those who had done wrong and encouraged them to repent through their suffering. On the other hand, when he brought them back and saved them, it wasn't out of pity, but rather it hardened them - meaning that his kindness and compassion actually caused them to become more stubborn.

So, sending Jesus Christ as the Savior into the world shouldn't be considered an act of mercy from God, but rather an act of hardening. This is because his mercy gave people a chance to become even more stubborn. On the other hand, by destroying Jerusalem and punishing the Jews to this day, he is actually showing them mercy, as he is disciplining them for their sins and encouraging them to repent.

When God takes his saints to heaven on Judgment Day, it won't be an act of mercy, but of hardening. This is because he will give them an opportunity to misuse his kindness. In sending the wicked to hell, he will actually be showing mercy, as he will be punishing them for their sins. I ask you, have you ever heard of such compassion and wrath from God as these?

We can say that good people are improved by both God's patience and strictness. However, when we talk about good and bad people together, these figures of speech can twist God's mercy into anger and His anger into mercy in a very confusing way. They say it's anger when God is giving blessings, and they call it mercy when He is delivering punishments. Now, if God is said to harden when He is giving blessings and tolerating evil, and He is said to have mercy when He is causing suffering and disciplining, then why is He said to have hardened Pharaoh instead of the Israelites or even the whole world? Didn't He bless the Israelites? Doesn't He bless the entire world? Doesn't He tolerate the wicked? Doesn't He send rain on both the evil and the good?

Why is He said to have had compassion on the Israelites rather than Pharaoh? Didn't He cause suffering to the Israelites in Egypt and in the desert? I agree that some people misuse God's anger and kindness, while others use it correctly. But you define hardening as 'God's tolerance and kindness towards the wicked.' You define 'God's compassion' as not tolerating, but disciplining and cutting short. So, from God's perspective, He hardens through constant kindness, and He shows mercy through constant strictness.

SECTION 6: ERASMUS' INTERPRETATION DOESN'T MAKE SENSE AND DOESN'T SOLVE THE PROBLEM.

The best part is when Erasmus claims that 'God hardens people's hearts when he tolerates their sins, and shows mercy when he punishes and causes suffering, urging them to repent through harsh treatment.' I ask, what did God leave out when he punished, disciplined, and called Pharaoh to repentance? Weren't there ten plagues brought upon that land? If your explanation is correct - that 'showing mercy means immediately punishing and calling the sinner to repent' - then God definitely showed mercy to Pharaoh. So why doesn't God say, 'I will have mercy on Pharaoh,' instead of saying, 'I will harden Pharaoh's heart?' Because when God is supposedly showing mercy to Pharaoh - that is, according to you, punishing and disciplining him - he says, 'I will harden his heart;' which, according to you, means 'I will be kind to him and be patient with him.' How absurd does that sound? What happened to your clever interpretations, your Origen, your Jerome, and your highly respected scholars, whom the lone individual, Luther, dares to disagree with? It's the foolishness of human thinking that forces you to speak this way - playing with God's words, which you can't accept as being said seriously.

The text itself, as written by Moses, clearly shows that these interpretations are just made up and don't apply here. It also shows that something much more significant is meant by the words, "I will harden Pharaoh's heart" - beyond just giving blessings along with punishment and discipline. We can't deny that both of these approaches were used in Pharaoh's case, with great effort and care.

What could be more urgent than the wrath and punishment he had to endure, being struck with so many signs and plagues that even Moses himself said they were never seen before? Even Pharaoh himself was moved by them more than once, as if he regretted his actions - but he didn't truly change or stay committed. At the same time, what could be more generous and kind than the way his plagues were removed, his sins forgiven, his blessings restored, and his disasters taken away?

However, neither approach seems to work. The Lord still says, "I will harden Pharaoh's heart." So even if we accept your interpretation of hardening and mercy (that is, your explanations and figures of speech) as they are shown in Pharaoh's case, there is still an act of hardening. The hardening that Moses talks about must be one thing, and what you're imagining must be another.

SECTION 7: NECESSITY STILL REMAINS, AND YOU DON'T CLEAR GOD OF RESPONSIBILITY.

But since I'm arguing with people who make up stories and with imaginary ideas, let me also create my own imaginary scenario and consider something impossible: that the figure of speech Diatribe dreams about is actually used in this passage. This way, I can see how she avoids saying that we do everything solely by God's will and under a necessity imposed on us. I can also see how she tries to excuse God from being the one responsible and deserving blame for our hardening.

If it's true that God is said to harden us when he tolerates us through his patience and doesn't punish us quickly, then the following two principles still hold:

First, humans still inevitably serve sin. Since it's agreed that free will cannot choose anything good (which is what Diatribe argues), it doesn't improve through God's patient tolerance. Instead, it gets worse unless God, in his mercy, adds the Spirit to it. So, everything still happens by necessity concerning us.

Secondly, God may seem as cruel in tolerating people out of patience as he is thought to be when he hardens them through his mysterious will. Because he knows that free will can't choose anything good and gets worse through his patience, this very patience makes him appear cruel, as if he enjoys our suffering. He could heal us if he wanted to, and he could choose not to tolerate us if he wanted to. In fact, he couldn't tolerate us unless he wanted to, because no one can force him to do something against his will. So, if his will remains unchanging, and if it's agreed that free will can't choose anything good, then all the arguments excusing God and blaming free will are pointless.

Free will always says, "I can't, and God won't. What can I do? I wish he would show me mercy by punishing me. I don't improve from his patience, but I get worse unless he gives me the Spirit. He doesn't give it, which he would if he wanted to. So, it's clear that he doesn't want to give it."

SECTION 8: DIATRIBE'S SUN AND RAIN SIMILES DON'T HOLD UP.

Diatribe's comparison of the sun hardening mud and melting wax, and rain causing cultivated ground to produce fruit while untilled ground produces thorns, doesn't really work. She's trying to say that God's patience can either harden or convert people, depending on their nature.

But we don't see free will as being divided into two types, like mud and wax or cultivated and untilled ground. We believe there's only one kind of free will, and it's equally powerless in everyone. In these comparisons, free will is nothing more than mud or untilled ground, since it can't choose good.

Paul doesn't say that God, as the potter, makes one vessel for honor and another for dishonor from different lumps of clay. Instead, he says that the potter makes both from the "SAME lump." So, just as mud always gets harder and untilled ground gets thornier with sun and rain, free will always gets worse with both the hardening sun and the softening rain.

If there's only one definition of free will and its powerlessness is the same in everyone, then there's no reason why one person's free will can achieve grace while another's can't – unless there's some other factor besides God's patience and compassion. Since the definition doesn't make distinctions, it's assumed that free will in everyone is a power that can't choose anything good.

So, if we follow this line of thinking, it would mean that God doesn't actually choose anyone, and there's no room for divine selection.

Instead, it's all up to a person's free will to decide whether they accept or reject patience and anger. But if you take away God's wisdom and power in making these choices, what are you left with? Just a vague idea of fate, where everything is decided on a whim.

In the end, this would lead us to believe that people are saved or damned without God even being aware of it, since there's no clear distinction between the two. Instead, God just treats everyone the same, first with tolerance that can make them stubborn, and then with compassion that can discipline and punish them. It's up to each person to decide if they'll be saved or damned, while God is off doing something else, maybe attending a feast with the Ethiopians, like Homer described.

Aristotle also describes a God for us, similar to one who sleeps, for example, and allows anyone who wants to, to take advantage of and misuse his kindness and strictness. And how can logic think differently about God than what Diatribe does here? Just as she snores away and disregards divine matters, she assumes that God is also somewhat dozing off. She believes that God, having no involvement in the practice of wisdom, will, and present power in selecting, separating, and inspiring, has entrusted humans with the busy and challenging task of accepting or rejecting His patience and anger. This is what happens when we try to measure and justify God using human reasoning. Instead of respecting the mysteries of His Majesty and being overwhelmed by His glory, we intrude to examine them. Instead of offering a single excuse for Him, we spew out countless blasphemies! In the process, we also forget ourselves and babble like crazy people, speaking against both God and ourselves simultaneously, even though our intention is to speak wisely on behalf of both God and ourselves.

You can see, first of all, what Diatribe's interpretation does to God's image. But don't you also notice how consistent she is with herself? Previously, she had made Freewill equal for everyone by including everyone in one definition. But now, as she argues, she forgets her own definition and creates distinctions between a cultivated Freewill and an uncultivated Freewill, presenting a variety of Freewills based on different actions, habits, and personalities. There is one that can do good, another that cannot do good, and this is done through its own abilities before grace is received. According to these abilities, she had defined that Freewill could not, by itself, desire anything good.

As a result, if we don't allow God's will alone to have the power to harden, show mercy, and do everything, then we must attribute to Freewill the ability to do everything without grace, even though we have denied that it can do any good without grace.

So, the comparison of the sun and rain doesn't really work for this point. A Christian might use that comparison more appropriately by thinking of the Gospel as the sun and rain (like in Psalm 19 and Hebrews 6), the cultivated ground as the chosen ones, and the uncultivated ground as the rejected ones. The chosen ones are built up and improved by the word, while the rejected ones are offended and made worse. On the other hand, when left to its own devices, free will is like the uncultivated ground in everyone, and is actually the realm of Satan.

SECTION 9: ERASMUS' TWO REASONS FOR INTERPRETING THIS FIGURATIVELY ARE EXAMINED.

Now let's look at the reasons for interpreting this passage figuratively. Diatribe thinks it's absurd that God, who is not only just but also good, would be said to have hardened someone's heart just to show off his own power through that person's wickedness. So, Diatribe turns to Origen, who admits that God provided the opportunity for the hardening, but puts the blame back on Pharaoh. Origen also points out that the Lord said, "For this reason I have raised you up," not 'for this reason I have made you.' Because if Pharaoh was wicked just because of how God made him, then God wouldn't have seen all his works as very good. That's Diatribe's argument.

So, absurdity is one of the main reasons for not taking Moses' and Paul's words literally. But what belief is threatened by this absurdity, and who is bothered by it? Human reason is bothered. And it's true that human reason, which is blind, deaf, foolish, disrespectful, and sacrilegious when dealing with all of God's words and actions, is brought in here to judge God's actions and words. By the same logic, you would deny all the beliefs of the Christian faith, because it's incredibly absurd (and as Paul says, "a stumbling block to Jews and foolishness to Gentiles") that God would become human, born of a virgin, be crucified, and sit at the right hand of the Father.

It's ridiculous, I say, to believe such things. So let's come up with some ideas like the Arians did, to stop Christ from being considered God without any doubt. Let's also create ideas like the Manicheans did, to prevent him from being a real man; and let's portray him as a kind of ghost, which passed through the Virgin like sunlight through a piece of glass, and was crucified. What a great way to interpret the Scripture!

However, these ideas don't really help us progress, and they don't avoid the absurdity: it still seems unreasonable that a just and good God would demand impossible things from free will. When free will can't choose good and is forced to serve sin, it's still blamed. As long as God withholds the Spirit, he wouldn't be any kinder or more merciful than if he hardened people's hearts or allowed them to be hardened. Reason keeps insisting that these actions don't seem like those of a kind and merciful God.

These concepts are so beyond our understanding, and we lack the ability to even control our own thoughts, that we struggle to believe God is good if he were to act and judge in this way. Putting faith aside, we want to be able to touch, see, and understand how God can be just and not cruel. We would have this kind of understanding if it were said about God, "He hardens no one, he condemns no one; on the contrary, he has compassion for everyone, he saves everyone." This would mean that hell would be destroyed, the fear of death removed, and no future punishment would be feared.

This is why we become so passionate and insistent on excusing and defending the idea of a just and benevolent God.

Faith and the Spirit, however, have a different perspective. They believe that God is good, even if he were to destroy all humans. And what's the point of exhausting ourselves with these complex speculations, just so we can shift the blame of hardening from God to free will? Let free will do its best, using all its resources and exerting all its strength, but it will never provide an example of avoiding being hardened where God has not given his Spirit, or of earning mercy where it has been left to its own devices. Because, according to Diatribe, what difference does it make whether free will is hardened or deserves to be hardened, since hardening is inevitably part of it as long as it lacks the ability to desire good?

These rhetorical devices don't resolve the absurdity; if anything, they only make way for even greater absurdities and attribute all power to free will. So let's forget about these unhelpful and misleading devices and stick to the clear and straightforward word of God.

SECTION 10: THE FACT THAT GOD MADE EVERYTHING VERY GOOD ISN'T A SUFFICIENT REASON.

The other main reason for accepting this interpretation is that the things God created are very good. And God doesn't say, "I made you for this very purpose," but rather, "For this very purpose, I have raised you up."

First, let me point out that this statement was made before humanity's fall, when the things God had created were indeed very good. But in the third chapter, we quickly see how humans became evil, abandoned by God, and left to their own devices. All people are born from this corrupted state, and as a result, they are born wicked - including Pharaoh.

In this long note, the author discusses the idea of "the perfectibility of man." He believes that this concept is not only impossible but also dangerous. He argues that if people were to become perfect, they would no longer have any reason to improve themselves, and society would stagnate. The author also points

As Paul says, "We were all by nature the children of wrath, even as others." God, therefore, made Pharaoh wicked by creating him from a wicked and corrupted seed. This is in line with the Proverbs of Solomon, which state, "The Lord has made all things for himself, yes, even the wicked man for the day of evil." God didn't create wickedness in Pharaoh, but rather formed him from an evil seed and governed him. So, it's not accurate to say that because God formed the wicked man, he isn't wicked. How can he not be wicked when he comes from a wicked seed? As mentioned in Psalm 51, "Behold I was conceived in sins." Job also asks, "Who can make clean that which has been conceived of unclean seed?"

Although God doesn't create sin, he continues to form and multiply a nature that has been corrupted by sin due to the absence of the Spirit. It's like a carpenter making statues out of rotten wood. In this way, people are created with the same nature they were formed from by God.

Secondly, I'd like to point out that if you interpret the words "very good" to refer to God's works after the fall, remember that these words are about God, not us. It doesn't say that humans saw the things God made and thought they were very good.

Many things may seem good to God and actually are, but they might appear bad to us and indeed are. For example, afflictions, calamities, errors, and hell - all of these are considered God's best works, but they are seen as terrible and damnable by the world. What could be better than Christ and the Gospel? Yet, what is more despised by the world? How these things are good in God's eyes but evil in ours is a mystery known only to God and those who see with His eyes, meaning those who have the Spirit. But there's no need for such complex arguments right now. The previous answer is enough for now.

SECTION 11: HOW GOD WORKS EVIL IN US, CONSIDERED.

You might wonder how God can be said to work evil in us, like hardening our hearts, giving people over to their desires, tempting them, and so on. Honestly, we should be satisfied with God's words and simply believe what they say, as God's works are beyond our understanding. But to indulge reason, which is just another term for human folly, I'm willing to play the fool and try to address this question, even if it means babbling a bit.

Firstly, even reason and Diatribe agree that God works all things in all things, and that nothing happens or has any effect without Him. He is all-powerful, and this is part of His omnipotence, as Paul says in his letter to the Ephesians (Ephesians 1:21).

So, Satan and humans, having fallen from God and being abandoned by Him, cannot desire good; meaning, they cannot desire things that please God or that God wants. People are constantly focused on their own desires, so they can only seek what is their own, not God's. However, this will and nature of theirs, which is against God, still exists. Satan and evil people are not nothing, as they have a nature and will, even though their nature is corrupt and against God. This remaining nature in evil people and Satan, being God's creation and work, is no less subject to God's power and actions than all of God's other creations and works.

Since God moves and influences everything, it must be that He also moves and influences Satan and evil people. But He acts in them according to what they are and what He finds them to be. That is, since they are against Him and evil, and are driven by this force of God's power, they only do things that are against Him and evil. It's like a horse rider driving a horse that is lame in one or two of its legs; the rider drives the horse according to its abilities and condition. So, the horse moves awkwardly. But what can the rider do? They drive the lame horse among healthy horses, making the lame horse move awkwardly while the others move well. It cannot be any other way unless the horse is healed. This example shows how when God works in and through bad people, the result is evil; but it doesn't mean that God is doing evil, even though He works through evil people. This is because, being good Himself, He cannot do evil.

However, God still uses flawed tools that cannot avoid being controlled and influenced by His power. The fault of evil actions lies in these tools, which God does not let remain idle. At the same time, God is the one who drives them. It's like a carpenter who cuts poorly because they're using a jagged and serrated axe. This is why wicked people can't help but constantly go astray and commit sins. They are seized and driven by God's power, and they are not allowed to remain idle. Instead, they think, want, and act according to their nature.

SECTION 12: HOW GOD HARDENS

These truths are certain and established if we first believe that God is all-powerful, and secondly, that wicked people are God's creations. However, when people are opposed to God and left on their own without His Spirit, they cannot want or do good. God's omnipotence makes it impossible for wicked people to escape His influence and guidance. Yet, being under God's control, they obey Him. However, their corruption and opposition to God make them unable to be guided and pulled towards goodness.

God cannot stop using His omnipotence just because wicked people don't like Him, and wicked people can't change their dislike into good-will. So, it's inevitable that people keep making mistakes and sinning until they are set right by God's Spirit. However, in all of this, Satan still rules peacefully and maintains his control, following the push of God's divine power.

Next comes the process of hardening, which happens like this: Wicked people are completely focused on themselves and their own concerns, just like Satan, their leader. They don't care about God or His matters; instead, they seek their own wealth, glory, achievements, wisdom, power - basically, their own kingdom. And they want to enjoy these things peacefully. But if anyone opposes them or tries to take away any of their possessions, their anger and fury against their enemy are just as strong as their desire to pursue these things. They are just as unable to control their anger as they are to control their desires and pursuits, and they are just as unable to control their desires as they are to end their existence. They can't do any of this because they are God's creations, even if they are flawed ones.

This is the story of the world's anger against God's Gospel. The Gospel, which is stronger than any creature, comes to challenge this peaceful ruler of the palace. It condemns the desires for glory, wealth, and personal wisdom and righteousness - in short, everything that people rely on. This provocation of the wicked, caused by God saying or doing something against their wishes, is what hardens and burdens them.

So, even though people are naturally inclined to resist and go astray due to the corruption of their nature, they are made even worse when they are opposed and deprived of what they want. For example, when God was trying to take back control from the evil Pharaoh, He made Pharaoh even more stubborn and weighed down his heart. God did this by having Moses confront him with words, threatening to take away his kingdom and free the people from his rule. At the same time, God didn't give Pharaoh the Spirit within, but let his own wicked and corrupt nature, ruled by Satan, grow more intense, filled with arrogance and contempt.

SECTION 13: AVOIDING MISUNDERSTANDINGS

Don't think that when we say God hardens or causes evil in us (since to harden is to make evil), He is creating new evil within us. It's not like imagining a malicious wine maker who mixes poison into the wine. There's no evil in the container itself; the container just receives or endures the harmful actions of the one mixing. But when people hear that God works both good and evil in us, and that we are subject to God's actions passively, they might think that humans are either good or at least not bad, and that somehow they become the subject of God's bad actions. These people don't fully understand how active God is in all His creations and how He doesn't let any of them rest. So, anyone who wants to understand such statements should remember this: God works evil in us (or through us), not because of His own fault, but because of our own flaws.

Since we are naturally evil and God is good, He guides us through His own power (that's just how His omnipotence works). And because He is good, He can only do evil through an evil instrument. However, He uses it wisely by turning it to His own glory and our salvation.

Similarly, God finds Satan's will to be evil without creating it as evil. It became evil when God abandoned Satan and Satan sinned. God then takes this evil will and uses it in His actions, moving it wherever He wants. But Satan's will doesn't stop being evil just because God moves it this way. Just like David said about Shimei in 2 Samuel 16:10, "Let him curse, for God has commanded him to curse David." How does God command him to curse? Such a hateful and wicked act! There was no external commandment like this to be found anywhere. David must have thought about this: the all-powerful God speaks, and it happens; He does everything through His eternal word.

So, God's power and omnipotence take control of Shimei's will and all his actions - that will which was already evil and had been turned against David before. Shimei met David at just the right moment, deserving such a curse - and even the good God commands this curse (meaning, He speaks the word and it happens) which is unleashed by a wicked and blasphemous tool. For He takes control of that tool and brings it with Him in His actions.

SECTION 14: CONSIDERING PHARAOH'S CASE

So, God hardens Pharaoh by showing him His words and actions, which Pharaoh's wicked and evil will naturally hates - most likely due to his inherent flaws and natural corruption.

Now, God doesn't change His will internally through His Spirit; instead, He continues to present and enforce His words and actions. On the other hand, Pharaoh, considering his strength, wealth, and power, relies on them due to his natural flaws. As a result, he becomes arrogant and conceited because of his perceived greatness. At the same time, he becomes a proud mocker of Moses, who approaches him humbly and with the straightforward word of God. This is how Pharaoh's hardening begins.

Then, the more Moses pushes and warns him, the more Pharaoh gets irritated and aggravated. His evil will wouldn't be activated or hardened on its own, but since the all-powerful God drives it forward with an unavoidable force, like He does with the rest of His creations, it has to happen. Additionally, God presents external factors that naturally provoke and upset Pharaoh's will. As a result, Pharaoh can't avoid being hardened any more than he can avoid the influence of divine omnipotence or the dislike and evilness of his own will. This is how God completes Pharaoh's hardening.

He presents his harmful intentions towards something that, by his own nature, he dislikes from the outside. After this, he doesn't stop encouraging that evil desire, as he discovers it, through his own powerful influence within. In the meantime, due to the wickedness of his will, the man can't help but despise what goes against him and rely on his own strength. As a result, he becomes so stubborn that he neither listens nor understands, but is swept away under the control of the devil, like someone who is insane and ranting.

If this perspective on the situation is acceptable, then I have made my point. We agree to dismiss the interpretations and explanations of people and take God's words literally, so we don't have to make excuses for God or accuse him of being unfair. When he says, "I will harden Pharaoh's heart," he's speaking clearly, as if to say, "I will make Pharaoh's heart hard" or "it will become hard because of my actions and influence." We've discussed how this happens: by God stirring up Pharaoh's own evil desires from within, using the same general force that moves everything, so that Pharaoh continues to act according to his own inclinations and desires. God won't stop pushing him, and he can't do otherwise. At the same time, God will present Pharaoh with a message and an action that will clash with his evil desires. Pharaoh won't be able to do anything but make bad choices while God strengthens the evil within him through his omnipotence.

In this way, God was absolutely certain that Pharaoh's heart would become hard. He knew for sure that Pharaoh's will couldn't resist the power of God's influence, nor could it let go of its own wickedness or accept Moses as a friend when he appeared as an enemy. Instead, Pharaoh's will would remain evil, and he would inevitably become worse, more stubborn, and more arrogant as he followed his own natural tendencies and faced opposition that he didn't like and looked down upon because of his self-confidence.

So, as you can see from this statement, it's clear that free will can only lead to evil. This is because God, who never makes mistakes due to ignorance or lies out of wickedness, confidently promises that Pharaoh's heart will be hardened. God knows for sure that an evil will can only desire evil, and if something good is presented to it that goes against its own desires, it can only make the situation worse.

SECTION 15: PEOPLE MIGHT STILL ASK IRRELEVANT QUESTIONS.

So, someone might ask, "Why doesn't God just stop using his power to provoke the wicked person's will to continue being evil and getting worse?" My response is, "To ask this is to want God to stop being God just to accommodate the wicked. It's like wishing for God's power and actions to stop. In fact, it's like wanting God to stop being good so that the wicked don't get worse."

But why doesn't God change those evil desires that he stirs up at the same time? This relates to the hidden aspects of his greatness, where his decisions are beyond our understanding. We shouldn't be asking this question; instead, we should be in awe of these mysteries. And if people get upset and complain about this, let them complain. It won't change anything, though. God won't be altered by these complaints. And what if many ungodly people are scandalized and leave? The chosen ones will still remain, regardless.

The same answer will be given to those who ask, "Why did he allow Adam to fall? And why does he continue to create all of us, who are tainted by the same sin - when he could have prevented Adam from sinning, and could have either created us from a different source or cleansed the tainted seed first?" He is God, whose will has no cause or reason that can dictate it as a rule or measure since it has no equal or superior, but is itself the guiding principle for everything. If it didn't have any rule or measure, nor any cause or reason, then it could no longer be the will of God. For what He wants is not right because he should want it or should have wanted it. On the contrary, it is right simply because He wants it; therefore, whatever is done must be right. Cause and reason are applied to a creature's will, but not to the Creator's; unless you were to place another Creator above Him.

SECTION 16: COMPARING THE TROPE TO THE TEXT

I believe the "trope-making" Diatribe has been adequately refuted by the points I've made so far. But let's now examine the text itself and see how well it aligns with the Diatribe's interpretation.

It's common for people who avoid arguments by focusing on specific words to completely ignore the actual text and its context. Instead, they choose a word they don't like and twist its meaning to fit their own interpretation, without considering how it relates to the surrounding text or the author's intent. This is what Diatribe does here, taking the phrase "I will harden" out of context and molding it to suit their own view, without thinking about how it fits back into the text as a whole. This is why even the most learned scholars, who have been widely respected for centuries, often find Scripture unclear. It's no surprise, really - even the sun wouldn't be able to shine if people treated it this way.

But I've already pointed out that Pharaoh isn't said to be hardened simply because God is patient with him and doesn't punish him right away. After all, Pharaoh was afflicted with many plagues. If "hardening" means being patient and not immediately punishing someone, then why would God repeatedly promise to harden Pharaoh's heart (as a future action) while the miracles were already happening?

All this time, before these miracles and this hardening occurred, Pharaoh was a man who had caused so much suffering to the Israelites due to his extreme pride, which stemmed from his prosperity and wealth. However, this idea doesn't really fit the purpose here, because it could be applied to anyone who sins while experiencing God's patience and leniency. In that case, we could say that all people are hardened, since everyone commits sins, and no one could do so without God's patience. So, this hardening of Pharaoh is something different and beyond the general patience of God's leniency.

SECTION 17: MOSES' MAIN GOAL IN REPEATEDLY EMPHASIZING GOD'S PLAN AND ACTIONS IN HARDENING PHARAOH'S HEART IS TO STRENGTHEN THE ISRAELITES' FAITH.

In fact, Moses' main focus is not to highlight Pharaoh's wickedness, but to confirm God's truth and mercy, so that the Israelites don't doubt God's promises to free them. Since this liberation is a huge deal, God warns them about the challenges they'll face, so their faith doesn't waver. This way, they'll know that everything that's happening was predicted and is being carried out by the very same God who made those promises to them. It's as if God is saying, "I am freeing you, and that's the truth. But it will be hard for you to believe because Pharaoh will resist and delay the process. Don't doubt my promises at all. All this resistance is part of my plan, so I can perform even more amazing miracles to strengthen your faith and show my power. This way, you'll trust me even more in the future when it comes to other things."

This is similar to what Christ does when he promises the kingdom to his disciples during the Last Supper. He predicts many challenges, including his own death and their various struggles, so that once these events occur, their faith in him will grow even stronger.

Moses also illustrates this concept when he says, "But Pharaoh will not let you go, so that many signs may be performed in Egypt." And again: "I have provoked you for this purpose: to demonstrate my power through you and to make my name known throughout the earth." You can see that Pharaoh's stubbornness serves a specific purpose: to resist God and delay Israel's redemption, providing an opportunity to display numerous signs and demonstrate God's power. The ultimate goal is for God's name to be recognized and believed in all over the world. This is all done to strengthen faith and comfort the weak, so they can confidently trust in God as the true, faithful, powerful, and compassionate One.

It's as if God is gently telling his followers, "Don't be frightened by Pharaoh's hardened heart; I am the one who controls it, and I will use it for a greater purpose. As your deliverer, I will perform many signs and reveal my greatness, so that you may believe in me."

So, we have that saying which Moses repeats after almost every plague, "And Pharaoh's heart was hardened, and he did not let the people go, as the Lord had spoken." What does this phrase, "As the Lord had spoken," mean if not that God's truthfulness was shown, as He had already predicted that Pharaoh would be stubborn? If there was any possibility of change or any freedom of will in Pharaoh, such that he had the power to lean towards either side, God could not have predicted his stubbornness with such certainty. But since the one making the promise here can neither be mistaken nor lie, it was absolutely and undoubtedly going to happen that Pharaoh would be stubborn. And this could not be the case unless the stubbornness was completely beyond human control and only within God's power. This is just as I described it earlier: in other words, either God was certain that He would not stop using His omnipotence in Pharaoh's case or because of Pharaoh, since He cannot even stop using it.

Moreover, God was also sure that Pharaoh's will, being naturally evil and opposed to Him, could not agree with God's word and work, which was contrary to it.

So, even though God's omnipotence preserved Pharaoh's inner desire to make decisions, when a contradictory message and action from God was presented to him, the only possible outcome was for Pharaoh's heart to become hardened. If God had not used his omnipotence on Pharaoh at the moment he received Moses' contradictory message, and if Pharaoh's will had been left to act on its own, then there might have been room for debate about which direction his will would have taken.

However, in this situation, Pharaoh is pushed and rushed into making a decision. His will isn't forced against his wishes, but rather, God's natural influence leads him to act according to his own nature, which is a negative one. As a result, he can't help but clash with the message, and in doing so, his heart becomes hardened. This passage strongly argues against the concept of free will, as God, who makes promises, cannot lie. If God doesn't lie, then it's inevitable that Pharaoh's heart will become hardened.

SECTION 18: PAUL'S REFERENCE TO THIS PASSAGE IN ROMANS 9. DIATRIBE STRUGGLES AND ULTIMATELY CONCEDES.

Now let's examine Paul's use of this passage from Moses in Romans 9. Diatribe is really struggling here, twisting and turning in every possible way to avoid losing the concept of Free Will. At one point, she claims it's the necessity of a consequence, but not the necessity of a consequent. Another time, she says it's an ordered will or a signified will, which can be resisted, while a will of good pleasure cannot be resisted. Sometimes, she argues that the passages from Paul don't oppose Free Will because they don't address human salvation. On other occasions, she claims that God's foreknowledge either presupposes necessity or it doesn't. Sometimes, she says grace comes before the will, causing it to desire, accompanying it on its journey, and ensuring a successful outcome. Other times, she argues that the first cause brings about everything, while at other times it acts through secondary causes, doing nothing itself.

Diatribe uses these confusing and contradictory statements to buy time and distract us from the real issue at hand. She assumes we are as disinterested or clueless about the matter as she is. It's like little children who cover their eyes when they're scared or playing, thinking that no one can see them because they can't see anyone else. In the same way, Diatribe tries to avoid the bright light (or rather, the lightning) of the clearest possible words by using various excuses to pretend she doesn't see the actual truth. She hopes to convince us to cover our own eyes so we won't see it either. But all these tactics are signs of a mind that knows it's been defeated and is desperately fighting against an unbeatable truth.

The idea that the necessity of a consequence is somehow different from the necessity of a consequent has already been disproven (Part 1, Section 11). Let Diatribe argue and debate as much as she wants. If God knew beforehand that Judas would betray Jesus, then Judas had no choice but to become a traitor. Judas, or any other creature, couldn't have done otherwise or changed his will, even though he acted willingly and not by force. But the act of willing was set in motion by God's omnipotence, just like everything else.

It's an undeniable fact that God doesn't lie or make mistakes. The words we're discussing aren't unclear or ambiguous, even if all the scholars throughout history have misunderstood them. No matter how much you try to argue, everyone's conscience must admit that if God's foreknowledge is accurate, then what He knows must happen. Otherwise, how could we trust His promises or fear His warnings if they don't necessarily come true? And how could He make promises or warnings if His foreknowledge could be wrong or if we could change the outcome?

This undeniable truth clearly ends all debate and overcomes any clever arguments. We know that human foresight can be wrong. We know that an eclipse doesn't happen because we predict it, but we predict it because it's going to happen. But what does this have to do with God's foreknowledge? That's what we're discussing here.

SECTION 19: DIATRIBE'S CONCESSIONS AND RETRACTIONS EXPOSED.

If you deny the necessity of something foreknown happening, you take away faith and fear of God. You also destroy all of God's promises and threats, and even deny the existence of God. But even Diatribe, after a long struggle and trying all her tricks, is finally forced by the truth to admit our point of view. She says:

"The question about the will and purpose of Diatribe's God is a more difficult one. For God wants the same things that he foreknows. And this is what Paul adds: 'Who can resist his will, if he has mercy on whom he wants, and hardens whom he wants?' (Romans 9:18-19) For if he were a king, he would do whatever he wants, so that no one could resist him; he would be said to do what he wants. Thus, the will of God, being the main cause of all events, seems to impose a necessity on our will."

This is what she says. And I thank God that Diatribe has finally come to her senses. What happened to free will now? But this slippery eel escapes our grasp again by saying: "But Paul doesn't answer this question; instead, he scolds the person asking it, saying, 'But who are you, a human being, to talk back to God?' (Romans 9:20)"

Oh, what a clever dodge! Is this how you handle the word of God? To just assert something like this on your own authority, without providing any scriptural evidence or performing miracles? Or rather, to twist some of the clearest words God ever spoke? "Paul doesn't answer this question," she says. What is he doing then? "He scolds the person asking it," she says. Isn't this scolding actually the most complete answer to the question? What was really being asked in this question about God's will? Wasn't it whether he imposes a necessity on our will? Paul answers, "This is why (meaning, because God does this) he has mercy on whom he wants to have mercy, and he hardens whom he wants to harden. It doesn't depend on human desire or effort, but on God's mercy." (Romans 9:18)

Paul isn't just satisfied with answering the question; he also brings up those who argue for free will. These people claim that there's no such thing as merit, and we aren't condemned by our own faults, among other things. Paul brings them up to put an end to their complaints and grumbling.

Paul says, "You ask me, then, why does God still find fault? For who can resist His will?" Do you see how he's personifying the argument? When people hear that God's will forces a certain outcome on us, they disrespectfully complain, asking why God still finds fault. In other words, why does God push us, demand things from us, and condemn us, as if we could do what He wants if we just decided to? God doesn't have a good reason for these complaints. Instead, He should blame His own will and take issue with that, since no one can resist His will. Who can receive mercy if God doesn't choose to give it? Who can change themselves if God wants to harden them? We can't change or resist God's will. If His will is for us to be hardened, then we have no choice but to be hardened, whether we want it or not.

If Paul hadn't resolved this question or clearly determined that divine foresight imposes a necessity on us, then why bring up people who complain and argue that it's impossible to resist God's will? No one would complain or be upset if they didn't think this necessity had been established. Paul's words about resisting God's will are not unclear. Is there any doubt about what he means by "resisting" or "will," or who he's talking about when he mentions God's will? Let countless highly respected scholars be blind to this and pretend that the Scripture is unclear, and let them be afraid of a tough question. We have some very clear words on this topic: "He has mercy on whom he wants to, and he hardens whom he wants to." Also, "You might say to me, then, why does he still find fault? Who can resist his will?" This question isn't difficult; in fact, nothing could be more obvious to common sense than this conclusion: 'If God knows something will happen beforehand, it will definitely happen.' This logically follows once we accept, based on Scripture, that God neither makes mistakes nor is deceived.

I admit that the question is difficult, even impossible to resolve, if you try to maintain both God's foreknowledge and human freedom at the same time. What's more difficult, or rather more impossible, than arguing that contradictions and opposites don't conflict with each other, or that a number can be both ten and nine at the same time? The question we're discussing isn't difficult. Instead, the difficulty is sought out and brought in, just like ambiguity and obscurity are forced into the Scriptures through violent means.

So, he silences those wicked people who are offended by those straightforward words. And why are they offended? Because they realize that the divine will is fulfilled by our necessity, and because they see that it has been clearly determined that they have no freedom or free will left – but everything depends on God's will alone. He silences them, I say, by telling them to be quiet and to respect the majesty of the divine power and will, over which we have no control. Meanwhile, it has complete power over us to do what it pleases. It's not that we are harmed by its actions since it owes us nothing. It has received nothing from us, and it has promised nothing to us beyond what it chose and was pleased to do.

SECTION 20: WHERE TRUE REVERENCE FOR THE SCRIPTURES LIES.

This is the place and time to worship not the imaginary inhabitants of those Corycian caves, but the real majesty of God in his awe-inspiring wonders and his incomprehensible judgments – and to say, "Your will be done, in heaven, so on earth." On the other hand, we are never more disrespectful and reckless than when we try and criticize these very mysteries and judgments, which are unfathomable. Meanwhile, we think that we are incredibly reverent in examining the holy Scriptures. We don't search those Scriptures, which God has commanded us to search, in one direction, but in another – a direction in which he has forbidden us to search them. So, we do nothing but search them with constant recklessness, if not blasphemy.

Isn't it a misguided quest when we try to reconcile God's all-knowing foresight with our own free will? And when we're willing to diminish God's foresight if it doesn't allow us our freedom or if it implies fate? Isn't it like saying, with those who complain and blaspheme, "Why does He still find fault? Who can resist His will? What happened to the most merciful God? What happened to the One who doesn't want the death of a sinner? Did He create us just to take pleasure in our suffering?" and similar things. Won't these be the cries heard forever among the devils and the damned?

But even our natural reasoning has to admit that the living and true God must be the kind of being who imposes some sort of necessity on us, given that He Himself is free. For example, He would be a laughable God, or more accurately an idol, if He were to foresee the future with uncertainty or be surprised by what happens. Even the pagans have attributed an unstoppable destiny to their gods. He would be just as ridiculous if He didn't have the power to do everything and didn't make everything happen; or if anything actually happened without His involvement. Now, if we accept God's foresight and omnipotence, then it logically follows, without a doubt, that we didn't create ourselves, we don't live by ourselves, and we don't do anything by ourselves, but it's all through His all-powerful nature. And since He knew in advance what kind of people we would be, and He continues to shape us that way, and to guide and govern us as such — what can we possibly imagine within us that is free to have a different outcome than what He already knew or is now bringing about?

So, God's foreknowledge and omnipotence directly contradict human free will. Either God will be wrong in his foreknowledge and fail in his actions (which is impossible), or we will act according to his foreknowledge and influence. By God's omnipotence, I don't mean the power to do many things he doesn't do, but the active omnipotence by which he does everything in all things. This is how the Scripture refers to God as omnipotent. This omnipotence and foreknowledge of God, I argue, completely negates the idea of free will.

We can't use the complexity of Scripture or the difficulty of the subject as an excuse here. The words are very clear, even children understand them. The subject matter is simple and straightforward, and it's something that even common sense can grasp. So, no matter how many people throughout history have written and taught otherwise, it won't help you.

SECTION 21: WHAT OUR NATURAL REASON DISLIKES

Our natural reason is deeply offended by the idea that God would abandon people, harden them, and damn them purely based on his own will, as if he took pleasure in their sins and suffering, which are so immense and eternal. God is described as being incredibly merciful and good, so it seems unjust, cruel, and unbearable to think of him in this way. This idea has upset many great individuals throughout history - and who wouldn't be offended?

I've been deeply upset by this issue myself, to the point of despair, wishing I had never been born a man - until I realized how beneficial that despair was and how closely related it is to grace. That's why there's so much effort put into promoting the goodness of God and blaming human will. This led to the discovery of distinctions between God's regulated and absolute will, the necessity of consequences and consequents, and other similar concepts. However, these ideas have only resulted in confusing the ignorant with "vain babblings, and oppositions of science, falsely so called." Yet, the troubling thought remains deeply rooted in the hearts of both the educated and uneducated (if they ever become serious) that they cannot believe in God's foreknowledge and omnipotence without acknowledging our necessity.

Even natural reason, though offended by this necessity and trying hard to eliminate it, is forced to accept its existence due to personal conviction. This would still be the case even if there were no Scripture.

Everyone can find this belief deep within their hearts, and they can't help but acknowledge and accept it when they hear it discussed, even if they don't want to:

First, that God is all-powerful, not just in what He is capable of doing, but also in what He actually does, as I've mentioned before; otherwise, He would be a ridiculous God. Secondly, He knows and foresees everything, and He can't be mistaken or misled.

Once people accept these two things through the testimony of their hearts and senses, they are eventually forced to admit that we were not created by our own will, but by necessity. As a result, we don't do anything by our own free will, but rather as God has foreseen and directed us with a plan and power that is both infallible and unchangeable. So, we find it written in everyone's hearts that there is no such thing as free will, even if this belief is clouded by so many opposing arguments and the teachings of so many influential people throughout history.

Similarly, every other law that has been written in our hearts (according to Paul's testimony) is recognized when properly under- , stood. However, it becomes obscured when twisted by ungodly teachers and influenced by other opinions.

SECTION 22: PAUL'S ARGUMENT CONTINUES. DIATRIBE IS DISHONEST AND COWARDLY, TRYING TO ESCAPE BUT FAILING.

Now, let's return to Paul. If he isn't addressing this question and concluding that human necessity comes from God's foresight and will, why does he need to use the analogy of the potter who makes one vessel for honor and another for dishonor from the same lump of clay (Romans 9:21)?

However, the created thing does not say to its creator, "Why have you made me like this?" (Romans 9:20). Paul is talking about people, whom he compares to clay, and God to the potter. The comparison doesn't make sense unless he means that our freedom is insignificant; otherwise, it's pointless and irrelevant. In fact, Paul's entire argument in favor of grace falls flat. The main purpose of his letter is to show that we are powerless, even when we seem to be doing good. He also says that Israel, by pursuing righteousness, did not achieve it, while the Gentiles, who did not pursue it, did achieve it (Romans 9:30-31). I will discuss this in more detail when I present my own arguments.

However, Diatribe, ignoring the overall context and purpose of Paul's argument, finds comfort in cherry-picked and distorted words. Diatribe doesn't care that later in Romans 11:20, Paul warns them, "You stand by faith; be careful not to become arrogant." And again, in Romans 11:23, "They too, if they believe, will be grafted in," etc. He doesn't mention anything about human abilities here, but uses imperative and subjunctive verbs, the significance of which has already been explained.

Indeed, Paul himself, in the same place, seems to prevent those who boast about free will, by not saying that they can believe, but "God is able to graft them in." In short, Diatribe seems unsure and hesitant when discussing these texts from Paul's writings, to the point where it seems like she doesn't even agree with her own words. In the places where she should be proving her doctrine, she often stops the discussion with phrases like 'But enough of this,' or 'I won't investigate this now,' or 'This isn't part of the subject,' or 'They would say this,' and many similar expressions. This leaves the matter unresolved, making it unclear whether she is defending free will or just trying to deflect Paul's arguments with empty words.

She does all this in her own unique way, as if she isn't really committed to the cause. But we shouldn't be so indifferent; we shouldn't just skim the surface or be swayed like a reed in the wind. Instead, we should confidently, firmly, and passionately assert our beliefs, and then back them up with solid, relevant, and ample evidence.

Furthermore, Diatribe tries to cleverly balance the ideas of liberty and necessity when she says, 'Not all types of necessity eliminate free will. For example, God the Father necessarily begets the Son, but He does so willingly and freely, as He is not forced to do so.'

Are we debating now, I ask, about compulsion and force? Haven't I always made it clear in my writings that I'm talking about a necessity of immutability? I know that the Father willingly begets; I know that Judas betrayed Christ through an act of his will. But I claim that if God foreknew it, then this will was definitely and infallibly going to arise in Judas. If what I'm saying isn't clear enough, let's distinguish between two types of necessity: one of force, which relates to the action, and another of infallibility, which relates to the timing. Let anyone who listens to me understand that I'm talking about the necessity of infallibility, not of force. In other words, I'm not discussing whether Judas became a traitor willingly or unwillingly, but whether it was absolutely certain that Judas would betray Christ at the time appointed by God, through an act of his own will.

But look at what Diatribe says here: "If you consider God's infallible foreknowledge, Judas was bound to become a traitor; but Judas could have changed his will." Do you even know what you're saying, my Diatribe? Leaving aside what has already been proven—that the will can only choose evil—how could Judas change his will while still being consistent with God's infallible foreknowledge? Could he change God's foreknowledge and make it fallible? At this point, Diatribe gives up, abandons her position, drops her weapons, and retreats. She leaves the debate to those scholastic subtleties that distinguish between the necessity of a consequence and the necessity of a consequent. This is the kind of wordplay she doesn't want to engage in.

No doubt, it's wise of you to bring your case to the center of a crowded court - when a skilled speaker is most needed - only to turn your back and leave the task of responding and clarifying to others. You should have followed this advice from the beginning and refrained from writing altogether, as the saying goes, "The man who doesn't know how to fight, stays away from the weapons of the field."

No one expected Erasmus to solve the difficult question of "how God can know everything for certain, yet our actions are still uncertain." This issue has been around long before Diatribe's time. However, people did expect him to respond and clarify. But, being a skilled speaker himself and knowing that we're clueless about it, he uses a clever rhetorical trick to help him. He takes us, the uninformed, along with him - as if the matter being debated isn't important and the whole discussion is just a trivial argument - and he boldly leaves the crowded scene, wearing his crown of ivy and laurel.

But your strategy hasn't worked, my friend! There's no rhetorical skill powerful enough to deceive a sincere conscience. Conscience's sting is stronger than the most eloquent speech with all its techniques and figures. We won't let the rhetorician move on to another topic just to hide from the issue at hand. This isn't the place for such a show. The crux of the matter, the heart of the debate, is being challenged here. This is where Free Will is either defeated or triumphs completely.

But instead of facing this critical moment, as soon as you sense danger - or rather, see that victory over Free Will is certain - you claim to see only metaphysical subtleties in the question. Is this how a trustworthy theologian should act? Are you truly committed to the cause? If so, why do you leave your listeners hanging and the debate in a state of chaos and frustration? Yet, you still want to be seen as having done your job honorably and having won the victory. Such cunning and deception might be acceptable in worldly matters, but it's absolutely unacceptable in theology, where the goal is to seek simple and honest truth in order to save souls.

SECTION 23: CONGRATULATIONS TO THE SOPHISTS AND DIATRIBE ON THEIR DESPERATE NEED FOR A DISTINCTION BETWEEN THE NECESSITY OF A CONSEQUENCE AND THAT OF A CONSEQUENT.

The Sophists have also felt the unstoppable and overwhelming force of this argument, so they've come up with this distinction between the necessity of a consequence and that of a consequent. However, it has already been demonstrated how pointless this distinction is. Just like you, they don't realize what they're saying and how much they're admitting against themselves. Because if you accept the necessity of a consequence, free will is defeated and brought down, and it doesn't matter whether the consequence is necessary or contingent. Why should I care if free will acts willingly and not by force? It's enough for me that you agree, "Judas must necessarily do what he does willingly, and the outcome cannot be different if God has foreknown it." If God foreknows either that Judas will betray the Lord or that he will change his mind about betraying him - whichever of the two He foreknows, it will necessarily happen. Otherwise, God would be wrong in his fore-knowledge and prediction, which is impossible. The necessity of the consequence achieves this: if God foreknows an event, that event necessarily occurs. In other words, free will is nothing. This necessity of the consequence is neither unclear nor vague. Even if the great scholars throughout history have been blind, they must still acknowledge its existence, as it is so evident and certain that it can be felt.

However, the necessity of the consequent, which they find comforting, is nothing more than an illusion; as the saying goes, it directly contradicts the necessity of the consequence. For example, if I say "God fore-knows that Judas will be a traitor; therefore, it will definitely and infallibly happen that Judas is a traitor," this is the necessity of a consequence.

In response to your argument about necessity, you try to comfort yourself by saying, "But since Judas can change his decision to betray, there is no necessity in the outcome." I ask you, how can these two statements coexist: "Judas might not want to betray" and "it is necessary for Judas to want to betray"? Don't they directly contradict each other? You say, "He won't be forced to betray against his will." But how does that help your case? You've been talking about the necessity of an outcome, claiming that the outcome isn't made necessary by the necessity of the consequence. But you haven't said anything about forcing the outcome. Your response should have addressed the necessity of the outcome, but instead, you give an example that demonstrates force in the consequence. I ask one question, and you answer another. All of this comes from a state of mind where you're not fully awake or aware, and you don't realize how ineffective your argument about the necessity of an outcome is.

SECTION 24: THE OTHER ACCEPTED TEXT IS DEFENDED. IT HAS NOTHING TO DO WITH SALVATION.

This is what Jerome had said. As for the first of the two passages, it concerns the hardening of Pharaoh's heart and includes all similar texts, forming an unbeatable group.

Now let's look at the second example, involving Jacob and Esau. Before they were even born, it was said, "The elder shall serve the younger." Diatribe tries to avoid this passage by claiming that it doesn't really relate to the topic of human salvation. They argue that God may decide that someone should be a servant or poor, regardless of the person's will, without necessarily condemning them to eternal damnation.

Notice how a slippery mind, determined to avoid the truth, seeks out various detours and escape routes. But still, they don't quite manage to get away. Let's assume, for the sake of argument, that this text doesn't directly concern human salvation (which I'll address later). Does that mean Paul brought it up for no reason? Are we supposed to believe that Paul would make himself look foolish or absurd in the middle of such a serious discussion?

This idea actually comes from Jerome, who, with an air of arrogance and while speaking sacrilegiously, dares to claim in multiple instances that the Scriptures Paul cites to argue against free will don't actually oppose free will in their original context. What does this imply, if not that Paul is twisting the divine Scriptures and misleading the faithful by imposing his own ideas onto them when establishing the foundations of Christian doctrine? This is hardly the respect that the Holy Spirit should receive through Paul, who is a chosen and holy instrument of God!

Now, Jerome should be read with discernment. And this statement of his is to be considered among the many that he has written disrespectfully, due to his lack of effort in studying and his difficulty in understanding Scripture. Diatribe quickly accepts this statement without any discernment and doesn't bother to soften it with any explanation. Instead, she judges and defines the Scriptures by this statement, as if it were an unquestionable truth. This is how we end up using the inappropriate statements of people as guidelines for interpreting God's word. Can we still be surprised that God's word has become "ambiguous and obscure," and that many of the Fathers are blind to its true meaning when it is treated with such disrespect?

SECTION 25: PAUL DEFENDED IN HIS USE OF GENESIS 25:21-23. NOTHING IS GAINED BY ASSUMING THE SERVICE IS ONLY TEMPORAL.

Therefore, let anyone who says, "those words do not oppose the doctrine of Freewill in their original context, which oppose what is quoted by Paul," be condemned. This is said, but it is not proven. And it is said by those who neither understand Paul nor the passages he cites, but deceive themselves by interpreting the words in their own, disrespectful way. Even if this particular text (Genesis 25:21-23) were only about temporary servitude (which is not the case), Paul still rightfully and effectively quotes it to prove that when it was said to Rebekah, "The older will serve the younger," it is not because of the merits of Jacob or Esau, but through the One who calls.

Paul's question is about whether they achieved what is said of them through their own free will. He argues that it wasn't due to their own free will, but rather by the grace of the one who called them, that Jacob achieved what Esau did not. He supports this with strong evidence from Scripture, such as the fact that they were not yet born and had done neither good nor evil. The main focus of the argument lies in this proof, and this is the topic being debated.

However, Diatribe, with her clever rhetorical skills, avoids and disguises these points, and doesn't really address the issue of merits (even though she claimed she would, and even though Paul's discussion of the topic demands it). Instead, she argues about temporary servitude (which isn't really relevant) just so she can appear not to be defeated by Paul's powerful words.

What could she possibly argue against Paul in support of free will? What did free will do for Jacob, and how did it harm Esau, when God's foreknowledge and plan had already determined what each of them would receive? Specifically, that one would serve and the other would rule, even before they were born or had done anything. The rewards were decided before the individuals were born and had started to act. Diatribe should have addressed this point. This is what Paul emphasizes: that they had not yet done anything good or evil, but still, one is chosen to be the master and the other the servant by divine judgment. The question isn't whether this servitude relates to eternal salvation, but rather what merit led to this servitude being imposed on someone who hadn't earned it.

But it's incredibly frustrating to argue with these twisted attempts to manipulate and evade Scripture.

SECTION 26: THE SERVICE IS NOT REALLY ABOUT EARTHLY MATTERS, BUT SPIRITUAL ONES.

It is clear from the text itself that Moses is not only talking about their earthly servitude and rule; and that Paul is also correct in understanding Moses to be referring to their eternal salvation. Even though this isn't so crucial to the main point, I won't allow Paul to be slandered by disrespectful people. The divine response given to Rebekah in the book of Moses is this: "Two types of people will be separated from your womb; and one group will overcome the other, and the older will serve the younger." (Genesis 25:23) Here, two distinct groups of people are clearly differentiated from each other. One is accepted into God's grace, allowing them to overcome the older group, even though they are younger. This victory is not achieved through physical strength, but rather through God's support. How else could the younger group conquer the older one, if not for God's presence with them?

Now, as the younger is about to become part of God's people, it's not just about external rule or servitude being discussed here, but everything related to being God's people - like God's blessing, the word, the Spirit, the promise of Christ, and the eternal kingdom. This idea is further supported by Scripture later on, where it talks about Jacob being blessed and receiving the promises and the kingdom. Paul briefly touches on these points when he says, "the elder will serve the younger," referring us back to Moses for a more detailed explanation. So, contrary to the disrespectful interpretation by Jerome and Diatribe, we can argue that all the passages Paul cites actually argue even more strongly against the concept of free will in their original context than they do in his writings.

This observation is not only true for Paul but also for all the Apostles who use Scripture to support their teachings and confirm them. Wouldn't it be absurd to quote something as evidence if it doesn't actually support the argument or address the issue at hand? It's considered foolish among philosophers to try to prove an unknown thing with something even more unknown or with an unrelated argument. So, how can we attribute such nonsense to the main teachers and authors of Christ's doctrine, upon which the salvation of souls depends? This is particularly relevant when they discuss the core aspects of faith. But should we really be surprised by such insinuations from those who don't truly respect the divine Scriptures?

SECTION 27: DIATRIBE'S EVASIONS OF MALACHI 1:2-3. LOVE, AS A FIGURE OF SPEECH, IS USED FOR THE EFFECT OF LOVE.

Malachi's statement, which Paul quotes, "Jacob I have loved, but Esau I have hated," is twisted by Diatribe in three different ways. The first argument is, 'If you take the words literally, then God does not love as we do; nor does He hate anyone, since God is not subject to emotions like these.'

What am I hearing? Hasn't the question been changed from why God loves and hates to how He loves and hates? The real question is, on what basis does He love or hate us? We know very well that God does not love or hate in the same way we do; we love and hate changeably, but He loves and hates according to His eternal and unchangeable nature. That's how far He is from being affected by emotions. And it's this very fact that forces the concept of free will to be nothing more than an illusion – the love of God towards people is eternal and unchangeable, and His hatred towards them is eternal as well. This is true not only before we have done anything to deserve it, but even before the creation of the world. And everything that happens to us is determined by whether He has loved us or not loved us from eternity. This is so true that not only God's love, but even the way He loves, brings necessity upon us.

Look at what Diatribe's attempts to escape have gotten her. No matter how much she tries to avoid it, she keeps coming back to the same point, proving that it's pointless to fight against the truth. But let's accept your argument: let God's love be the result of love, and God's hatred be the result of hatred. Are these outcomes created outside or alongside God's will? Will you also argue that God doesn't will things the way we do, and that He isn't influenced by the desire to will something?

If these outcomes happen, they only happen when God wills them. And whatever God wills, He either loves or hates. So tell me, what did Jacob and Esau do to deserve God's love and hatred, respectively, before they were even born and had done anything? It seems that Paul is right to use Malachi to support Moses' idea that God chose Jacob before he was born because He loved him, not because Jacob loved Him first or because God was influenced by any merit of Jacob's. This example of Jacob and Esau demonstrates what our free will can truly accomplish.

SECTION 28: MALACHI DISCUSSES TEMPORARY SUFFERING.

The second of these complex interpretations is that Malachi doesn't appear to be talking about the eternal hatred that leads to damnation, but rather a temporary suffering. It is a criticism of those who would rebuild Edom. This is another instance where Paul is accused of misusing Scripture. It seems that we completely disregard our respect for the Holy Spirit's majesty if it means we can support our own ideas about it.

But we'll put up with this insult for now and see what good it does. Malachi talks about temporary affliction. So what? What does this have to do with the matter at hand? Paul is using Malachi to show that this affliction was brought upon Esau without any merit of his own, simply because of God's hatred. Paul does this to argue that free will is meaningless. This is where you're being challenged, so you should focus your response on this issue. We're discussing merit, and you bring up reward. But you do so in a way that doesn't avoid what you intended to avoid. In fact, by mentioning reward, you're actually acknowledging merit. But you pretend not to see this. So tell me, what was the reason in God's mind for loving Jacob and hating Esau when they didn't even exist yet?

Also, it's not true that Malachi only talks about temporary affliction, nor is he concerned with the destruction of Edom. You're twisting the whole meaning of the prophet with this forced interpretation. The prophet makes his point very clear by using straightforward language. He wants to call out the Israelites for their ingratitude; even though God has loved them, they don't love Him as a father or fear Him as a master in return. He proves that God has loved them both through Scripture and actual events. For example, even though Jacob and Esau were brothers (as Moses writes in Genesis 25), God still loved and chose Jacob before he was born (as we've just shown); but He hated Esau so much that He turned his land into a wasteland.

Moreover, God hates, and He continues to hate, with such persistence that even after bringing Jacob back from captivity and restoring him, He still did not allow the Edomites to be restored. If they even say they will build, He threatens their destruction. If the Prophet's own clear text does not contain these things, let the whole world accuse me of lying. So, it's not the boldness of the Edomites being criticized here, but the ingratitude of Jacob's descendants (as I mentioned earlier). They don't realize that what God is giving them and taking away from their brothers, the Edomites, is for no other reason than He loves one and hates the other.

How can it be argued now that the Prophet is only talking about temporary suffering? For he clearly states that he is discussing two different nations of people who descended from the two Patriarchs. God had chosen one of these to be His people and had preserved them; the other had been abandoned and eventually destroyed. Now, the act of choosing a people as His own, or not doing so, is not only about temporary good or evil, but about everything. For our God is not just the God of our temporary possessions, but of everything we have and hope for. He won't choose to be your God or be worshiped by you with half-hearted effort or a limp, but with all your strength and heart - so as to be your God both now and in the future, in all situations, cases, times, and actions.

SECTION 29: JACOB AND ESAU AS A METAPHOR FOR JEWS AND GENTILES

The third of these complex interpretations is this:

"Using a metaphorical form of expression, it is said that God doesn't love all the Gentiles nor hate all the Jews; but rather, some from each group. By this metaphorical interpretation, it becomes clear [she says] that this statement doesn't prove necessity, but rather counters the arrogance of the Jews."

Having created this escape route for herself, she then goes on to argue that God is said to hate those who aren't even born yet, because He knows in advance that they will do things deserving of hatred. In this way, God's hatred and love don't interfere with free will. In the end, she concludes that the Jews have been removed from the olive tree due to their lack of belief; that the Gentiles have been added to it because of their faith — attributing this idea to Paul — and she offers hope to those who have been removed, that they may be added back; and she warns those who have been added, that they may be removed.

I swear, I don't think Diatribe even knows what she's saying! But maybe there's some rhetorical technique at play here, which teaches scholars to obscure the meaning when there's any risk of being caught by the words. I don't see any of those metaphorical expressions here; Diatribe might imagine them in her dreams, but she doesn't prove them. It's no surprise, then, that the statement from Malachi doesn't contradict her when taken metaphorically, since it doesn't have that meaning at all. Also, our debate isn't about that removal and addition that Paul talks about later, when he encourages.

We know that people are joined to the faith through belief and are separated from it by disbelief, and they should be encouraged to believe so they don't get cut off. However, this doesn't mean or prove that they can choose to believe or disbelieve through their own free will. It's this free will that we're debating. We're not talking about who are believers and who aren't, who are Jews and who are non-Jews, or what happens to believers and unbelievers; that's for the person giving advice. Our question is, by what merit or action do people gain the faith that connects them or the disbelief that separates them? This is the teacher's role. Describe this merit to us! Paul teaches that this happens not because of anything we do, but only because of God's love and hatred. When people come to believe, he encourages them to keep going so they don't get cut off. But encouragement doesn't prove what we can do, only what we should do.

I have to use almost more words to keep my opponent from going off track and leaving their argument than in arguing the case itself.

However, keeping them on point is like winning the debate, because the words we're discussing are so clear and undeniable. So, my opponent mostly tries to avoid the issue, quickly moving out of sight and arguing a different case than the one they started with.

SECTION 30: PAUL DOESN'T USE THE ANALOGY OF CLAY IN THE POTTER'S HAND. TEMPORAL AFFLICTIONS DON'T AVOID ITS MEANING.

The third passage is taken from Isaiah 45:9, "Does the clay say to its potter, what are you making?" and from Jeremiah 18:6, "As the clay is in the hand of the potter, so are you in my hand." Then it says,

"These words seem to have a stronger impact when used by Paul than when they appear in the Prophets. In the Prophets, they refer to temporary suffering, but Paul uses them to discuss eternal election and rejection." This makes it seem like Paul is being criticized for his boldness or for not fully understanding the original context. However, before we look at how these passages don't exclude free will, let's first note that Paul doesn't seem to have taken this passage directly from the Prophets, and the Diatribe doesn't prove that he did. Paul usually mentions the author's name or states that he's quoting from the Scriptures, but he doesn't do either here. So, it's more likely that Paul uses this common analogy (which different writers use to explain various ideas) in his own way to illustrate his point. This is similar to how he uses the saying, "A little leaven corrupts the whole lump," in 1 Corinthians 5:6 to talk about bad influences, and in other places to criticize those who distort the word of God. Jesus also refers to the leaven of Herod and the Pharisees in Mark 8:15.

So, even if the Prophets mainly discuss temporary suffering, Paul still uses the analogy in his own way to argue against free will. However, I won't go into detail on this point right now, as I don't want to get sidetracked by unrelated questions. But I'm not sure how it can be proven that free will isn't taken away if we're like clay in the hands of a God who causes suffering. I also don't understand why the Diatribe insists on making this distinction. It's clear that we experience hardships from

God against our will, and we have no choice but to endure them, whether we want to or not. We don't have the power to avoid them, even though we're encouraged to bear them with a willing attitude.

SECTION 31: ADDRESSING THE OBJECTION FROM 1 TIMOTHY 2:20

It's worth discussing Diatribe's objection to the idea that Paul's use of a simile in his argument doesn't exclude the concept of free will. Diatribe points out two supposed absurdities, one from Scripture and one from reason. The Scriptural objection is based on 2 Timothy 2:20, where Paul says that in a large house there are vessels of gold, silver, wood, and clay, some for honorable purposes and some for dishonorable ones. He then adds, "if a man cleanses himself from these, he will be a vessel for honor," etc. Diatribe argues that it would be ridiculous to say to a clay pot, "if you clean yourself, you'll be a vessel of honor." However, this would make sense if said to a barrel with the ability to understand and adapt to its master's will when instructed.

From this, Diatribe concludes that the simile doesn't perfectly align in all aspects, and therefore doesn't prove anything. In response, I would first point out that Paul doesn't say "if a man cleanses himself from his own filth," but rather "from these," meaning the dishonorable vessels. The intended meaning is that if a person remains separate from these ungodly teachers and doesn't associate with them, then they will be a vessel of honor, etc. But even if I were to concede that this passage from Paul has no more significance than Diatribe wants to give it - that is, that the simile doesn't prove anything - what then?

How can she prove that Paul means the same thing in that passage from Romans 9:13, which we are discussing? Is it enough to just quote another passage, without considering whether it has the same purpose or a different one? There's no easier or more common mistake in interpreting Scripture, as I've often pointed out, than to assume different passages are the same just because they seem similar. So, the similarity of texts (which Diatribe relies on here) is even less effective than our own analogy that she's trying to refute. But, to avoid being argumentative, let's assume that both of these passages in Paul's writings mean the same thing, and that an analogy doesn't always perfectly match the thing it's illustrating (which is undoubtedly true). In fact, if it did, it wouldn't be an analogy or a metaphor, but the actual thing itself, as the saying goes, "An analogy limps and doesn't always stand on all fours."

But here's where Diatribe goes wrong and offends: she ignores the main reason for the comparison, which should be the main focus, and instead nitpicks about the words used. Instead, we should try to understand the meaning, as Hilary suggests, not only from the words themselves but also from the reasons behind them. That's where the strength of an analogy lies - in the reason for using it. So why does Diatribe focus on the words Paul uses, rather than the reason he uses the analogy in the first place?

When Paul says, "If a man cleanses himself," he's giving an exhortation; when he says, "In a great house there are vessels," and so on, he's providing instruction. So, considering the context of Paul's words and thoughts, you'd understand that he's talking about the variety and purpose of vessels.

So, the meaning is basically this: "Since so many people are losing their faith these days, our only comfort is knowing that God's foundation is solid and has this guarantee: the Lord knows who truly belongs to Him, and anyone who calls on His name will turn away from evil." This explains the reason and power behind the comparison that the Lord knows who belongs to Him.

Next comes the actual comparison, which is that there are different types of people, some meant for good and some for bad. The main point of this teaching is that people don't determine their own purpose, but rather, it's up to their creator. This idea is also found in Romans 9:21, which says that the potter has the power to decide the purpose of each creation. So, Paul's comparison stands strong and effectively proves that free will doesn't really matter to God.

Finally, there's the encouragement to "cleanse oneself from these things." The significance of this phrase is already clear from what we've discussed earlier.

This doesn't mean that someone can cleanse themselves. In fact, if anything is proven by these words, it's that free will can cleanse itself without grace - since Paul doesn't say, "if grace has cleansed anyone," but "if he cleanses himself." However, there's been a lot of discussion about imperative and conjunctive verbs. And the comparison isn't expressed in conjunctive verbs, but indicative. Just as there are chosen and rejected people, there are vessels of honor and dishonor. In short, if this explanation is accepted, Paul's entire argument falls apart. But why would he bring up people complaining against God as the potter if the fault was seen to be in the vessel, not the potter? Who would complain about hearing that someone deserving of damnation is damned?

SECTION 32: REASON'S OBJECTION TO THIS COMPARISON, PRESENTED BOLDLY.

Diatribe brings up a second absurdity from Madam Reason, also known as Human Reason: "The fault shouldn't be blamed on the vessel, but on the potter, especially since he's the kind of potter who creates the clay itself and shapes it. Here's a vessel thrown into eternal fire, which has done no wrong except not being in control of itself."

Nowhere does Diatribe reveal itself more openly than here. This is where we hear what Paul says profane people argue: "Why does he find fault? Who can resist his will?" (It's said differently, but with the same meaning.) This is the truth that reason can't understand or tolerate. This is what offends so many talented people, accepted for so many ages! Here, they truly demand that God should act according to human laws and do what seems right to them, or stop being God.

The secrets of God's majesty won't benefit God at all. Let God explain why He is God, or why He wants or does things that don't seem fair - as if you were calling a shoemaker or a tailor to come and stand at your judgment seat. Our human nature doesn't think it's right to give God the honor of believing that He is just and good when He speaks and acts beyond the rules found in Justinian's Codex or in Aristotle's

Ethics. Let God's creative power give in to just one tiny part of His creation, and let the famous Corycian cave switch places with its observers, so that it stands in awe of them, not the other way around!

So, it's ridiculous for God to condemn someone who can't help but deserve such condemnation. And because this idea is so absurd to our human nature, it must be false that "He has mercy on whom He will have mercy, and whom He wills He hardens" (Romans 9:18). But we need to set some rules for God, so He doesn't condemn anyone who hasn't first deserved it according to our judgment. Only then can people be satisfied with Paul and his analogy; they allow Paul's reminder to have no meaning. Instead, they modify it so that, according to Diatribe's explanation, the potter here makes a dishonorable vessel based on previous wrongdoings - just as God rejects some Jews for their unbelief and accepts the Gentiles for their faith.

But if God's work is such that He considers our merits, then why do people complain and argue? Why do they say, 'Why does He find fault? Who can resist His will?' What's the point of Paul trying to silence them? After all, who can be surprised (I won't even ask, who is angry or argues) if someone is condemned because they deserve it? Also, what happens to the potter's power to create whatever he wants if he's subject to merits and laws? He's not allowed to do what he wants, but he's required to do what he should.

Respecting merits is entirely different from having the power and freedom to do whatever one wants. This is demonstrated by the homeowner in the parable, who exercises his freedom to distribute his wealth as he pleases, despite the complaints of his workers who demand a fair distribution based on their rights. These factors undermine Diatribe's interpretation.

SECTION 33: WHY NOT QUESTION THE SALVATION OF THE SAVED?

But let's assume for a moment that God does consider the merits of the damned. Wouldn't we also have to accept that he looks at the merits of the saved? If we follow reason, it is just as unfair to reward the undeserving as it is to punish the undeserving. So, we must conclude that God must justify people based on their previous merits; otherwise, we would be accusing him of being unjust, enjoying the company of evil and wicked people, and encouraging them to be impious by rewarding them for it. But woe to us - we would be truly miserable if this were our God. For who would be saved then?

Look at how useless the human heart is! When God saves the unworthy without merit - in fact, when he justifies the ungodly despite their many faults - the human heart does not accuse him of being unfair. It does not arrogantly demand an explanation for his actions, even though they may seem unjust according to its own judgment. But because it benefits and pleases the heart, it considers it fair and good. However, when God condemns the undeserving - since it is disadvantageous to the heart - it is deemed unfair and intolerable. This is when people start to complain, grumble, and blaspheme.

So, you can see that Diatribe and her friends don't make fair judgments in this situation, but instead, they base their decisions on how it affects their own interests. If they truly cared about fairness, they would argue with God for rewarding those who don't deserve it, just as much as they argue against condemning those who don't deserve it.

She would also praise and celebrate God for condemning those who don't deserve it, just as much as she does for saving the unworthy. There is equal injustice in each case if you base it on our own judgment - unless it's not equally wrong to praise Cain for his murder and make him a king, as it would be to throw innocent Abel into prison or put him to death. So, when it's found that reason praises God for saving the unworthy but criticizes him for condemning the undeserving, she is proven guilty of not praising God as God, but as someone who supports her own personal interests. In other words, she focuses on herself and her own things in God and praises them, not on God and the things of God.

The truth is, however, that if you are happy with God for rewarding the unworthy, then you shouldn't be unhappy with him for condemning the undeserving. If he is just in one case, then why not in the other? In the first case, he showers favor and compassion on the unworthy; in the second, he pours out anger and harshness on the undeserving. In both cases, it seems excessive and unjust according to human judgment, but it is fair and true according to His own.

For now, it's impossible to understand how it's fair that He rewards the unworthy - but we will see how when we reach that place where we will no longer just believe in Him, but we will see Him clearly (2 Corinthians 3:18). Similarly, it's currently impossible to understand how it's fair that he condemns the undeserving; but we accept it as a matter of faith until the Son of man is revealed.

SECTION 34: SCRIPTURE MUST BE UNDERSTOOD WITH QUALIFICATIONS.

Diatribe is quite unhappy with the potter and clay analogy and feels quite cornered by it. In the end, it resorts to bringing up various passages from Scripture, some of which seem to give all credit to humans, and others that give all credit to grace. Diatribe passionately argues that both of these interpretations should be understood with a reasonable explanation and not taken literally. Otherwise, if we insist on using the potter and clay analogy, Diatribe is ready to challenge us with other texts, particularly this one from Paul: "If a man purges himself from these." Here, Diatribe claims that Paul is contradicting himself and gives all credit to humans, unless a reasonable explanation comes to his rescue. 'If, then, an explanation of the text is allowed here, so as to leave room for grace, then why can't the potter and clay analogy also allow for some qualification, so as to leave room for Free Will?'

My response is that it doesn't matter to me whether you interpret the words in a simple way, a double way, or in a hundred different ways. What I'm saying is that you don't achieve anything, and you don't prove anything (of what you're trying to achieve and prove) with this "reasonable" explanation. It should be proven through this explanation that Free Will can't will anything good.

In this case, when Paul says, "If a man purges himself from these," he is simply encouraging people to do so. However, if we follow Diatribe's logic and claim that Paul's encouragement is pointless if a person cannot cleanse themselves, then it would mean that free will can do everything without grace. This would contradict Diatribe's own argument.

I am still waiting for a passage from the Bible that supports this interpretation. I don't trust those who come up with explanations on their own. I don't believe there is any passage that gives all the credit to humans. I also disagree that Paul contradicts himself when he says, "If a man cleanses himself from these." I believe that the supposed contradiction in Paul's words is just as made up as Diatribe's forced explanation, and neither of them can be proven.

I admit that if we were allowed to expand the meaning of the Bible with Diatribe's additional claims - like saying that commands are useless if we don't have the power to follow them - then Paul would indeed be contradicting himself, and the entire Bible would be in conflict. In that case, Diatribe could also argue that free will can do everything. But wouldn't that also contradict her other statement that God is the one who does everything? This expanded interpretation of the Bible not only conflicts with our views but also with Diatribe's own belief that free will can't choose anything good.

So, Diatribe should first explain how these two ideas can coexist with Paul's teachings: free will can't choose anything good, and 'if a man cleanses himself, he can do so, or else it's said in vain.' As you can see, Diatribe is struggling with the example of the potter and is trying to avoid its implications. Meanwhile, she doesn't realize how much her interpretation harms the cause she's trying to defend, and how she's contradicting and making a joke of herself.

SECTION 35: LUTHER HAS ALWAYS MAINTAINED THE PERFECT CONSISTENCY OF SCRIPTURE - ILLUSTRATES IT IN AFFIRMED OPPOSITES.

On the other hand, as I mentioned earlier, I've never been too concerned about interpretations, nor have I ever said things like "extend the hand;" meaning 'grace shall extend it.' These are Diatribe's made-up claims about me, said to help her own cause. My belief has always been that there is no inconsistency in the words of Scripture, and no need for an 'explanation' to untangle a knot. It's the supporters of Free Will who create knots where there are none, and imagine contradictions for themselves. For example, those two statements, "If a man cleanses himself," and "God works all in all," are not at all opposite. Nor is it necessary (to untangle a knot) to say, God does something, and man does something.

The first of these texts is a conjunctive sentence, which neither affirms nor denies any work or power in man, but it describes what work or power there should be in a person. There's nothing figurative here, nothing that needs explanation: the words are simple, the meaning is simple, if you don't add consequences and corruptives like Diatribe does. Then, indeed, the meaning would become unsound. But whose fault would that be? Not the text's, but the one who corrupts it.

The second text, "God works all in all," is an indicative sentence, stating that all work, all power is God's. So, in what way do these two passages disagree, when one has nothing to do with the power of man, and the other attributes everything to God?

Don't they actually agree with each other quite well? However, Diatribe is so overwhelmed and choked by the idea that "it is pointless to command the impossible" that she can't help herself. Whenever she encounters an imperative or conjunctive verb, she immediately adds her own conclusions, saying, "Something is commanded, so we must be able to do it, otherwise it would be foolish to command it." With this, she goes around boasting about her victories, as if her conclusions and imagination were as certain as divine authority. Based on this, she doesn't hesitate to claim that some parts of Scripture attribute everything to humans, or that there is inconsistency in those passages that must be resolved through interpretation. She doesn't realize that all of this is just her own invention, without any support from Scripture, and that if accepted, it would actually refute her own argument more than anyone else's. Wouldn't she be proving (if she proves anything) that free will can do everything? This is the exact opposite of what she set out to prove.

SECTION 36: DIATRIBE CONTRADICTS HERSELF, ARGUES ABSURDLY, AND DOESN'T KNOW WHAT SHE'S TRYING TO PROVE. IN THE END, SHE DOESN'T PROVE ANYTHING, AND PAUL'S POSITION REMAINS STRONG.

Diatribe keeps repeating the same idea: "If humans do nothing, there is no merit; and where there is no merit, there is no punishment or reward." Yet again, she fails to see how much more strongly her own arguments refute her position than mine.

So, what do these consequences show, other than that all possible merit comes from free will? If that's the case, then where does grace fit in? Moreover, if you claim that free will earns just a little bit and grace earns the rest, why does free will get the entire reward? Should we also create a tiny reward for it? If there must be a place for merit in order to have a place for reward, then the merit should be as significant as the reward. But why am I wasting my words and time on something that doesn't matter? Even if all of Diatribe's arguments were valid and could stand on their own, and even if our merit was partly due to human effort and partly to God's work, they still can't define what this merit consists of, what kind it is, and how extensive it is. So, we're just arguing about trivial matters.

In the end, Diatribe doesn't prove any of the things she claims - neither inconsistency nor a nuanced interpretation - nor can she provide a scriptural text that attributes everything to humans. Instead, all these ideas are just figments of her imagination. Paul's analogy of the potter and his clay remains unharmed and undeniable, showing that it's not up to our own will what kind of vessels we are shaped into. And those exhortations from Paul, like "If a man purifies himself" and similar ones, serve as examples we should follow, but they don't prove our ability or effort to do so. Let this be enough regarding the passages about Pharaoh's hardening, Esau, and the potter.

SECTION 37: GENESIS 6:3 EXPLAINED

Diatribe eventually addresses the passages that Luther cites against free will, intending to refute them as well. The first of these is Genesis 6:3, "My Spirit shall not always abide in man, for he is flesh." Diatribe attempts to refute this passage in several ways.

First, she argues that "flesh" in this context doesn't mean 'sinful desire,' but rather 'weakness.'

Secondly, she elaborates on Moses' words. She believes his statement applies only to the men of that time, not the entire human race. So, she would say 'in those men;' but she doesn't even think it applies to all the men of that era, since Noah is excluded.

Lastly, she points out that this phrase has a different meaning in Hebrew; it refers to God's mercy, not his harshness, according to Jerome. Maybe she's trying to convince us that, since this statement doesn't apply to Noah but to the wicked, God's harshness is meant for Noah, while his mercy is meant for the wicked!

But let's ignore these silly ideas from Diatribe, who seems to treat the Scriptures like a story. I don't care about Jerome's opinion on this matter. It's clear he doesn't prove anything. We're not looking for Jerome's thoughts, but the true meaning of Scripture. Let those who twist Scripture claim that the Spirit of God represents his anger. I assert that she fails to prove this in two ways: first, she can't provide a single Scripture passage where the Spirit of God means God's anger; instead, kindness and gentleness are consistently attributed to him. Secondly, even if she could somehow prove that it represents anger in some instances, she still can't directly prove that it must be interpreted that way here.

Also, let her claim that "flesh" represents weakness; she still doesn't prove anything. For example, when Paul calls the Corinthians "carnal," he's not accusing them of weakness, but of wrongdoing – he complains that they're divided into factions. This isn't a weakness or an inability to understand deeper teachings, but rather the old malice that he tells them to get rid of.

Let's take a look at the Hebrew text: "My Spirit shall not always judge man, because he is flesh." This is exactly what Moses says. If we set aside our own interpretations, the words are quite clear and straight-forward, I believe. However, the surrounding text, which discusses the onset of the flood, clearly indicates that these words come from an angry God. The reason for this anger was that people were marrying for lustful reasons and then ruling the earth with tyranny. This forced God to bring about the flood in anger, barely allowing a hundred-year delay for something that would otherwise never have happened. If you read Moses carefully, you'll see that this is his intended meaning.

If you treat the Scriptures like a game, searching for bits and pieces of Virgil within them, then it's no surprise that they seem obscure, or that you can find support for not only free will but even divine will within them. This approach to "qualified interpretation" really just unties knots and ends discussions! Jerome and his friend Origen have filled the world with these trivial ideas and set a harmful example by not respecting the simplicity of Scripture.

For me, it's enough to prove from this text that divine authority refers to people as flesh - and a type of flesh that is so incompatible with God's Spirit that it must eventually be withdrawn from them. The meaning of the statement that God's Spirit will not always judge among humans is clarified by the mention of a 120-year period during which judgment would still occur. The Spirit is contrasted with the flesh because people, being flesh, do not receive the Spirit, and the Spirit, being divine, cannot approve of the flesh.

From this, we can understand that he must be removed after 120 years. So, we can interpret the passage in Moses like this: 'My Spirit, which is in Noah and my other saints, condemns those wicked people through the word they preach and the holy life they lead (for to judge among people means to exercise the ministry of the word among them - to reprove, rebuke, and entreat, both when it's convenient and inconve-nient). But it was all in vain. Being blinded and hardened by their physical desires, they only got worse the more they were judged. This is just like when the word of God enters the world: people become worse the more they are taught. Romans 7:7. And this is why God's anger is now speeding up, just like the flood did back then. Not only do people sin nowadays, but they also despise grace, and as Christ says, "Light has come, but people hate the light." John 3:20.

Therefore, since people are flesh, as God himself testifies, they can only focus on their physical desires. This means that free will can only lead to sin. And since people become worse even when God's Spirit is among them and teaching them, what would they do if they were left on their own without God's Spirit? It doesn't matter here that Moses is talking about the people of that time. The same is true for everyone, as we are all flesh. As Christ says in John 3:6, "That which is born of the flesh is flesh." At the same time, he teaches us how serious this problem is when he says, "No one can enter the kingdom of God unless they are born again."

So, Christians should be aware that Origen, Jerome, and others like them are making a harmful mistake by claiming that "flesh" doesn't refer to ungodly desires in these instances. For example, in 1 Corinthians 3:3, when it says "you are still carnal," it's talking about ungodliness. Paul is saying that there are still ungodly people among them, and even the godly can be considered carnal when they focus on worldly things, even if they've been justified by the Spirit.

In general, when you read the Bible and see "flesh" being contrasted with the "Spirit," you can usually understand that "flesh" represents everything that goes against the Spirit. For example, "The flesh profits nothing." But when "flesh" is mentioned on its own, it usually refers to our physical nature and condition, like in "The two shall be one flesh," "My flesh is food indeed," and "The word was made flesh." In these cases, you can replace the Hebrew term for "flesh" with "body."

The Hebrew language uses one word, "flesh," to express what we mean by both "flesh" and "body." I wish that translators had used separate terms for these concepts throughout the entire Bible. That way, my quote from Genesis 6:3 would stand strong as an argument against free will, since it's clear that the "flesh" mentioned here is the same as what

Paul talks about in Romans 8: "it cannot be subject to God's will." We'll discuss this more when we get to that passage. And even Diatribe admits that our fleshly nature can't desire anything good on its own.

SECTION 38: GENESIS 8:21 AND 6:5 EXPLAINED.

The second passage comes from Genesis 8:21, which says, "The imagination and thought of man's heart are prone to evil from his youth." And in Genesis 6:5, it says, "Every thought of man's heart is intent upon evil continually." Diatribe tries to brush this off by saying that just because most people have a tendency towards evil, it doesn't completely eliminate free will.

But I ask, does God speak about most people rather than all people when, as if regretting after the flood, He promises to the remaining humans and those who would come after, that He would no longer bring a flood because of humanity? He adds the reason, saying that humans are prone to evil. It's as if He said, 'If human wickedness were taken into account, there would never be an end to floods. But from now on, I don't intend to focus on what humans deserve,' etc. So you see, God states that people were evil both before and after the flood, making Diatribe's claim about most people irrelevant.

Moreover, Diatribe seems to think that this tendency or inclination towards evil is a minor issue, as if it were within our power to overcome or restrain it. But Scripture describes this inclination as a constant pull and drive of the will towards evil. Why didn't Diatribe consult the Hebrew text here as well? Moses doesn't mention inclination in it, so there's no basis for arguing. In chapter 6, it is written: "Every imagination of the thoughts of his heart is only evil all his days." It doesn't say inclined to or prone to evil, but absolutely evil; and nothing but evil is imagined and thought of by humans all their lives. The nature of this wickedness is described: it neither does nor can do anything else, seeing that it is evil. For an evil tree cannot bear any fruit other than evil, according to Christ's testimony in Matthew 7:17.

As for Diatribe's objection, 'Why is there room for repentance if repentance doesn't depend on the will, but everything happens out of necessity?' I would respond by asking the same about all of God's commands. Why does He command if everything happens by necessity? He commands to teach and warn people about what they should do so that, after realizing their own wickedness, they may receive grace, as I have explained earlier. So, this text also remains an unshakable argument against the idea of free will.

SECTION 39: ISAIAH 40:2 EXPLAINED

The third passage is from Isaiah 40:2: "She has received from the Lord's hand double for all her sins." The person claims that Jerome interprets this verse as referring to divine vengeance, not as grace given in return for evil deeds. This means that if 'Jerome says so, it is therefore true.' I argue that Isaiah clearly states a specific idea in this verse, yet the person brings up Jerome's opinion – a man who, to put it mildly, lacks judgment and diligence. What happened to our agreement that we would rely on the Scriptures themselves, not human interpretations?

The entire chapter of Isaiah, according to the Gospel writers, discusses the forgiveness of sins as announced by the Gospel. They claim that "the voice of him that cries" refers to John the Baptist. Now, can we tolerate Jerome imposing Jewish blindness on us regarding the historical meaning of this passage, and then imposing his own foolish ideas as allegory? This would mean that, through a distortion of grammar, we might understand a verse about forgiveness to instead be about vengeance. I ask, what kind of vengeance has been fulfilled by preaching Christ?

Let's take a look at the Hebrew words themselves. "Be comforted, He says; be comforted, O my people;" or, "Comfort, comfort my people, says your God." (Isaiah 40:1) I don't think the one who commands consolation would inflict vengeance. It then follows, "speak to the heart of Jerusalem and proclaim to her." To speak to the heart is a Hebrew expression meaning "to speak good, sweet, and soothing things," as in Genesis 34:3. Sichem speaks to the heart of Dinah, whom he had defiled. In other words, he comforted her in her sadness with gentle words, as our translation puts it.

He explains what those good and sweet things are, which God has commanded to be spoken for their consolation, by saying, "For her warfare is finished, in that her iniquity is pardoned; seeing that she has received from the Lord's hand, double for all her sins." The term 'warfare,' which our manuscripts mistakenly translate as 'malice,' seems to the bold Jewish grammarians to denote a fixed time. They understand Job 7:1 in this way: "The life of man on the earth is warfare;" meaning, there is a set time appointed to him.

I prefer to interpret the term 'warfare' literally, according to its grammatical meaning, understanding Isaiah to be talking about the course and labor of the people under the law, which was similar to that of competitors in a stadium.

So, Paul compares both preachers and listeners of the word to soldiers, like when he tells Timothy to fight as a good soldier and wage a good war. He also describes the Corinthians as running in a race. Similarly, "No man is crowned unless he strives lawfully." He equips both the Ephesians and Thessalonians with armor and proudly says that he himself has fought the good fight, and there are similar examples in other places. In 1 Kings (or 1 Samuel), the Hebrew text says that Eli's sons slept with the women who were serving (or warring) at the entrance of the covenant tabernacle. Moses also talks about their warfare in Exodus. That's why their God is called the Lord of Sabaoth, meaning the Lord of warfare or armies.

Isaiah announces that the legal people's warfare, which they struggled with under the law, would come to an end. As Peter says in Acts 15:8-10, it's like an unbearable burden - being freed from the law, they've been moved to the new service of the Spirit.

This end of their tough service and the start of a new, more free one isn't given to them because they deserve it (since they couldn't even handle that service), but rather because they don't deserve it. Their sins were freely forgiven, so their warfare is over. There's no confusion or unclear words here. He says their warfare is finished because their sins are forgiven - clearly implying that, as soldiers under the law, they hadn't fulfilled the law and couldn't have, but they had been fighting in the service of sin and had been sinful soldiers.

It's as if God is saying, "If I want them to fulfill the law, then I have no choice but to forgive their sins. In fact, I have to remove the law itself, because I can see that they can't help but sin. And they do this the most when they're trying their hardest to follow the law through their own strength."

The Hebrew phrase "her iniquity has been forgiven" means that God forgives sins out of pure grace, without any merit on our part – in fact, even when we don't deserve it at all. This is what the next part means: "For she has received from the Lord's hand double for all her sins." As I mentioned earlier, this not only refers to the forgiveness of sins, but also to the end of the struggle to follow the law.

This is nothing less than a double freedom – the removal of the law, which was the power of sin, and the forgiveness of sin, which was the cause of death – all achieved through the victory of Jesus Christ. This is what Isaiah means when he says, "from the hand of the Lord." We didn't achieve these things through our own strength or merits, but received them as a gift from Christ's victory.

"In all their sins" is another Hebrew expression, similar to the Latin phrase meaning "for" or "on account of" their sins. Just like in Hosea 12:12, where it says that Jacob served for his wife, and in Psalm 17, where it says that enemies surround me for my soul. So Isaiah is saying that our sins, and only our sins, are the reason we receive this double freedom: the end of the struggle with the law and the forgiveness of sin. As Isaiah 64:6 says, all our merits are like filthy rags – they're all sins.

Should we allow this incredibly beautiful and powerful argument against free will to be tainted with outdated ideas, like those Jerome and Diatribe have smeared on it? Absolutely not! Instead, my friend Isaiah stands firm as the one who defeats the concept of free will. He makes it clear that grace is given not because of any merits or efforts of free will, but rather because of its sins and shortcomings. Free will, by its own abilities, can only continue the battle of sin. Even the very law, which was supposedly given to help, turned out to be an unbearable burden; it only made free will even more sinful while struggling under it.

SECTION 40: EPISODE ON GOD'S HELP – CORNELIUS RESCUED.

Diatribe argues that,

"Even though sin increases through the law, and where sin has increased, grace also increases — it doesn't mean that a person, with God's help (even before grace makes them acceptable), can't prepare themselves for God's favor through morally good actions."

I wonder if Diatribe is just making this up, or if she got this idea from somewhere else and added it to her own collection. She doesn't seem to understand what her own words mean. If sin increases by the law, how can a person prepare themselves for God's favor through moral actions? How can actions be helpful when the law isn't helpful? Or what does it mean for sin to increase by the law, if not that actions done according to the law are sins? But we'll discuss this more later. Then, what is she saying? That "a person, with God's help, can prepare themselves through good actions?" Are we debating about God's help or about free will? What isn't possible with God's help? But this is exactly what I said: Diatribe doesn't take her own argument seriously; that's why she seems so disinterested and unfocused while discussing it. She brings up Cornelius the centurion as an example of someone whose prayers and charity pleased God before he was baptized and filled with the Holy Spirit.

I've also read Luke's account in Acts, but I haven't found any mention that Cornelius' good deeds were done without the Holy Spirit, as Diatribe seems to think. On the contrary, Luke describes Cornelius as a just and God-fearing man. To call someone just and God-fearing without the Holy Spirit would be like calling Belial Christ.

The whole argument in that passage actually shows that Cornelius was considered clean in God's eyes. Even the vision sent from heaven to

Peter, which also corrected him, confirms this. Luke praises Cornelius' righteousness and faith with such strong words and actions that it's impossible to doubt them. However, Diatribe and her Sophist friends somehow manage to see the opposite, even with the clear evidence of words and facts. This just shows their lack of diligence in reading and understanding the Scriptures, which they then criticize as obscure and ambiguous.

So what if Cornelius hadn't been baptized yet or hadn't heard about Christ's resurrection? Does that mean he didn't have the Holy Spirit? If you follow that logic, you'd have to say that John the Baptist, his parents, Christ's mother, and Simeon didn't have the Spirit either! But let's not entertain such absurd ideas!

SECTION 41: ISAIAH 40.6-7 EXPLAINED.

My fourth text comes from the same chapter of Isaiah, "All flesh is grass, and all its glory as the flower of grass; the grass withers, and its flower falls, because the Spirit of the Lord blows upon it;" etc. My Diatribe thinks that this passage is being misused when applied to the topic of grace and free will. Why, I ask? Because, she says, Jerome interprets the Spirit as indignation and the flesh as the weak state of humanity, which cannot stand against God. Once again, I am presented with Jerome's opinions instead of Isaiah's words. I find it more challenging to deal with the weariness caused by Diatribe's carelessness than with Diatribe herself. But I have already shared my thoughts on Jerome's interpretation.

Let's compare Diatribe's own words. She says that flesh represents the weak state of humanity and the Spirit represents divine indignation. Does divine indignation have nothing else to dry up, then, but only this miserable and weak state of humanity, which it should rather lift up than destroy?

But this is an even more interesting point:

"The flower of grass is the glory that comes from success in physical things. The Jews took pride in their temple, circumcision, and sacrifices; the Greeks in their wisdom."

So, the flower of grass and the glory of the flesh are the righteousness of works and the wisdom of the world. How can Diatribe call righteousness and wisdom physical things? What should we say to Isaiah, who uses clear, non-figurative language when he says, "Truly the people are grass."? He doesn't say, 'Truly the weak state of humanity is grass,' but "the people are grass;" and he confirms it with an oath. What are the people, then? Just the weak state of humanity? Honestly, I'm not sure what Jerome means by 'the weak state of humanity,' whether he's referring to the creature itself or the miserable situation and condition of humanity.

But, whether it's one or the other, the divine anger certainly "carries off wonderful praise and ample spoils" by drying up a miserable person, or people who are unhappy, instead of breaking down the proud, pulling down the powerful from their positions, and sending the wealthy away with nothing; just as Mary sings.

SECTION 42: THE TRUE INTERPRETATION.

But let's say goodbye to our ghosts and follow Isaiah. He says that people are like grass. Now, people are not just flesh or the weak state of human nature. Instead, the word includes everything that is found among people: rich people, wise people, just people, holy people - unless the Pharisees, elders, princes, chiefs, rich, and so on were not part of the Jewish people. Their glory is rightly called the flower of grass because they boasted about their power, their government, especially their law, of God, of righteousness, and wisdom, as Paul argues in Romans 2, 3, 9. So when Isaiah says "all flesh," what else could he mean if not all the grass or all the people? He doesn't just say "flesh," but "all flesh." Now, what belongs to people is their soul, body, mind, reason, judgment, and anything else that can be mentioned or discovered as the best in a person. For the one who says "all flesh is grass" doesn't exclude anyone, except the Spirit that dries up the grass. And the one who says "the people are grass" doesn't leave anything out. So let there be Free Will and let there be whatever is considered the highest and lowest among people; Isaiah calls all of this "flesh" and "grass," seeing that these three words - flesh, grass, people - mean the same thing in this context, according to the interpretation of the author of the book.

Then again, you yourself agree that the wisdom of the Greeks and the righteousness of the Jews, which were dried up by the Gospel, are grass or the flower of grass.

Do you think wisdom wasn't the most excellent thing the Greeks had? Or that righteousness wasn't the most excellent thing the Jews could achieve? Show me something more excellent than these. What happened to your confidence, which I assume even gave Philip Melancthon a black-eye?

"If anyone argues that the best part of a person is just flesh, meaning wickedness, I'd be willing to agree, as long as they can prove it with evidence from the Scripture."

You have Isaiah loudly declaring that people without the Lord's Spirit are just flesh, but even this loud voice doesn't make you listen. You also admitted (maybe without realizing it) that the wisdom of the Greeks is like grass or the glory of grass, which is the same as calling it flesh. Unless you want to argue that Greek wisdom doesn't relate to reason or "the leading thing," as you call it using a Greek term - the main part of a person. At least listen to yourself - if you don't care about my opinion - when you're forced to admit the truth. You have John saying, "That which is born of the flesh is flesh; and that which is born of the Spirit is Spirit." This verse clearly shows that anything not born of the Spirit is flesh. Otherwise, Christ's division of all people into two groups, flesh and Spirit, wouldn't make sense. You dare to ignore this verse, as if it doesn't teach you what you're asking for.

So, you quickly change the subject, as you usually do. Meanwhile, you mention how John says, "Believers are born of God, and made sons of

God; indeed, gods and new creatures." But you don't pay attention to the conclusion that this division leads to. Instead, you just tell us in unnecessary words who the other part of the division includes. You rely on your persuasive skills, as if no one would notice your sneaky change of topic and deception.

It's hard to believe that you're not being cunning and adaptable in this situation. Anyone who studies the Scriptures with the slyness and dishonesty that you use can confidently claim that they haven't learned from the Scriptures yet, but that they want to be taught.

On the other hand, he doesn't want anything less than to undermine the clear light found in the Scriptures and to justify his own stubbornness. This is similar to how the Jews still argue today that the teachings of Christ, the Apostles, and the Church are not supported by the Scriptures. Heretics can't be taught anything by the Scriptures, and the Papists haven't learned from them either, even though the truth is as clear as day.

Maybe you're waiting for a passage from the Scriptures that specifically says, "The most important part of a person is their flesh," or "The best thing about a person is their flesh." And until you find that, you plan to walk away as an unbeatable winner. This is like the Jews demanding a prophecy that explicitly states, "Jesus, the carpenter's son, born of the Virgin Mary in Bethlehem, is the Messiah and the Son of God." Here, when you should accept our conclusion based on the obvious meaning, you instead demand that we provide you with specific words and phrases. In other situations, when you're defeated by both the words and the meaning, you resort to your tropes, your tangled arguments, and your "sober explanations." You always find something to argue against the divine Scriptures, which isn't surprising since you're constantly looking for ways to oppose them. Sometimes you turn to the interpretations of ancient scholars, other times to the absurdities of reason. And when neither of those work, you talk about unrelated things or focus on minor details to avoid addressing the main point. What can I say? You're more slippery than Proteus himself. But rest assured, we won't let you escape our grasp with these tricks.

What victories did the Arians claim, just because the word "homoousios" was not found in the Scriptures? They didn't care that the meaning behind the word was clearly proven by other words. But let's ask even the most wicked person whether this is the behavior of a good person - I won't even say a religious one - who wants to learn.

Go ahead, take your victory - I admit I'm defeated - the phrase "the most excellent thing in man is but flesh" is not in the Scriptures. But do you see what kind of victory you have when I show that there are countless examples proving that not just one part, or the most excellent part of a person, is flesh; but that the whole person is flesh? And not just that, but the entire population is flesh. And if that's not enough, the whole human race is flesh. For Christ says, "That which is born of the flesh is flesh." Untangle your arguments, come up with your metaphors, follow the interpretations of the ancient scholars, or talk about something else like the Trojan War, just so you don't have to face the text in front of you.

We don't just believe it, but we see and feel that the entire human race is born of the flesh. So, we are forced to believe what we can't see: that the whole human race is flesh, based on Christ's teachings. Now, we'll leave it to the clever debaters to argue whether the most important part of a person is included in the whole person, the whole population, or the entire human race. We know that in the phrase "whole human race," both the body and soul are included, along with all their abilities and actions, all their vices and virtues, all their foolishness and wisdom, and all their justice and injustice. All things are related to the physical body because they are focused on their own physical existence. They lack the glory of God and the Spirit of God, as Paul mentions in Romans 3.

SECTION 43: GOD HATES THE VIRTUES OF NON-BELIEVERS.

Regarding your statement that not all human emotions are related to the physical body, and that there are emotions connected to the soul and spirit, through which we strive for honorable things - just like the philosophers who believed that one should face death a thousand times before committing a dishonorable act, even if no one would know about it and God would forgive it:

I respond by saying that it's easy for someone who doesn't believe in anything to confidently believe and say anything. Let your friend Lucian, not me, ask you if you can show us even one person from the entire human race (you can be twice or seven times a Socrates if you want) who has demonstrated what you're talking about and what you claim they taught. Why do you tell stories with empty words? How can someone strive for honorable things if they don't even know what honorable means? You might consider it honorable, for example, that they died for their country, their spouses and children, or their parents; or that they endured extreme pain to avoid lying or betraying their loved ones. Such were the cases of C. Scaevola, M. Regulus, and others. But what can you show in all these examples, other than an outward appearance of good deeds? Have you looked into their hearts?

No, it seems that at the same time, on the surface of their actions, they were doing all these things for their own glory. They weren't ashamed to admit and even brag about seeking their own glory. It was this desire for glory that drove the Romans, according to their own words, to do whatever virtuous deeds they did. This is also true for the Greeks, Jews, and the entire human race.

Now, even though this pursuit of personal glory is considered honorable among people, nothing could be more dishonorable in the eyes of God. In fact, it was the most disrespectful and ultimate act of sacrilege in His sight that they didn't act for God's glory or give Him the praise He deserves. Instead, they committed the most blasphemous form of theft by taking God's glory and attributing it to themselves. So, they were never less honorable and more despicable than when they were displaying their most exceptional virtues. But how could they act for God's glory when they knew nothing of God and His glory? It's not because God's glory wasn't visible, but because their human nature didn't allow them to see it due to their obsession with their own glory. This is where you find the leading spirit, that main part of a person striving for honorable things – in other words, acting as a thief of God's glory and pretenders to His Majesty – especially in those who are most honorable and famous for their outstanding virtues. Try to deny now, if you can, that these people are driven by their human nature and are lost due to their ungodly desires.

I think Diatribe might not have been so bothered by the statement that a person is either driven by their human nature or by the spirit when she read it in the Latin translation, which says 'a person is either carnal or spiritual.'

We must acknowledge that the Hebrew language has its unique features, just like any other language. For instance, when it says, "Man is flesh or spirit," it conveys the same meaning as when we say, "Man is carnal or spiritual." Similarly, the Latin language has expressions like, "The wolf is a sad thing for the folds," "Moisture is a sweet thing to the sown corn," or "Man is wickedness and malice itself." In the same way, the Holy Scripture uses intense expressions, calling man "flesh" as if he were the embodiment of carnality. This is because man has a strong preference for the things of the flesh and no interest in anything else. Likewise, it calls him "spirit" because he is drawn to, seeks, does, and endures only the things of the Spirit.

Now, one might ask this question: "Even if the whole man, and that which is most excellent in man, is called flesh, does it mean that whatever is flesh must immediately be called ungodly?" My response is that anyone who does not have the Spirit of God is ungodly, as the Scripture states that the Spirit is given to justify the ungodly. Furthermore, when Christ distinguishes the Spirit from the flesh by saying, "That which is born of the flesh is flesh," and adds that one who is born of the flesh cannot see the kingdom of God, it clearly implies that whatever is flesh is ungodly, under God's wrath, and far from the kingdom of God.

Now, if something is far from God's kingdom and spirit, it must necessarily follow that it is under Satan's kingdom and spirit - since there's no middle ground between God's kingdom and Satan's kingdom; these two are constantly battling each other. These considerations show that even the most exceptional virtues among non-believers, the wisest sayings of their philosophers, and the most outstanding actions of their citizens - no matter how well-spoken or honorable they may seem in the world's eyes - are actually just flesh in God's sight and services rendered to Satan's kingdom. In other words, they are impious, sacrilegious, and entirely evil.

SECTION 44: CONSEQUENCES OF THIS ASSUMPTION REGARDING A PART IN MAN THAT IS NOT 'FLESH.'

But let's assume for a moment that Diatribe's claim is true: that not all of a person's nature is flesh (i.e., wicked); but part of it, which we call spirit, is honest and sound. Look at the absurdity that follows from this - not in the eyes of human reason, but in relation to the entire religion of Christ and the main articles of faith. For if the most excellent part in a person is not ungodly, lost, and damned, but only the fleshly part - that is, the more base and inferior desires - then what kind of Redeemer would we make Christ out to be? Would we portray the value of his most precious blood-shedding as so small that it only redeemed the lowest part in a person, while the most excellent part is strong on its own and doesn't need Christ? From now on, we must preach Christ not as the Redeemer of the whole person, but of the person's most worthless part, that is, the flesh; while the person is their own redeemer in their better part.

Choose whichever of the two options you prefer. If the better part of a person is sound, it doesn't need Christ as a Redeemer.

If a person doesn't need Christ, then they are essentially triumphing over Christ with a superior glory by healing themselves, which is considered the better part. In contrast, Christ only heals the less valuable part. Furthermore, Satan's kingdom would also be insignificant. It would rule over the less valuable part of a person, while the person's better part would actually rule over Satan. So, according to this belief about the main part of a person, humans are elevated above both Christ and the devil, making them the ultimate God and ruler.

What happened to the widely accepted opinion that free will can't do anything good? Here, Diatribe argues that free will is the main, healthy, and honest part of a person, which doesn't even need Christ and can do more than God and the devil. I bring this up, as I have before, to show you, Erasmus, how dangerous it is to approach sacred and divine matters without the guidance of God's Spirit and relying solely on human reason.

If Christ is the Lamb of God who takes away the sin of the world, then the entire world is under sin, damnation, and the devil's control. The distinction between main parts and less important parts doesn't matter. The term "the world" refers to people who are focused on worldly things in every aspect of their lives.

SECTION 45: LUTHER FALSELY CHARGED. THE AUTHORITY OF THE ANCIENTS IS MISUSED AND WORTHLESS, BUT IF IT'S GOOD, IT CONTRADICTS ERASMUS.

If a person, even when regenerated by faith, is entirely made of flesh, what happens to the spirit born of the Spirit? What about the Son of God and the new creation? I would like to know more about these matters.

So much for the rant. Where are you going so quickly, my dear Rant? What's on your mind? You want to know how the spirit in a person, born from the Spirit of God, can be flesh? Oh, how happy and confident you are in this victory, as you mock your defeated opponent, as if it were impossible for me to hold my ground here! In the meantime, you'd love to misuse the authority of the ancient scholars, who mention certain seeds of goodness being naturally planted in the minds of people. First of all, if you want and as far as I'm concerned, you can use or misuse the authority of the ancient scholars.

It's up to you what you choose to believe when you listen to people who share their own opinions without any basis in the word of God. Maybe you're not really that concerned about what anyone else believes. You seem to easily trust people without considering whether what they say is true or false in God's eyes.

I have a question for you too: when did I ever teach what you so openly and publicly accuse me of? Would anyone be crazy enough to say that someone born of the Spirit is nothing but flesh? I clearly distinguish between flesh and Spirit as substances that are in conflict with each other. In line with the sacred teachings, I say that a person who hasn't been born again through faith is flesh. I also say that a reborn person is flesh only insofar as there's still a part of their flesh in them that fights against the Spirit they've received. I can't believe you'd intentionally make up something like this just to create hostility towards me. Otherwise, what worse thing could you accuse me of? But maybe you're just not familiar with my teachings, or you're not able to handle the complexity of the topic. You seem so overwhelmed by it that you can't even remember what you're arguing against me or in favor of yourself.

For example, you say that you believe, based on the authority of ancient scholars, that there are some seeds of goodness in people's minds by nature. But then you contradict yourself by saying that free will can't choose anything good. I don't see how these two ideas can coexist. So, I constantly have to remind you of the main issue we're discussing, which you keep forgetting and end up arguing something completely different.

SECTION 46: JEREMIAH 10:23-24 DEFENDED.

Regarding Jeremiah 10:23-24, you claim that this passage is more about the success of events rather than the power of free will. But once again, you're just imposing your own interpretation on the Scripture without any solid basis. Why should we accept your view just because you say so? If we let opponents of the truth twist the Scriptures like this, what won't they be able to achieve? Show us how your interpretation comes from the context, and then we'll believe you. On the contrary, I can demonstrate from the same context that the Prophet, while trying to teach the ungodly with great persistence and without success, realizes that his words are useless unless God teaches them internally. This means that it's not up to humans to hear and desire what is good.

Realizing this and feeling alarmed at the thought of God's judgment, he asks God to correct him justly, if correction is absolutely necessary. However, he pleads not to be subjected to God's wrath along with the ungodly, whom God allows to become hardened and persist in their disbelief.

But let's assume that this passage refers to both favorable and unfavorable events. What if this interpretation actually undermines the concept of free will? This new explanation is created so that those who are inexperienced and unskilled in deception may think they have received a satisfactory understanding of the text. This is similar to the trick used to avoid the necessity of a consequence. They don't realize that they are even more trapped by these evasions than by the straightforward meaning of the words, so misled are they by these new terms!

If we don't have control over the outcome of our earthly affairs, over which we are supposed to be lords and masters (Genesis 1), then how can we have control over the divine grace of God, which depends solely on God's will? Can the effort of free will achieve eternal salvation when it can't even stop a physical attack or keep a single hair on our heads in place? Do we have no power to possess the created world, yet somehow have the power to possess the Creator? Why are we so deluded?

Striving for good or evil implies a much greater degree of control over events. This is because, in pursuing either of the two, one is more likely to be deceived and has less freedom than when striving for money, fame, or pleasure.

So, what incredible escape has your interpretation achieved? While it denies human freedom in trivial matters, it proclaims it in the significant matters of God. It's like saying, 'Codrus can't pay half a crown, but he can pay millions of guineas.' I'm also surprised that Diatribe, who has been so critical of Wickliff's statement, 'all things happen by necessity,' now willingly admits that events are necessary for us.

'Furthermore, no matter how much you force the issue,' she says, 'to relate it to the topic of free will, doesn't everyone agree that no one can live a righteous life without God's grace? However, we also make an effort according to our own abilities, to the point where we pray daily, "O Lord my God, guide my path in your sight." The person who asks for help doesn't stop trying.'

Diatribe believes that her response isn't just a weak argument; as long as she speaks up and says something, she thinks she has satisfied everyone. She's so confident in her own authority.

The thing we need to prove is whether we strive using our own strength. What she proves is that she tries by praying. Is she mocking us? Is she making fun of the Catholics? Whoever prays, prays with the help of the Spirit; in fact, the Spirit himself prays within us (Romans 8:26). How does the power of free will get proven by the effort of the Holy Spirit? Is free will the same as the Holy Spirit in Diatribe's opinion? Are we currently discussing the power of the Spirit? Diatribe leaves me with this passage from Jeremiah, untouched and unbeatable, and only offers her own interpretation: "We also strive with our own strength," and Luther has to believe her - if he wants to.

SECTION 47. PROVERBS 16:1 DEFENDED.

She also argues that the saying in Proverbs 16:1 refers to events: "The preparation of the heart belongs to man, but the answer of the tongue is from the Lord." As if we should be satisfied with her word alone and not need any other authority! And it's more than enough to respond that even if we accept this interpretation, which applies it to events, then the victory is clearly mine, as I said before: since free will is nothing in our own actions and events, it's even less in God's actions and events. But notice how clever she is: "How can preparing the heart be a person's work when Luther says everything happens by necessity?" I respond, "Since events are not in our control, as you admit, how can it be a person's work to bring things to their conclusion?"

SECTION 48: PROVERBS SUPPORTING FREE WILL

For my response, I'll use the same answer you provided me. No, really, we need to work on this topic because all future events are unknown to us. As the Preacher says, "In the morning sow your seed, and in the evening do not withhold your hand, because you do not know whether this or that will spring up." I'm saying that these events are uncertain to us in terms of knowledge, but they are necessary in terms of outcome. Their necessity instills in us a fear of God, which protects us from arrogance and complacency, while their uncertainty creates a sense of hope that strengthens our minds against despair.

But she goes back to her old argument that many statements in the book of Proverbs support Free Will, like this one: "Commit your works to the Lord." Do you hear that? Your works. She points out that there are many imperative and conjunctive verbs in the book, as well as many second-person pronouns, which she believes prove the existence of Free Will. For example, "commit" implies that you can commit, and "your works" implies that you do them. So, when it says, "I am your God," you would interpret it as 'you make me your God,' and "Your faith has made you whole." Do you hear that? "Your faith." If you inter-pret it this way, then you believe that you create your own faith. And now you have proven Free Will. I'm not mocking here, but rather demonstrating that Diatribe isn't taking this argument seriously.

Regarding the statement in Proverbs 16:4, "The Lord has made all things for himself; even the wicked for the day of evil," she completely changes its meaning by adding her own words, defending God by saying that He hasn't created any evil creatures. It's as if I was talking about creation itself, rather than God's ongoing influence on created beings, through which God even affects the wicked, as I've already mentioned with the example of Pharaoh.

God creates a wicked person, not by making evil or an evil being (which is impossible), but when the seed upon which God works is corrupted, an evil person is created. This is not the fault of the Creator, but rather the result of the corruption within the material. The saying from Proverbs 21:1, "The heart of the king is in the hand of the Lord; he inclines it wherever he will," doesn't necessarily mean that God forces the king's heart, as if we were talking about compulsion, but rather about an unchangeable necessity.

When we say that God inclines the heart, it doesn't mean a lazy or passive action, as Diatribe suggests. Instead, it refers to God's powerful influence, which a person cannot avoid or change. This means that a person will have the will that God has given them, and that will is guided by God's own actions. I have already discussed this point.

Diatribe argues that since Solomon is talking about the king's heart, this text shouldn't be used to express a general idea. Instead, it should be understood in the same way as Job 33:30, which says, "He makes a hypocrite reign for the sins of the people." Eventually, Diatribe admits that God does move the king to do evil, but in a way that allows the king to be driven by his passions so that God can punish his people.

I respond by saying that whether God permits or inclines the king's heart, the very act of allowing or influencing comes from God's will and actions. This is because the king's will cannot escape the influence of the all-powerful God, who guides every person's will to do good or evil.

Regarding my statement about making a general proposition from the specific one about the king's will, I believe I did so appropriately and wisely. If the king's heart, which appears to be particularly free and in control of others, cannot will anything other than what God desires, then how much less can anyone else do so? This same conclusion applies not only to the king's will but also to any person's will. If one individual, no matter how private, cannot will anything except as God influences them, the same must be said for all people. The fact that Balaam could not say whatever he wanted is clear evidence from the Scriptures that humans are not free to choose or do their own laws or actions. Otherwise, there would be no such thing as examples in the Scriptures.

SECTION 49: JOHN 15:5 EXPLAINED

After acknowledging that many testimonies, like those Luther gathers from the Book of Proverbs, could indeed be collected, it is claimed that they could be interpreted in a way that supports both Freewill and the opposing view. Finally, the powerful argument from John 15:5 is mentioned, where it says, "Without me, you can do nothing," etc.

I must say, I'm impressed by the skill of this eloquent speaker on the topic of Freewill. They teach us to interpret the testimonies of Scripture in a way that suits our own understanding, so that they appear to support Freewill. In other words, they make the Scriptures say what we want them to say, rather than what they should say. And then, they pretend to be extremely afraid of one specific argument, which they call "Achillean," so that the unsuspecting reader might think the rest of the arguments are not worth considering once this one has been defeated.

But I'll be keeping a close eye on this grandiose and heroic Diatribe, to see how it manages to defeat my "Achilles" argument when it hasn't even managed to address a single common soldier – no, not even a "Thersites" – and has only ended up destroying itself with its own weapons.

So, she takes this little word 'nothing' and kills it with the help of many words and examples, leading it to the conclusion that 'nothing' can mean small and imperfect. In other words, she's saying what the Sophists have already taught about this passage: "without me, you can do nothing;" meaning, you can't do anything perfectly. Her persuasive skills are so strong that she makes this old, worn-out interpretation seem fresh and new. She's so confident in her argument that you might think she's the first one to ever suggest it, as if it's never been heard before and is almost a miracle for her to present it. All the while, she doesn't pay much attention to the actual text and its surrounding context, which is where the true understanding should come from.

Not to mention that her goal is to demonstrate, using many words and examples, how this word 'nothing' can be understood as 'something small and imperfect.' It's as if we were really arguing about what could be interpreted this way when the actual issue is whether it should be interpreted this way. So, her entire impressive interpretation only amounts to this, if anything: that this passage from John becomes uncertain and ambiguous. And it's no surprise, since Diatribe's main goal is to argue that the Scriptures are always ambiguous (so she doesn't have to rely on them) and that the testimonies of the Fathers are definitive - this way, she can freely misuse the Scriptures. It's strange to show such reverence for God by making His words useless and human words valuable!

SECTION 50: INCONSISTENCY CHARGED. AN ADVANTAGE IS GIVEN TO HERETICS.

But the most amusing part is seeing how consistent she is with herself. 'Nothing' can be understood as 'a little.' And in this sense, she says, it's absolutely true that we can do nothing without Christ. He's talking about the fruits of the Gospel, which only come to those who remain in the Vine, meaning Christ.

Here, she admits that fruit only comes to those who stay in the Vine, and she does this using the same convenient interpretation that proves 'nothing' means the same as 'small and imperfect.' Maybe we should also conveniently interpret the adverb 'not' to mean that the fruits of the Gospel come to people outside of Christ to some extent, or in a small and imperfect way. This way, we could claim that ungodly people, without Christ and with the devil ruling them and fighting against Christ, can produce some portion of the fruits of life. In other words, Christ's enemies can work for Christ. But let's not go any further with this.

I'd like to know how we should respond to heretics who use this law to interpret the Scriptures, insisting that 'nothing' and 'not' imply an imperfect substance. For example, when it says 'without him was nothing made,' they argue it means 'very little' was made. Or when it says 'the fool has said in his heart there is no God,' they claim it means 'God is imperfect.' And what about 'He has made us and not we ourselves,' which they say means we made a tiny bit of ourselves? There are countless passages in the Scriptures where 'nothing' and 'not' appear. Should we consider the appropriateness of the interpretation in these cases? But which heretic doesn't think their interpretation is suitable?

What! I guess this is a way to untangle knots, by giving such freedom to corrupt minds and deceptive spirits! To those of you who undermine the certainty of sacred Scripture, I can easily believe that this freedom of interpretation would be convenient. But for us who are working to establish people's consciences, nothing could be more inconvenient, harmful, or dangerous than this convenience you recommend.

So listen up, great conqueror of Luther's Achilles. Unless you can prove that 'nothing' in this context not only can but must be understood as 'a little,' you'll gain nothing from all these words and examples, other than showing that you've been fighting fire with dry stubble. What does your "maybe" matter to me when you need to prove that it "must be"? Until you do that, I'll stick to the natural and grammatical meaning of the word, laughing at your armies as much as your triumphs!

So, what happened to that widely accepted belief that Free Will can't will anything good? Maybe it's time for a convenient interpretation to step in. It seems that 'nothing good' now means 'something good,' thanks to an entirely new approach to grammar and logic that claims 'nothing' means the same as 'something.' This would be considered impossible by logicians since they are contradictory terms.

What about the claim that we believe Satan is the ruler of this world, reigning over the wills and minds of people, who are his captives and serve him? According to Christ and Paul, that fierce lion (1 Peter 5:8) is indeed the relentless enemy of God's grace and human salvation. Would he really allow a person, who is his slave and part of his kingdom, to strive for good by making any effort towards it, even for a moment, so they could escape his tyranny? Wouldn't he instead do everything in his power to encourage and push people to will and do things that go against grace?

You argue that human will exists in a free environment and is left to its own devices. You have no problem claiming at the same time that the will's effort can lean towards either side. This is because you picture both God and the devil as distant observers of this changeable and free will. You don't think they actively influence and stir up our bound will, each of them being fierce warriors for their respective sides. Just believe this fact, and our viewpoint stands strong, with Free Will defeated and humbled, as I've already demonstrated.

So, either Satan's kingdom in people is non-existent, and therefore Christ is lying, or if his kingdom is as Christ describes it, then Free Will is nothing more than Satan's captive servant, which can't be free unless the devil is first removed by God's power.

Can you see from this, my Diatribe, what you're implying and how powerful it is when you criticize Luther's confidence in his claims by saying, "Luther uses strong scriptural evidence, but all his scripture is torn apart by one small word?" Who doesn't know that the entire body of Scripture could be torn apart by one small word? We knew this long before we ever heard of Erasmus. But the real question is whether it's acceptable for Scripture to be torn apart by one small word. The dispute is about whether it's done correctly and if it must be done this way. If someone focuses on this issue, they'll see how easy it is to tear apart the Scriptures and how terrible Luther's confidence is. But in reality, they'll see that it's not a bunch of small words or even all the gates of hell that can achieve this goal.

SECTION 51: LUTHER PROVES THE NEGATIVE.

Let's do what Diatribe can't do for her positive claim. Even though it's not our responsibility, let's prove our negative. Through strong reasoning, we'll force the admission that the word 'nothing' here not only can, but must mean not 'a little,' but its natural meaning. I'll do this with additional arguments, on top of the unbeatable one I've already used to win: that words should keep their natural meaning unless proven otherwise. Diatribe hasn't done this and can't do it here.

First, I must emphasize this point based on the nature of the situation. It has been proven through clear and unambiguous scriptural evidence that Satan is the most powerful and cunning ruler of this world's princes, as I mentioned earlier. Under his rule, human will is no longer free and in control, but instead is enslaved to sin and Satan. As a result, people can only desire what Satan allows them to desire, and he won't let them desire anything good. Even if Satan didn't control them, sin itself, which humans serve, would be enough to stop them from desiring good things.

Secondly, the continuation of the discussion, which Diatribe boldly disregards, supports this point as well. In John 15:6, Christ says, "If a man does not abide in me, he is cast out as a branch, and he withers, and they gather him up, and cast him into the fire, and he burns." Diatribe has ignored these words, using clever rhetorical tactics, hoping that this transition would be too difficult for uneducated readers like the Lutherans to understand.

You'll notice that Christ, explaining his own metaphor of the branch and the vine, clearly states what he wants the word 'nothing' to mean: that without Christ, a person is cast out and withers. And what else could 'cast out' and 'withers' mean, if not being handed over to the devil's control and continually getting worse? To get worse and worse is not to have power or to strive. The more a withering branch withers, the more it's prepared for burning. If Christ hadn't explained this metaphor like this, no one would have dared to interpret it this way. So, it's clear that the word 'nothing' should be taken literally here, based on its natural meaning.

Now, let's also examine the examples Diatribe uses to prove that 'nothing' sometimes means 'a little,' to show that even in this part of her argument, she is nothing and achieves nothing.

Even if she had proven something here, it wouldn't have made a difference - she's completely ineffective in all aspects and methods. She claims, "It is a common saying that a man does nothing if he doesn't achieve what he's after; but the person who tries often makes some progress towards their goal." I must say, I've never heard this saying before; it seems like you're just making it up.

Words (as far as they name things) should be understood based on the topic at hand and in relation to the speaker's intention. When someone is actively trying to do something, they don't call their efforts "nothing." They're not talking about their attempt when they mention "nothing," but rather the outcome. That's what someone means when they say, "that person does nothing or achieves nothing;" in other words, "they haven't reached their goal; they haven't succeeded."

Moreover, if your example proves anything (which it doesn't), it actually supports my argument more than yours. This is precisely what I'm arguing and want to demonstrate: that free will can do many things, but they amount to nothing in God's eyes. What's the point of trying if you don't get what you're after? So, no matter which way Diatribe turns, she stumbles and contradicts herself. This usually happens with lawyers defending a weak case.

SECTION 52: 1 COR 3:7; 13:2; JOH 3.:27.

Again, Diatribe refers to a passage from Paul, "Neither is he that plants anything, nor he that waters, but God who gives the increase" (1 Cor 3:7). Diatribe claims that Paul is saying something of little importance and useless by itself is considered 'nothing.'

But wait, are you calling the ministry of the word 'useless of itself' and 'of small importance'? That same ministry that Paul praises so highly everywhere else, especially in 2 Cor 3:5-8, where he calls it the ministry of life and the ministry of glory? It seems you're not considering the context or the speaker's intention.

When it comes to giving the increase, the planter and the waterer are indeed nothing. But when it comes to planting and watering, they are not nothing. The main work of the Spirit in the church of God is to teach and exhort. This is what Paul means, and his words clearly express this.

But even if we accept this example as relevant (like the others), it still supports my argument. I'm saying that Free Will is 'nothing' - meaning it's 'useless of itself' before God, as you interpret this passage. We're talking about this kind of existence, fully aware that the ungodly will is 'something' and not 'mere nothing.'

As for the quote from 1 Cor 13:2, "If I do not have charity, I am nothing," I'm not sure why Diatribe brings this up. Maybe she's just looking for more examples or thinks we don't have enough arguments to counter her. But the person who doesn't have charity is truly and strictly 'nothing' before God.

I still maintain the same stance regarding Freewill. This example also supports my argument against Diatribe, unless Diatribe still doesn't understand what our debate is about. We're not talking about a natural existence, but rather an existence of grace, as they call it. We know that Freewill performs certain natural actions, like eating, drinking, having children, and managing a household. So, Diatribe could have avoided mocking us with that nonsensical statement, which seems like delirious rambling, that if we insist on the word "nothing," then a person can't even sin without Christ. On the contrary, even Luther admits that Freewill has the power to commit sin, though it has no other power! It seems that the wise Diatribe must have her joke, even on a serious topic.

What we're saying is that without God's grace, a person still remains under the control of God's general omnipotence, which performs, moves, and carries away all things in a necessary and infallible course. But what the person does while being carried away is "nothing" - meaning, it's nothing in the eyes of God, and it's considered nothing but sin. So, in terms of grace, a person who doesn't have charity is nothing. After Diatribe admits on her own that we're discussing the fruits of the gospel in this verse, fruits that aren't produced without Christ, why does she then immediately change the subject, start a different discussion, and argue about natural actions and human fruits? It's probably because someone who lacks the truth is never consistent with themselves.

So, let's look at that quote from John 3:27 again: "A man can receive nothing unless it is given to him from heaven." John is talking about a man who already has something, and he's saying that this man doesn't receive anything else - meaning, he doesn't receive the Spirit and its gifts. He's talking about this, not about the man's nature. John didn't need Diatribe to tell him that the man already had eyes, nose, ears, mouth, mind, will, reason, and all the other human traits. Maybe Diatribe thinks that when John mentioned a man, he was actually talking about some abstract concept like Plato's chaos, Leucippus' vacuum, Aristotle's infinite, or some other "nothing" that would eventually become "something" through a gift from heaven. Seriously?

Why is Diatribe even bringing up examples from Scripture just to play around with such an important topic? What's the point of providing so much information? Is it to teach us that fire, escaping from evil, striving for good, and everything else comes from heaven - as if anyone didn't already know or agree with that?

I'm talking about grace, or as she puts it, "Christ and gospel fruit." But in the meantime, she keeps going on about nature, just to buy time, prolong the argument, and confuse those who aren't well-versed in the subject. Despite all this, she doesn't provide a single example of 'nothing' meaning 'a little' - which is what she said she would do. Instead, she clearly shows that she doesn't know or care about Christ, grace, or the difference between grace and nature. This is a distinction that even the most basic Sophists understood and frequently discussed in their schools.

She doesn't realize that all her examples actually support my argument and go against hers. Even this quote from John the Baptist, "A man can receive nothing unless it is given to him from heaven," shows that free will is nothing. Ah, this is how she plans to defeat me: Diatribe gives me the weapons to destroy her when she's defenseless. So, it seems that those Scriptures that the stubborn Luther uses to support his arguments are somehow dismissed by a single word from her.

SECTION 53: DIATRIBE'S USE OF SIMILES IS POINTLESS AND WORKS AGAINST HER - WHAT SHE SHOULD HAVE FOCUSED ON.

Diatribe uses many similes, which only serve to distract the naive reader, as is her style, and make them focus on unrelated topics while forgetting the main issue at hand. For example, she says that God protects the ship, but the sailor guides it to the harbor, implying that the sailor has a role to play. This simile assigns distinct tasks to God (preserving) and the sailor (guiding), suggesting that both have their own responsibilities. If it proves anything else, it shows that God is responsible for preservation, while the sailor is responsible for guidance. What a fitting and clever simile!

Similarly, the farmer brings the crops to the barn, but God provides them. Again, this assigns separate tasks to God and humans - unless Diatribe wants to make the farmer a creator and co-provider of the crops. But even if these similes do assign the same tasks to God and humans, what do they prove other than that the creature works together with the Creator? Is our debate about cooperation? Aren't we discussing the power and function of free will instead? What a detour! The speaker was supposed to talk about a palm tree but only mentioned a gourd. A barrel was to be made, so why did a pitcher appear instead?

I also know that Paul collaborates with God in teaching the Corinthians. He preaches externally, while God teaches internally, with each having a different role. Similarly, Paul works with God when he speaks through the Holy Spirit, and in this case, both have the same role.

I firmly believe and maintain that God, when working outside the boundaries of the grace of His Spirit, is involved in everything, even in the actions of the wicked. As the sole creator of all things, He alone moves, drives, and propels everything through the power of His omnipotence. Nothing can escape or change this, but must follow and obey according to the capacity God has given it. This means that even all wicked acts work together with Him.

Similarly, when God acts through the Spirit of grace in those He has made righteous - that is, in His own kingdom - He also drives and moves them. As new creations, they follow and work together with Him, or as Paul says, they are led by Him (Romans 8:14).

However, this is not the main focus of our discussion. Our question is not about what we can do when God works, but rather, what can we do on our own? In other words, as beings created from nothing, can we do or strive for anything through the general movement of God's omnipotence to prepare ourselves for the new creation of His Spirit? This is the question that should have been addressed, instead of diverting us to another topic.

Our answer to this question is: before a person is created, they do nothing and strive for nothing to make themselves a creature; and after they have been created, they do nothing and strive for nothing to maintain themselves as a creature. Both of these events occur solely through the will of God's omnipotent power and goodness. He creates and sustains us without our involvement, but He does not work within us without our participation. This is because we are created and preserved for the very purpose of allowing God to work within us and for us to work together with Him (Colossians 1:29). This is true whether it happens outside the boundaries of His kingdom through the action of His general omnipotence, or within the boundaries of that kingdom through the special power of His Spirit.

So, we're saying that before a person is transformed into a new creation in the spiritual kingdom, they don't do anything or make any effort to prepare themselves for that change and kingdom. And even after they've been made new, they still don't do anything or make any effort to stay in that kingdom. Instead, it's the Spirit alone that does both of these things in us - creating us anew without our input and keeping us in that state once we're there. As James says, "Of his own will he begat us by the word of his power, that we might be the beginning of his creation;" (James 1:18), referring to the renewed creation. However, the Spirit doesn't work in us without our involvement, since we are the ones being transformed and preserved for the purpose of working together with the Spirit. Through us, the Spirit preaches, shows compassion to the poor, and comforts the afflicted. But what role does free will play in all of this? What's left for it but nothing; absolute nothing?

SECTION 54: INCONSISTENCY AND AUDACITY OF DIATRIBE; TAKES UP ONE SUBJECT AND PURSUES ANOTHER; ARGUES BY INVERSION.

If you read the Diatribe in this part for five or six pages, you'll see that all it does is bring in examples like these and then quote some of the most beautiful passages and parables from Paul's writings and the Gospels. The point seems to be to teach us that there are countless texts in the Scriptures (as the Diatribe puts it) that talk about the cooperation and supporting gifts of God.

Now, if I understand from these testimonies that humans can't do anything without God's help, then no human actions are good. But she, on the other hand, using a rhetorical twist, concludes: "No, actually, there's nothing humans can't do with God's help; therefore, all human actions can be good. So, as many times as the word of God mentions divine assistance, that's how many times it supports free will. Now, there are countless such passages. So, I've won if the question is decided by the number of testimonies."

That's what she says. But do you think she was really clear-headed or in her right mind when she wrote this? I won't accuse her of being malicious or wicked for consistently discussing different topics than what she intended to (unless maybe she wants to wear me out with her constant rambling). However, if she enjoys talking nonsense about such a serious subject, I'll gladly expose her absurd claims for everyone to see.

First, I don't doubt or question that all human actions can be good if done with God's help. Second, I don't doubt or question that there's nothing humans can't do with God's help. But I'm amazed at your carelessness, since you started writing about the power of free will but ended up writing about the power of divine grace. After doing this, as if everyone were clueless, you boldly claim that free will is supported by those Scripture passages that praise God's helping grace.

Not only do you have the nerve to do this, but you even sing your own praises, as if you're a glorious, triumphant conqueror! I now know firsthand, through your words and actions, what Freewill is and what its power is. "She is mad." What else could it be in you, I wonder, that speaks this way, if not this very Freewill?

But as crazy as you are, listen to your own conclusions: Scripture praises God's grace; therefore, Scripture supports Freewill. Scripture praises the help we receive from God's grace; therefore, Scripture establishes Freewill. I have to ask, what kind of logic did you learn to come up with such conclusions? Why couldn't it be the opposite? Grace is preached; therefore, Freewill is debunked. The help provided by grace is praised; therefore, Freewill is destroyed.

So, why is grace given? Is it so that the pride of Freewill, which is strong enough on its own, can have a wild party, adorned with grace as a kind of unnecessary decoration? Well then, I'll also make an inference by reversing the logic. Even though I'm not a skilled rhetorician, I'll do it with more solid reasoning than yours. For every passage in the divine Scriptures that mention divine help, that many exclude Freewill. There are countless such passages. If we're going to decide this based on numbers, then I've won.

Why do we need grace, and what is the purpose of receiving grace, if not because our free will is powerless and unable to desire good things, as the Diatribe itself has agreed with in its commendable opinion? When we praise grace and acknowledge the assistance it provides, we are simultaneously admitting the weakness of our free will. This is a solid conclusion and a logical outcome that even the forces of evil cannot overthrow (Matthew 16:18).

SECTION 55: LUTHER CONCLUDES HIS DEFENSE OF HIS OWN TEXTS.

At this point, I will stop defending my own texts against the Diatribe's attempts to refute them, so my book doesn't become excessively long. If there are any other points worth addressing, I will do so when presenting my own views. As for what Erasmus mentions in his conclusion - that if our view is correct, numerous commands, threats, and promises would be rendered meaningless, and there would be no room for merit or demerit, reward or punishment, along with other unpleasant implications - I have already responded to these concerns.

I neither accept nor endorse the so-called "golden mean" approach, which suggests (with good intentions, I presume) that we should grant a tiny amount of power to free will in order to more easily resolve the apparent inconsistencies in Scripture and the aforementioned issues. The truth is, this "golden mean" does not help the cause it intends to support, nor does it offer any real solutions to the difficulties we face. Unless we give complete control to free will, as the Pelagians do, the inconsistencies in Scripture remain, merit and reward are excluded, God's mercy and justice are nullified, and all the problems we hope to avoid by allowing a minuscule and ineffective power to free will persist, as I have already demonstrated.

So, we must completely deny the existence of free will and attribute everything to God. By doing this, we'll see that the Scriptures are consistent and our issues are either resolved or made bearable. However, there's one thing that bothers me, Erasmus. It's your belief that I'm arguing this point with more passion than reason. I can't stand being accused of hypocrisy, as if I believe one thing and write another. It's also not true what you say about me - that I've only recently started to completely deny free will because I've been defending myself so passionately. I know you won't find any evidence of this in my previous writings.

In fact, my theses and questions, which are still available, consistently state that free will is an illusion and just a name. This is the conclusion I've come to through truth, debate, and being challenged. I've argued this point with great intensity, and if that's a crime, then I'm guilty. But I'm overjoyed to bear witness to this truth for the world in the name of God. May God himself confirm this testimony on the final day!

No one will be more blessed than Luther, who is highly praised by his own time for not arguing the truth lazily or deceitfully, but with great, perhaps even excessive, intensity. Then, I'll gladly avoid the judgment mentioned by Jeremiah: "Cursed is the man who does the work of the Lord negligently."

Now, if I seem a bit harsh on your Diatribe, please forgive me. It's not because I have any ill-will towards you. Instead, I feel strongly that you're undermining this cause, which is Christ's cause, with your authority. Your knowledge and the content you present don't really warrant any special consideration. And honestly, who can keep their cool all the time without getting heated at some point?

You tried to be moderate in your treatise, but you ended up being almost as cold as ice. Yet, you still managed to throw some fiery and extremely bitter darts, making you seem quite hostile to your readers – unless they view you with particular favor and leniency. But all this is irrelevant to the cause at hand. We should both forgive each other for these rough edges, as we are only human, and nothing more than that can be expected from us.

PART FIVE
FREE WILL PROVEN TO BE A LIE

SECTION 1: HOW LUTHER PLANS TO CONDUCT THE FIGHT

We have now reached the final part of this discussion, where, as promised, I should present my own arguments against Free Will. However, I won't bring up all of them, because who could do that in a short piece when the entire Scripture supports my position? Moreover, there's no need to do so, since Free Will has already been defeated and brought down by a double victory: first, by proving that everything it thought supported it actually goes against it; and second, by showing that all the evidence it tried to refute remains unshakable. Furthermore, even if Free Will wasn't already defeated, it would be enough to bring it down with just one or two strong points. After all, why would you need to repeatedly stab an enemy who has already been killed by a single blow? So, I'll try to be brief now, as long as the topic allows me to be, and out of the countless arguments I could present, I will only call upon two main figures and a select few of their supporting points. These are Paul and John the Evangelist.

SECTION 2: ROMANS 1:18 PASSES JUDGMENT ON FREE WILL.

Paul, in his letter to the Romans, argues in favor of God's grace against Free Will. He says, "The wrath of God is revealed from heaven upon all ungodliness and unrighteousness of men, who hold the truth in unrighteousness." In these words, we hear a general judgment on all people, stating that they are under God's wrath. What else does this mean, if not that they are deserving of wrath and punishment? Paul gives the reason for this anger, saying that people do nothing but what is deserving of wrath and punishment; that everyone is ungodly and unjust, and holds the truth in unrighteousness. So where is the power of Free Will that strives for something good? Paul portrays it as deserving of God's wrath and judges it as ungodly and unjust. Now, something that is ungodly and deserving of wrath strives and has power not for grace, but against it.

Some might laugh at Luther for not examining Paul's text carefully enough and argue that in this passage, Paul is not talking about all people or all their efforts, but only about those who are ungodly and unjust – those who, as his words say, hold the truth in unrighteousness. Therefore, it doesn't mean that everyone is like this. However, I would like to point out that for Paul, saying 'upon all ungodliness of men' is the same as saying 'upon the ungodliness of all men,' since Paul often uses Hebrew expressions. So, his meaning is that all people are ungodly and unjust, and hold the truth in unrighteousness; therefore, all people are deserving of wrath.

Moreover, the Greek text doesn't use the relative term "of those who," but rather the article. So, it reads: "The wrath of God is revealed upon the ungodliness and injustice of people, as they hold the truth in unrighteousness." This phrase essentially serves as a label for all people: "That they hold the truth in unrighteousness." It's similar to when we say, "Our Father who is in heaven." We could also say, "Our heavenly Father," or "Our Father in the heavens," to differentiate them from those who believe and are godly.

However, if these ideas seem trivial or pointless, consider the very flow of Paul's argument, which supports and demonstrates them. Just before this, he said, "The Gospel is the power of God for salvation to everyone who believes; first to the Jew, and also to the Greek."

The words used here are clear and straightforward: "To the Jews and to the Greeks - that is, to everyone - the Gospel of the power of God is necessary so that believers can be saved from the wrath that is revealed." The author states that the Jews, who were superior to other nations in righteousness, in following God's law, and in the power of free will, are just like everyone else - lacking the power of God and needing it to be saved from the revealed wrath. When the author says that this power is necessary for them, doesn't that imply that they are under wrath?

Who would you think is not subject to God's wrath when you have to accept that even the greatest people in the world - like the Jews and the Greeks, for example - are not exempt? Furthermore, who would you exclude among those Jews and Greeks when Paul includes them all under one name, without any distinction, and subjects them all to the same judgment? Can we assume that there were no individuals in these two highly regarded nations who tried to be honest or who made the most of their free will? Yet, Paul doesn't care about that. He puts them all under wrath; he declares them all ungodly and unjust. Shouldn't we assume that the rest of the Apostles, with a similar judgment, also considered all other nations and each individual within them as part of a collective condemnation, under the curse and control of this wrath?

SECTION 3: A PUBLISHED GOSPEL SHOWS THAT NATURAL MAN LACKS BOTH KNOWLEDGE AND POWER.

Paul's passage in Romans 1:18 clearly states that free will, or the best quality in people - even in those who are highly regarded, those who possess law, justice, wisdom, and all virtues - is ungodly and unjust, deserving of God's wrath. If this argument doesn't hold, then Paul's point falls apart. But if it does stand, then his division of salvation for those who believe the Gospel and wrath for everyone else leaves no one in between. He portrays believers as righteous and unbelievers as ungodly, unrighteous, and subject to wrath. In essence, he's saying: "The righteousness of God is revealed in the Gospel, and it is by faith." Therefore, all people are ungodly and unrighteous, since it would be foolish for God to reveal righteousness to those who either already knew it or possessed its seeds. But since God is not foolish and still reveals a saving righteousness, it's clear that free will, even in the greatest individuals, not only has nothing and can do nothing, but also doesn't even know what is just in God's eyes. Unless you want to argue that God's righteousness is not revealed to the best of people, but only to the lesser ones, which would contradict Paul's claim that he is a debtor to both the Jew and the Greek, to the wise and the unwise, to the barbarian and the Greek. So, understanding that all people without exception are included here, Paul concludes that everyone is ungodly, unjust, and ignorant of righteousness and faith. This is how far they are from being able to desire or do any good thing.

This conclusion is firmly based on the idea that God reveals a path to salvation for those who are ignorant and living in darkness - which means they are unaware of it on their own. Now, those who don't know about this path to salvation are definitely under wrath and damnation. They can't free themselves from it due to their ignorance, and they can't even try to escape it. After all, how can you make an effort if you don't know what you're aiming for, where you're coming from, where you're going, or how far you need to go?

SECTION 4: EXPERIENCE SUPPORTS PAUL'S ARGUMENT. FREE WILL NEITHER UNDERSTANDS THE TRUTH NOR CAN TOLERATE IT.

Real-life examples support this conclusion. Can you find a single person among all humans - even the holiest and most righteous - who has ever thought that the way to righteousness and salvation is to truly believe in someone who is both God and man, who died for the sins of humanity, and who rose again and sits at the right hand of the Father? Or, who has ever imagined this wrath of God that Paul says is revealed from heaven? Look at the Jews, who have been taught by so many miracles and prophets. What do they think of this path? Not only have they refused to accept it, but they even hate it so much that no other nation on earth has persecuted Christ more severely to this day.

And yet, who would dare to say that there hasn't been a single person among such a large group of people who has tried to use their free will and attempted to achieve something through its power? So why do all people seek something different from this path? Why have the most exceptional individuals not only failed to pursue this way of righteousness and remained unaware of it, but also, once it was revealed and shared, rejected it with intense hatred and sought to destroy it?

In 1 Corinthians 1:23, Paul states that the way of salvation is a stumbling block for Jews and foolishness for Gentiles. He refers to both groups without distinction, and since Jews and Gentiles make up the majority of people on Earth, it's clear that free will is actually the greatest enemy of righteousness and human salvation. This is because some Jews and Gentiles must have used their free will to its fullest extent, yet they still ended up opposing grace.

So, how can we say that free will strives for good when it considers goodness and righteousness to be a stumbling block and foolishness? We can't claim that this verse only applies to some people and not all. Paul speaks of all Jews and Gentiles when he says, "to the Gentiles foolishness, and to the Jews a stumbling block." The only exception he makes is for those who believe. He says, "to us" – meaning the called and sanctified – "He is the power and wisdom of God." He doesn't specify 'some Gentiles' or 'some Jews,' but simply refers to all who are not believers.

Paul creates a clear division between believers and unbelievers, with no one in between. We're discussing Gentiles who don't have God's grace, and Paul says that God's righteousness is foolishness to them, and they reject it! This shows that free will's pursuit of goodness is not as admirable as it may seem.

SECTION 5: PAUL SPECIFICALLY MENTIONS THE MOST PROMINENT GREEKS AND THEN CRITICIZES THE JEWS WITHOUT EXCEPTION.

Moreover, observe how Paul himself brings up the most distinguished Greeks as examples to support his claim. He states that the wisest among them became foolish and their hearts were darkened (Romans 1:20-21). Additionally, they were led astray by their own reasoning, meaning their cunning arguments.

Doesn't Paul target the very best of the Greeks when he addresses their reasoning? This refers to their highest and most esteemed thoughts and beliefs, which they regarded as true wisdom. However, this wisdom, which Paul elsewhere calls foolish in them, is described as empty here. He explains that, despite their efforts, their situation only worsened: their hearts eventually darkened, they worshipped idols, and committed the shocking acts mentioned in the following verses.

So, if the best efforts and actions of the most virtuous non-believers are considered evil and wicked, what do you think of the rest of them, who are even worse? Paul doesn't make a distinction between the better ones; he condemns their pursuit of wisdom without any bias. Now, when the very act or effort is condemned, those who strive for it are also condemned, even if they do so with all their free will. Their very best effort, I say, is declared to be flawed - so how much more are the people involved in it?

Similarly, Paul also dismisses the Jews without any distinction, as being Jews only in their outward appearance and not in their hearts. In Romans 2:27, he says, "You, by the letter and circumcision, dishonor God." And again, in Romans 2:29, "For he is not a Jew who is a Jew outwardly, but who is a Jew inwardly." What can be clearer than this distinction? The outward Jew is a lawbreaker. But how many Jews do you think there were, who had no faith - men of great wisdom, devotion, and honesty, who pursued justice and truth with the utmost determination? Paul often acknowledges them: that they have a passion for God, that they seek the righteousness of the law, that they work day and night to achieve salvation, and that they live blamelessly! And yet, they break the law because they are not spiritually

Jewish, but instead stubbornly resist the righteousness that comes from faith. So, what's left to conclude other than that free will is at its worst when it's at its best, and the harder it tries, the worse it becomes? The words are clear, the distinction leaves no room for doubt, and there's nothing that can be argued against.

SECTION 6: PAUL'S CONCLUSION CONFIRMS HIS MEANING.

But let's listen to Paul himself as he explains his own words. Wrapping up his argument, he says in Romans 3:9, "So what then? Are we better than them? Not at all. For we have already made the charge that both Jews and Greeks are all under sin." So, what's the deal with free will now? According to Paul, all Jews and Greeks are under sin. Are there any hidden meanings or complications here? What good would a widely accepted interpretation do against such a clear statement? He says "all," which doesn't leave anyone out. By stating that they are under sin, meaning they are slaves to sin, he implies that there's nothing good in them.

But where does he make this claim that all Jews and Gentiles are under sin? It's only in the part where he says, "The wrath of God is revealed from heaven upon all ungodliness and unrighteousness of men" (Romans 1:18). In the following words, he supports this with real-life examples. Because they displeased God, they were subjected to many vices, as if their ungodliness was proven by the evil things they did. They only willed and did evil.

Paul then focuses on the Jews specifically, accusing them of breaking the law. He also supports this with their actions and experiences: "You preach that man should not steal, and you steal. You abhor idols, yet you commit sacrilege" (Romans 2:21-22). He doesn't make any exceptions, except for those who are spiritually Jewish.

You can't really argue here by saying, 'Even though they are under sin, the best parts of them, like reason and will, still strive for good.' If there's still some good effort in them, then Paul's statement that they are under sin would be false. When he talks about Jews and Gentiles, he includes everything about them. So, unless you twist his words and assume he meant, 'The flesh of all Jews and Greeks is under sin,' meaning their more base desires, there's no way around it. But God's wrath, revealed from heaven upon them, will condemn their entire being unless they are justified by the Spirit. This wouldn't be the case if their entire being wasn't under sin.

SECTION 7: PAUL'S QUOTATIONS ARE JUSTIFIED.

Now let's see how Paul supports his view from the Scriptures - whether the words make more sense as we read them in Paul's quotes than as we read them in their original context. Paul says, "As it is written, for there is no one righteous, not even one; there is no one who understands; there is no one who seeks after God. They have all gone astray; they have all become abominable; there is no one who does good, not even one," etc. (Romans 3:10-12).

Let anyone who can, provide a suitable interpretation here. Let anyone who dares, create their own explanations; complain that the words are ambiguous and unclear, and defend free will against these harsh condemnations. Then I will gladly give in and change my mind, and become a supporter and defender of free will. It's clear that these things are said about all people; for the Prophet presents God looking upon all people and declaring this judgment upon them. He says in Psalm 14:2-3, "The Lord looks down from heaven on all mankind to see if there are any who understand, any who seek God. But they have all turned aside," etc. And Paul prevents the Jews from thinking that these things don't apply to them by stating that they especially apply to them. "We know," he says, "that whatever the law says, it says to those who are under the law" (Romans 3:19). He meant the same when he said in Romans 1:16, "To the Jew first, and also to the Greek."

So, you see, all of humanity, everyone under the law - meaning both Gentiles and Jews - are considered unjust in God's judgment. They don't understand or seek God - not even one person - but instead, they all stray and become unproductive. I assume that among these people, those who are under the law, there are also those who are the best and most honorable. These are the ones who, through their own free will, strive for what is honorable and good. They are the ones Diatribe talks about, claiming they have a sense of decency and the seeds of honesty within them. That is, unless Diatribe believes that these people are actually the children of angels!

So, how can someone strive for goodness if everyone is universally ignorant of God and neither cares for nor seeks Him? How can someone have the power to do good if everyone turns away from goodness and is completely useless? Don't we know what it means to be ignorant of God, not understanding or seeking Him, not fearing Him - to turn away from the right path and be unproductive? Aren't these words clear, and don't they teach that all people are both ignorant of God and disrespect Him? And then, as the next step, that they turn towards evil and are useless for good? We're not talking about ignorance in seeking food or contempt for money, but ignorance and contempt for religion and piety. This ignorance and contempt are, without a doubt, not rooted in our physical bodies or our lower, base desires, but in the highest and most excellent parts of us where justice, piety, knowledge, and reverence for God should reign. That is, these exist in our rational minds and our will - and so, in the very power of free will itself; in the very essence of integrity, or in the very heart of what is most excellent in a person.

Where are you now, my Diatribe, who previously promised that you would willingly agree about the most excellent thing in a person, that it is flesh - that is, ungodly - if it were proven by Scripture? Agree to this now, then, as you hear that the most excellent thing in all people is not only impious but also ignorant of God, a despiser of God, turned towards evil, and unproductive for good. For what does it mean to be unjust, if not that the will, which is one of the most excellent things in a person, is unjust?

What does it mean to have no understanding of God and goodness, if not that our understanding, which is one of the most excellent things in us, is ignorant of God and goodness - in other words, it is blind to the knowledge of godliness? What does it mean to have gone astray and be unprofitable, if not for people to lack any ability in any part of themselves - and least of all in their most excellent parts - to do good, but only to do evil? What does it mean not to fear God, if not for people, in all their parts - especially in their better parts - to be disrespectful towards God? Now, to be disrespectful towards God is to be disrespectful towards all things related to God, such as His words, works, laws, commands, and will. What can our understanding dictate that is right when it is blind and ignorant? What can our will choose that is good when it is evil and unprofitable? Indeed, what can our will follow when our understanding dictates nothing but the darkness of its own blindness and ignorance? If our understanding is in error and our will is averse, what good can we do or attempt?

SECTION 8: THE PROPHET'S CONDEMNATION INCLUDES BOTH POWER AND ACTION.

But someone might try to make a clever distinction and say that, although our will turns aside and our understanding is ignorant in action, our will can still strive and our understanding can still gain knowledge by their own powers - considering that we have the power to do many things that we don't actually do, as our question is truly about power, not performance. I respond that the Prophet's words include both action and power, and it is the same thing to say, "People do not seek after God," as it would be to say, "People cannot seek after God." This can be inferred from the fact that if there were a power or force in us to desire good - given that we are not allowed to rest or take leisure due to the impulse of divine omnipotence, as I have shown earlier - it could only be that this power was directed towards something, or at least in some way, and it was demonstrated through some sort of use.

However, this is not the case because God looks down from heaven and doesn't see anyone who seeks after Him or tries to. Therefore, it follows that this power to seek after God is nowhere to be found; instead, all people go astray. Moreover, if Paul's words are not understood to mean a lack of power as well as a lack of action, then his argument would be useless. His main point is to prove that everyone needs grace. Now, if people could do anything on their own, they wouldn't need grace. But since they can't, grace is necessary for them. So, you see, free will is completely destroyed by this passage, and nothing good or honest is left in a person. They are declared to be unrighteous, ignorant of God, a despiser of God, opposed to Him, and useless in His sight. The Prophet is a strong opponent, both in his own text and under Paul's interpretation of it.

It's not a small thing when a person is said to be ignorant of God and to despise Him. These are the sources of all wickedness, the cesspool of sin, and the very essence of evil. What evil will be left undone when there is ignorance and contempt of God? In short, Satan's control over people couldn't have been described in fewer or more comprehensive words than by calling them ignorant and despisers of God. This includes unbelief, disobedience, sacrilege, blasphemy towards God, cruelty, and lack of compassion towards others. In this, self-love pervades everything, both divine and human.

SECTION 9: PAUL'S SIGNIFICANT STATEMENTS IN ROMANS 3:19-20 ARE EMPHASIZED.

Paul continues to clarify that he is referring to all people, particularly the best and most outstanding individuals. He states, "That every mouth may be stopped, and all the world may become guilty before God. Because by the deeds of the law, no flesh is justified before him." (Romans 3:19-20) I question how every mouth can be silenced if we still possess some power to accomplish something. A person might say to God,

"This is not entirely worthless. There is something here that you cannot condemn since it is what you have given me, so it can achieve some-thing. At the very least, this will not be silent, nor should it be held guilty before you."

If this power of free will is intact and capable of doing something, then it is false that the entire world is guilty or accused of guilt before God. This power is not insignificant, nor is it limited to a small part of the world. Instead, it is a highly valuable possession shared by everyone in the entire world, and its voice should not be silenced. Conversely, if its voice is silenced, then along with the whole world, it must be considered criminal and guilty before God. But on what grounds can it be deemed guilty unless it is unrighteous and impious, meaning deserving of punishment and retribution? I kindly request that she considers how this human power can be absolved from the guilt that the entire world faces in God's judgment, or by what means it can be excluded from being encompassed within the entirety of the world?

Paul's words are like powerful thunder and piercing lightning, truly acting as the "hammer which breaks the rock in pieces," as Jeremiah says (23:29). He states, "They are all gone out of the way," "The whole world is guilty," and "There is none righteous." These words shatter not just parts of some people, but everything in the entire world, in all people, without exception. They are so powerful that the whole world should tremble, fear, and flee from them.

What stronger words could be spoken than these: the whole world is guilty, all people have strayed and become unprofitable, no one fears God, no one is righteous, no one understands, and no one seeks after God? Yet, the human heart is so hard and stubborn that we don't hear or notice these thunderous and lightning-like words. Instead, we continue to praise and defend the idea of free will and its powers, even in the face of such powerful statements. This truly fulfills the saying from Malachi 1:4, "They may build, but I will throw down."

This statement also has a powerful message: "By the deeds of the law, no flesh is justified before him." (Rom 3:20) It's a strong statement, just like saying 'the whole world' or 'all the sons of men.' It's interesting to note that Paul doesn't talk about specific people but focuses on what they're striving for, which essentially includes everyone and their best qualities.

If Paul had said that only 'ordinary Jews,' 'Pharisees,' or 'some of the wicked' are not justified, it might seem like he's leaving some people out, as if they could still be somewhat useful through their own free will and by following the law. But when he condemns the very deeds of the law and calls them wicked before God, it's clear that he's condemning everyone who was passionate about the law and its deeds. And the only people who were truly passionate about the law and its deeds were the best and most outstanding individuals, using their intellect and willpower.

So, if those who were most dedicated to the law and its deeds, with the greatest passion and effort of their understanding and will - in other words, with the full power of their free will - and even with the law itself as a sort of divine helper that taught and encouraged them, are accused of being ungodly because they are not justified and are considered flesh in God's eyes, then what's left in the entire human race that isn't flesh and ungodliness? It seems that everyone involved in the deeds of the law is condemned, whether they are extremely zealous, moderately zealous, or not zealous at all. It doesn't matter because all they can do is perform the deeds of the law, and these deeds don't justify them. If they don't provide justification, they show that those who fulfill them are ungodly, and they remain that way. The ungodly are guilty individuals, deserving of God's wrath. These things are so clear, that no one can even whisper a word against them.

SECTION 10: THE ARGUMENT THAT PAUL IS ONLY REFERRING TO THE CEREMONIAL LAW

A common way to avoid Paul's message here is to claim that "the deeds of the law" refers only to the ceremonial ordinances, which have become harmful since Christ's death. However, this interpretation is based on an ignorant mistake made by Jerome. Despite Augustine's strong opposition, this error has spread throughout the world due to God's absence and Satan's influence. As a result, Paul's true meaning has been lost, and the understanding of Christ has been inevitably obscured.

In fact, if this were the only mistake in the church, it would still be a dangerous and powerful enough error to damage the Gospel's message. I believe that Jerome has earned hell rather than heaven for this mistake, and I am far from considering him a saint or canonizing him. Therefore, it is not accurate to say that Paul is only speaking about ceremonial works in this passage.

If we were to accept this interpretation, Paul's argument that all people are unrighteous and in need of grace would not make sense.

A person might argue, "I agree that we are not justified by ceremonial actions, but someone could be justified by the moral actions of the Ten Commandments. So, you haven't proven that we need grace through your argument." Moreover, what's the point of grace if it only frees us from ceremonial rules? Those are the easiest to follow and can be done out of fear or self-interest.

Also, it's incorrect to say that ceremonial rules became invalid after Jesus' death. Paul never claimed this. He said that they don't justify us and don't benefit us before God, meaning they don't make us innocent of ungodliness. This doesn't mean that following these rules is wrong. Just like eating and drinking don't justify us or make us more favorable to God, but it's not wrong to eat and drink.

Furthermore, they're mistaken in thinking that the ceremonial rules were as important as the Ten Commandments in the old law. Both had equal authority. Paul first addressed the Jews, as he mentioned in Romans 1:16. So, there's no doubt that "the deeds of the law" refers to all actions under the entire law. If the law was abolished and considered harmful, then these actions wouldn't even be called "works of the law." A repealed law is no longer a law, which Paul understood. So, when he talks about the deeds of the law, he's not referring to a nullified law but one that is still in effect and dominant.

In other words, it would have been so easy for him to say, "The law itself is now abolished!" which would have been straightforward and clear. But let's look at Paul's own words, as he is his own best interpreter. In Galatians 3:10, he says, "All who rely on observing the law are under a curse, for it is written: 'Cursed is everyone who does not continue to do everything written in the Book of the Law.'" You can see here that Paul, while discussing the same topic as in Romans and using similar language, refers to all the laws written in the Book of the Law whenever he mentions the works of the law.

What's even more surprising is that Paul actually quotes Moses when declaring a curse on those who don't continue in the law, while he himself declares a curse on those who rely on the works of the law, using a contrasting passage to support his opposing view. Just as Moses' statement is negative, Paul's is positive. But this is because, in God's eyes, those who are most passionate about the works of the law are the least likely to fulfill it – because they lack the Spirit, who is the one who fulfills the law. Sure, they might try to fulfill it through their own efforts, but they won't succeed. So, both statements are true: according to Moses, those who don't continue in the law are cursed, and according to Paul, those who rely on the works of the law are cursed. Both writers emphasize the need for the Spirit in carrying out the law. Without the Spirit, Paul says, the works of the law, no matter how much is done, don't justify. And for the same reason, without the Spirit, as Moses says, they don't continue in everything that is written.

SECTION 11: PAUL'S MEANING IS, "WORKS OF THE LAW, DONE IN THE FLESH, CONDEMN."

Paul categorizes people who follow the law into two groups: spiritual followers and carnal followers, with no one in between. He says, "By the deeds of the law, no flesh shall be justified." This means that those who follow the law without the Spirit are considered "flesh" - ungodly and ignorant of God - and their actions don't benefit them. In Galatians 3:2, Paul uses the same distinction, asking, "Did you receive the Spirit from the deeds of the law, or from the hearing of faith?" And again in Romans 3:21, he says, "Now the righteousness of God without the law is manifested." He also states, "We judge that a man is justified by faith without the deeds of the law." From all these statements, it's clear that Paul contrasts the Spirit with the works of the law, as well as with anything else that isn't spiritual and all the claims and powers of the flesh. This confirms that Paul's view aligns with Christ's words in John 3:6, which state that anything not of the Spirit, no matter how beautiful, holy, or excellent, is considered flesh. Therefore, even the most admirable actions according to divine law fall into this category, regardless of the efforts made to achieve them.

The Spirit of Christ is essential, for without it, everyone is only deserving of damnation. So, let's establish that when Paul talks about "the deeds of the law," he's not just referring to ceremonial acts, but to all actions under the entire law. At the same time, we should understand that anything done without the Spirit while performing these deeds is condemned.

Now, let's talk about the power of Freewill, which is truly the most exceptional quality in humans. We're discussing Freewill in its true sense, which exists without the Spirit. Even when someone is "of the works of the law," meaning they're the best kind of person, zealous for the law, and have been supported by the law through instruction and practice, Paul doesn't say they're "of sins and transgressions against the law." Instead, he says "as many as are of the deeds of the law," referring to the most righteous and law-abiding individuals.

SECTION 12: ALL THE LAW DOES IS SHOW US OUR SINS.

If our free will, even when aided by the law and putting all its effort into following the law, doesn't help us and doesn't justify us, but instead leaves us in ungodliness and fleshly desires, then what can we expect it to do on its own, without the law? "By the law," he says, "is the knowledge of sin." He shows here how much, and to what extent, the law benefits a person. In other words, our free will is so blind on its own that it doesn't even recognize sin and needs the law as a teacher. Now, what can someone do to get rid of sin if they don't even know what sin is? This is what they can do: they can mistake sin for something that isn't sin, and they can mistake something that isn't sin for sin - as we can see from our own experiences.

Look at how the world persecutes the righteousness of God that is preached in the Gospel! It labels it as heresy, error, and all sorts of terrible names, using the very people it considers to be the best and most zealous for righteousness and godliness. At the same time, the world boasts and brags about its own works and actions as if they were righteous and wise, but in reality, they are sinful and mistaken. Paul, therefore, silences the claims of free will with his words, by teaching that sin is revealed to us through the law. Free will itself is something that doesn't even know what sin is. This is how far Paul is from granting our free will any power to strive for goodness.

And here, we find the answer to Diatribe's frequently asked question throughout her entire treatise: "If we can do nothing, what is the purpose of having so many laws, precepts, threats, and promises?" Paul responds by saying, "By the law is the knowledge of sin." His answer is quite different from what humans or Free Will might think. Free Will, he says, is not proven by the law; it does not work together with the law to achieve righteousness. Righteousness comes not from the law, but from the knowledge of sin. This is the benefit, the effect, and the purpose of the law: to be a light for those who are ignorant and blind. The law serves as a light that reveals our diseases, sins, wickedness, death, hell, and the wrath of God. However, it does not help or free us from these things. The law is content with simply showing us our true state.

Upon realizing his sinful condition, a person becomes sad, troubled, and filled with despair. The law does not help him, and he certainly cannot help himself. Another light is needed to show him the solution. This light is the word of the Gospel, which presents Christ as the savior from all these problems. It is not Reason or Free Will that reveals Christ to us. How could they, when they themselves are shrouded in darkness and require the light of the law to expose their own sickness, which they mistakenly believe to be health?

SECTION 13: CONFIRMED BY GALATIANS 3:19 AND ROMANS 5:20.

In Galatians, Paul also discusses the same issue in a similar way. He asks, "What then is the law?" He answers this question, not like Diatribe would, by saying that it proves the existence of Free Will, but by saying, "It was added because of transgressions, until the Seed to whom the promise referred had come." He says it's for the sake of transgressions. It's not to restrain them, as Jerome imagines (since Paul insists that it was promised to the Seed who would come, that He would remove and restrain sin through the free gift of righteousness);

but to increase transgressions, as he writes in Romans 5:20, "The law was brought in so that the trespass might increase."

It's not that there were no sins without the law, or that sins weren't abundant. But because people didn't know that their actions were wrong or considered major offenses, most of these actions were seen as righteous. Now, if people don't know they're sinning, there's no chance for a solution or hope, because they wouldn't accept help from a doctor - they believe they're perfectly fine and don't need any assistance. The law is necessary to make people aware of their sins; so that, by understanding the severity and extent of their sins, the prideful person who thinks they're fine on their own can be humbled and may seek the grace offered to them through Christ. Look at this simple statement: "By the law is the knowledge of sin." This statement alone is powerful enough to challenge and overturn the concept of free will. For if it's true that people can't recognize sin and wickedness on their own, then as Paul says both here and in Romans 7:7 ("I would not have known lust to be sin, except the law had said, You shall not covet"), how will they ever know what righteousness and goodness are?

If she doesn't understand what righteousness is, how can she ever pursue it? We don't know the sin we were born into, the sin that surrounds and controls us; or rather, the sin that lives, moves, and rules within us. So how could we possibly know righteousness, which exists outside of us, in the heavens? These words make the concept of free will seem utterly insignificant and worthless.

SECTION 14: ROMANS 3:21-25 CONTAINS MANY POWERFUL THUNDERBOLTS AGAINST FREE WILL.

Given this, Paul confidently and authoritatively declares, "But now the righteousness of God without the law is revealed, being witnessed by the law and the prophets; the righteousness of God, I say, through faith in Jesus Christ, for all and upon all those who believe in him. For there is no distinction: for all have sinned and fall short of the glory of God; being justified freely by his grace, through the redemption that is in Christ Jesus; whom God has presented as a sacrifice of atonement, through faith in his blood," etc. In this passage, Paul only speaks of arguments that go against free will.

First thunderbolt: He says that the righteousness of God without the law is revealed. He distinguishes the righteousness of God from the righteousness of the law because the righteousness of faith comes by grace, without the law. When he says "without the law," he can only mean that Christian righteousness is entirely separate from the works of the law - so much so that the works of the law have no value or ability to achieve it.

He later says, "We believe that a person is justified by faith without the works of the law," and he has already said, "By the deeds of the law, no one is justified before God." From all of this, it's clear that the effort or desire of free will amounts to nothing. If God's righteousness exists without the law and without the works of the law, then wouldn't it exist even more so without free will? Since the highest effort of free will is focused on moral righteousness or the works of the law, its blindness and weakness are supported by this. The word 'without' removes morally good works, moral righteousness, and preparations for grace. In short, come up with any action that free will is capable of, and Paul will insist that God's righteousness has nothing to do with it.

Now, even if I were to accept that free will could make progress on its own – that is, towards good works, or the righteousness of civil law, or moral law – it still doesn't get any closer to God's righteousness, nor does God consider its efforts worthy of any recognition in obtaining his righteousness when he says that his righteousness is effective without the law. If free will doesn't move towards God's righteousness, what good would it do to advance through its own actions and efforts (if that were possible) even to the holiness of angels? These words are not obscure or ambiguous; there's no room for any misinterpretation here. Paul clearly distinguishes two types of righteousness. He attributes one to the law and the other to grace, stating that grace is freely given without the law and its works, but the law doesn't justify or accomplish anything without grace.

So, let me understand how Free Will can exist and be defended in the face of these objections.

SECTION 15: SECOND THUNDERBOLT

The second thunderbolt is that Paul states the righteousness of God is revealed and active for all who believe in Christ, and that there is no difference. In the clearest terms, he separates the entire human race into two groups: believers who receive God's righteousness and unbelievers who do not. Can anyone be so crazy as to doubt that the power or effort of free will is something different from faith in Christ? Now, Paul denies that anything outside the boundaries of this faith can be considered righteous before God. If it's not righteous before God, it must be sin. With God, there is nothing in between righteousness and sin, like a neutral substance that is neither righteous nor sinful. Otherwise, Paul's entire argument would collapse, which is based on this division of things: everything done and carried out among people is either righteous or sinful. It is righteous if done in faith; it is sinful if done without faith.

It's true that among humans, there are actions of a neutral nature, where they neither owe nor give anything to each other. However, the ungodly person sins against God, whether they eat, drink, or whatever they do, because they are constantly misusing God's creations wickedly and ungratefully, never giving glory to God from their heart at any moment.

SECTION 16: THIRD THUNDERBOLT

This is also a powerful statement when Paul says, "All have sinned and come short of the glory of God: nor is there any difference." I ask you, what could be said more clearly? Let's say someone acts according to their free will - tell me, does this person sin in their own efforts? If they don't sin, why doesn't Paul make an exception for them, but instead includes them with everyone else, without any distinction? Surely, saying "all have sinned" doesn't leave anyone out, regardless of their actions or efforts. If you make an exception for someone based on their actions or efforts, you're contradicting Paul, because this person who acts according to their free will is included among "all" and is considered a sinner like everyone else. Paul should have acknowledged this person, rather than grouping them so broadly with all the sinners.

Fourth thunderbolt:

Similarly, it's a powerful statement when Paul says that people are devoid of the glory of God. The glory of God can be understood in two ways here: actively and passively. Paul uses this distinction often in his writings, drawing from Hebrew idioms. Actively, the glory of God is what God takes pride in within us. Passively, it's what we take pride in regarding Him. I believe it should be understood passively in this context. In Latin, the phrase "faith of Christ" refers to the faith that Christ has. However, in Hebrew, the "faith of Christ" is understood to mean the faith that we have towards Christ.

So, the righteousness of God in Latin means the righteousness that God possesses. However, in Hebrew, it's understood to mean the righteousness that we receive from God and have before God. In the same way, I understand the glory of God not in the Latin sense, but in the Hebrew sense, as the glory we have in God and before God, which can be called glory in God. Someone who glories in God knows for sure that God favors them and considers them worthy of kindness. This means that what they do pleases God, or if they displease Him, it's freely forgiven and tolerated. If the efforts of free will are not sinful but good in God's eyes, then it can certainly boast. With confidence in that glory, one can say, "This pleases God," "God looks favorably upon this," "God values this and accepts it, or at least tolerates and forgives it." This is the kind of glory that the faithful have in God; those who don't have it are instead confounded before Him. However, Paul denies this glory to all people here. He claims that they are completely without this glory, which experience also proves. Ask any group of free will advocates, and if you can find one who sincerely believes that any of their desires and efforts are pleasing to God, I will admit defeat. But I know that no such person exists. If this glory is lacking, so that one's conscience doesn't dare to know for sure or be confident that a specific act pleases God, then it's certain that it doesn't please God. Because, as a person believes, so it is for them. They don't believe that they definitely please God, which is necessary since doubting God's favor is the very essence of unbelief. God wants us to have the utmost faith that He favors us. Thus, we prove through their own conscience that since free will lacks the glory of God, it constantly subjects itself to the accusation of unbelief, along with all its abilities, desires, and efforts.

Fifth thunderbolt:

But what will the defenders of Freewill say at last to the following statement: "being justified freely by His grace?" What does "freely" mean? What does "by His grace" mean? How can effort and merit fit with a freely-given righteousness? Maybe they will say that they only attribute a tiny bit to Freewill - definitely not a merit of worthiness. But these are just empty words; the whole point of Freewill is to make room for merit. This has been Diatribe's constant complaint and argument. 'If there is no freedom in the will, where is the place for merit? If there is no place for merit, where is the place for reward? To what can it be attributed if a person is justified without merit?'

Paul responds here, saying that there is absolutely no such thing as merit, and that everyone who is justified is justified freely. This is only attributed to the grace of God. But along with the gift of righteousness, the kingdom and eternal life are also given. So where are the effort, desire, hard work, and merit of Freewill? What is the purpose of these things? You can't complain about it being unclear or ambiguous; the matter and the words are very clear and simple. Even if they do attribute the smallest possible thing to Freewill, they still teach us that we can obtain righteousness and grace through this tiny bit.

The question of why God justifies one person and leaves another in their sins is often answered by pointing to free will. In other words, one person made an effort, while the other did not, and God rewards the one who tried and disregards the other. This way, God is not considered unjust. Even though these people claim they don't believe in earning grace through merit and don't call it that, their actions say otherwise.

What's the point of not calling it merit if they still attribute everything to it that merit entails? For example, the person who tries finds favor with God, while the one who doesn't try doesn't. Isn't this clearly a merit-based system? Doesn't this make God a judge of works, merits, and individuals? The person who lacks grace is blamed for not trying, while the one who does try receives grace – they wouldn't have gotten it if they hadn't tried. If this isn't merit, then what is?

You could play with words all you want, but the fact remains that even if you don't call it merit, it still functions like merit. It's like saying a thorn isn't a bad tree, but it does what a bad tree does, or a fig tree isn't a good tree, but it does what a good tree does. The argument for free will isn't inherently bad, but it follows the same logic as those who believe in merit-based salvation.

SECTION 17: SOPHISTS ARE WORSE THAN THE PELAGIANS.

These free will defenders have fallen into the trap of trying to avoid one extreme (Pelagianism) and ended up embracing another. In their attempt to distance themselves from the idea of merit, they end up affirming it even more, making them worse than the Pelagians they sought to oppose.

First, the Pelagians openly and honestly admit and claim a merit of condignity, calling things as they are, and teaching what they believe. However, our "friends" think and teach the same thing, but deceive us with false words and pretend to disagree with the Pelagians. In reality, they do the exact opposite - so if you look at the role we play, you'd see us as the most determined enemies of the Pelagians; but if you look at our true intentions, we are actually double Pelagians.

Secondly, by making this assumption, we value and obtain God's grace at a much lower price than the Pelagians. They argue that it's not just a small thing within us that allows us to receive grace, but many significant, complete, and perfect efforts and actions. Our "friends," on the other hand, consider it to be a very small thing, almost insignificant, by which we earn grace.

Therefore, if we must be mistaken, those who honestly and with less arrogance claim that God's grace is acquired at a high cost (considering it valuable and precious) are better than those who teach that it can be bought for a little, or even a very small amount, treating it as cheap and unworthy.

But Paul combines both ideas into one by simply saying that "all are justified freely." And again, he says "they are justified without the law" and "without the deeds of the law." By claiming free justification for all people, he doesn't leave room for anyone to work, earn, or prepare themselves, and he doesn't allow for any work to be considered fitting or deserving. In fact, he shatters both the Pelagians with their complete merit and the Sophists with their small amount of merit with this powerful statement. Free justification doesn't let you establish any kind of workers, since 'free gift' and 'prepare yourself by some work' are clearly opposites. Also, justification by grace doesn't allow for any personal worthiness, as Paul later says in Romans 11:6, "If by grace, then it is no longer of works; otherwise, grace is no longer grace." He also says in Romans 4:4, "Now to the one who works, the reward is not counted as grace but as debt." So, my friend Paul stands as the unstoppable destroyer of free will, defeating two entire armies with just one word. For if we are justified without works, all works are condemned, both small and great. He makes no exceptions, but strikes equally against all.

SECTION 18: THE FATHERS OVERLOOKED PAUL.

Look here, and see how all our friends have been asleep at the wheel, and how much it helps a person to rely on the authority of the ancient Fathers, even though they have been approved for so many ages. Haven't they all been equally blind, or rather, haven't they also overlooked Paul's clear and explicit words? Can anything be said more clearly and explicitly in favor of grace and against free will, if Paul's words are not clear and explicit?

The argument is made through comparison, boasting about grace as opposed to works. It is clearly and plainly stated that we are justified freely, and grace wouldn't be grace if it was earned by our works. All works are excluded from justification, so that only grace and free justification can be established. Yet, do we still search for darkness in the midst of this light?

When we can't claim great things and everything for ourselves, do we try to claim small and insignificant things just to argue that justification isn't free, without works, and by God's grace? It's as if someone who denies that we are provided with the greater things and all things necessary for justification, denies even more that we are provided with the little things and the few things. All the while, they maintain that we are justified only by God's grace, without any works, and even without the law itself, which includes all works, both great and small, and works of congruity and condignity.

Now, go ahead and boast about the authority of the ancient scholars and rely on their sayings, all of whom, as you can see, have overlooked Paul, the clearest and most explicit teacher. No, they have, in a way, deliberately avoided this bright star, or rather this sun, being so absorbed with the worldly idea that it seemed absurd to them that there could be no place left for merits.

SECTION 19: PAUL'S REFERENCE TO ABRAHAM'S EXAMPLE IS EXAMINED AND APPLIED

Let me use the example of Abraham, which Paul refers to later: "If Abraham was justified by works, he has glory; but not before God. For what does the Scripture say? Abraham believed God, and it was counted to him for righteousness." (Rom 4:2) Notice how Paul separates the two types of righteousness for Abraham. One is based on WORKS, which is moral and civil; but he says that Abraham wasn't justified before God by this, even though he was considered just by people because of it. He also has glory with people, but even with this righteousness, he falls short of God's glory. You can't argue that this is about the ceremonial law's works since Abraham lived long before the law. Paul is talking about Abraham's works in general, and those were his best. It would be absurd to debate whether someone is justified by bad works. So, if Abraham isn't just by any of his works and needs another righteousness, that of pure faith, then he remains accused of ungodliness in both his actions and character.

It's clear that no one can become righteous through their own works. Moreover, no works, desires, or efforts of free will are useful before God; they are all considered ungodly, unjust, and wicked. If a person isn't just, then their works and desires aren't just either; and if they aren't just, they are condemnable and deserving of wrath. The other righteousness is that of FAITH, which doesn't rely on any works but on God's favor and His way of considering us through grace. Notice how Paul emphasizes the word 'considering,' how he insists, repeats, and drives it home to us.

The passage says, "When someone works, their reward is considered a debt, not a gift. But when someone doesn't work and instead believes in the one who makes the ungodly righteous, their faith is considered righteousness, according to God's grace." (Romans 4:4-5 DRA) Then, it mentions David speaking similarly about grace, saying, "Blessed is the person whose sins the Lord doesn't hold against them" (Psalm 32:2).

In that same chapter, the word "imputation" is mentioned nearly ten times. In summary, Paul compares those who work and those who don't, leaving no one in between. He says that righteousness isn't given to the worker, but it is given to the non-worker if they believe. There's no way for free will to avoid this situation, as it must be either a worker or a non-worker. If it's a worker, then righteousness isn't given to it. If it's a non-worker who believes in God, then righteousness is given to it. But in that case, it wouldn't be free will; it would be a new creation, a soul renewed by faith. If righteousness isn't given to the one who works, it's clear that their works are nothing but sins, wicked and ungodly acts in God's eyes. No one can argue that even if a person is wicked, their work might not be wicked.

Paul focuses not just on the person, but on the person in action, specifically to emphasize that the person's actions and efforts are condemned, no matter what they may be or how they may be categorized. He discusses good works because he is talking about justification and merit. When he refers to a person who works, he means all people who work and all their works, especially good and honest ones. Otherwise, his distinction between workers and non-workers wouldn't make sense.

SECTION 20: LUTHER LEAVES OUT MANY POTENTIAL ARGUMENTS.

I'm not going to go into the strong arguments that could be made based on the purpose of grace, promise, the power of the law, original sin, and God's election. Each of these, on its own, completely negates the concept of free will. For example, if grace comes from God's purpose or predestination, then it must come by necessity, not through our efforts, as I've already explained. Also, if God promised grace before the law, as Paul argues here and in Galatians, then it doesn't come from our works or the law; otherwise, the promise would be meaningless. Similarly, if works had any power, then faith would be pointless (even though it's said that Abraham was justified by faith before the law).

Furthermore, since the law only reveals sin and doesn't remove it, it makes us feel guilty before God and threatens punishment. This is what's meant by the phrase "The law works wrath" (Romans 4:15). So, how could righteousness be obtained through the law? And if the law doesn't help us, then how can free will be of any use when acting without it?

So, considering that we are all under sin and damnation due to the one offense of Adam, how can we even try to do anything that isn't sinful and worthy of condemnation? When he says "all," he doesn't exclude anyone - not the power of free will, nor any person; whether they act or don't act, try or don't try, they will inevitably be included among everyone else. We couldn't have sinned and been condemned by Adam's single sin unless it was also our sin. After all, who could be condemned for someone else's sin, especially in God's eyes? But that sin isn't made ours by imitation or by something we do later, since it couldn't be that one sin of Adam as if we had committed it instead of him; it becomes ours by birth. However, this isn't the right time to discuss that topic. Nonetheless, original sin doesn't allow free will to do anything other than sin and be damned.

So, I'm leaving out these arguments because they're pretty obvious and strong. Plus, I've already mentioned them before. Now, if I wanted to list everything Paul said that goes against the idea of free will, I'd basically have to go through all of his writings and show how almost every single word he wrote challenges this highly praised concept of free will. That's what I've done in the third and fourth chapters.

The main reason I'm highlighting these chapters is to show, first, how we've all been kind of asleep at the wheel when it comes to reading Paul's writings, even though they're pretty clear. We haven't even realized that they contain some of the strongest arguments against free will. Second, I want to point out the foolishness of relying on the authority and writings of the old scholars. And third, I want to leave you with some food for thought about what these super clear arguments could do if they were used effectively and wisely.

SECTION 21: LUTHER'S OWN VIEW OF PAUL

As for my own take on Paul, I'm honestly amazed at how often he uses words like "all," "none," "not," "nowhere," and "without." For example, he says things like, "They have all gone astray," "There is none righteous," "There is none that does good, no not one," "All have become sinners and condemned by the offense of one." "We are justified by faith without the law, without works." It's so clear and straightforward that I can't help but wonder how, despite these all-encompassing words and ideas, opposing and even contradictory ideas have managed to take hold.

For example, there are some people who don't go out of their way to be unjust, wicked, sinful, or damned. There is something good in humans that leans towards goodness. It's as if those who incline towards good aren't included in the words "All," "None," and "Not." Personally, I wouldn't have anything to argue or respond to Paul if I wanted to. Instead, I would have to include the power of my free will and its efforts among those "alls" and "nones" that Paul talks about, unless there was some new grammar rule or way of speaking.

If Paul only used such expressions once or in just one place, maybe we could think it's a figure of speech and try to interpret the words I chose differently. But actually, Paul uses these expressions all the time. Not only that, but he uses both positive and negative statements together, contrasting and distributing his ideas. This way, he sets up opposing sides, and not just the words and sentences themselves, but also the context before, after, and around them, as well as the overall purpose and main point of the whole discussion, all come together to support one common conclusion: Paul means that "without faith in Christ, there is nothing but sin and damnation." In this way, I promised to disprove the concept of free will so that none of my opponents would be able to resist my arguments. I believe I have done so, even if they don't accept my point of view as the winning one or remain silent. It's not within my power to make them do so; that's a gift from God's Spirit.

SECTION 22: PAUL'S CROWN

But before we listen to the words of the Apostle John, let's consider how Paul concludes his argument on this topic. If this isn't enough, I'm ready to examine all of Paul's writings in opposition to free will through a continuous commentary. In Romans 8:5, after dividing the entire human race into two groups - flesh and spirit, just as Christ does in John 3 - Paul says: "Those who live according to the flesh have their minds set on what the flesh desires; but those who live in accordance with the Spirit have their minds set on what the Spirit desires."

Here, Paul refers to everyone as 'carnal' if they are not 'spiritual.' This is clear from the contrast between flesh and Spirit, as well as Paul's own words that follow: "You are not in the flesh, but in the Spirit, if the Spirit of Christ dwells in you. Now if anyone does not have the Spirit of Christ, they don't belong to him" (Romans 8:9). What else could he mean by saying, 'You are not in the flesh, but in the Spirit,' if not that those who don't have the Spirit are necessarily in the flesh? And if someone doesn't belong to Christ, who do they belong to, if not the devil? So, it's clear that those who don't have the Spirit are in the flesh and under Satan's control.

Now let's see what Paul thinks about the efforts and power of free will in those who are carnal. "Those who are in the flesh cannot please God" (Romans 8:8). And again, "The mind of the flesh is death" (Romans 8:6). And again, "The mind of the flesh is hostile to God" (Romans 8:7). Again, "It is not subject to the law of God, nor indeed can it be" (Romans 8:7). I'd like the free will advocate to explain how something that is death, displeasing to God, hostile to God, disobedient to God, and unable to obey Him can strive for good! Paul doesn't say that the mind of the flesh is dead or hostile to God, but rather "it is death itself; it is enmity itself." This makes it impossible for it to be subject to God's law or to please God, as Paul previously stated, "For what the law could not do, in that it was made weak by the flesh, God has done" (Romans 8:3).

I'm aware of Origen's idea about three types of affections: the flesh, the soul, and the spirit. According to him, the soul is in the middle and can be drawn to either the flesh or the spirit. However, these are just his own theories; he doesn't provide any evidence for them. As I've already demonstrated, Paul considers anyone who doesn't have the Spirit to be 'flesh.'

So, the highest virtues of the best people are "in the flesh," meaning they are dead, against God, not following God's law, and unable to follow it, and displeasing to God. Paul not only says that they don't follow the law, but they can't follow it. So, Christ says in Matthew 7:18, "A corrupt tree cannot bring forth good fruit." And in Matthew 12:34, "How can you, being evil, speak good things?" You see here that we not only speak evil, but we can't speak good. And in another place, he says that we, being evil, know how to give good gifts to our children (Matthew 7:11). But he still denies that we do good, even when giving good things. The thing we give (created by God) is good, but we ourselves are not good, nor do we give our good things well. And when saying this, he speaks to everyone, even his disciples. So, these two ideas from Paul remain true: "The just lives by faith" and "Whatever is not of faith is sin." In this, the latter comes from the former. If faith is the only way we can be justified, then it's clear that those who don't have faith are not yet justified.

Now, those who aren't justified are still sinners, and sinners are like corrupt trees that can only sin and produce bad fruit. So, Freewill is nothing more than a servant to sin, death, and Satan. It can't do anything good, and it's not even capable of trying to do anything but evil.

SECTION 23: GRACE IS SHOWN THROUGH THE REJECTION OF JEWS AND THE CALLING OF GENTILES.

Consider the example in chapter 10, taken from Isaiah: "I have been found by those who weren't looking for me; I have revealed myself to those who didn't ask about me." He talks about the Gentiles because they have been given the opportunity to know and hear about Christ, even when they couldn't even think of Him before, let alone seek Him or prepare themselves for Him through the power of free will. It's clear from this example that grace comes so genuinely without any strings attached that not even a thought about it, much less any effort or struggle, comes before it.

Take Paul, for example, when he was still known as Saul. What did he do with the high level of free will he had? Well, he was definitely thinking about the best and most honest things, if you ask mere reason. But look at his efforts to find grace: he's not seeking it. No, instead, he's furiously fighting against it like a madman, and that's when he receives his share.

On the other hand, when talking about the Jews in chapter nine, Paul says that the Gentiles, who didn't pursue righteousness, have achieved righteousness - the righteousness that comes from faith. But Israel, which tried to follow the law of righteousness, didn't reach that law. (Romans 9:30-31) What can anyone who supports free will say against these statements? The Gentiles, filled with ungodliness and all kinds of vices, receive righteousness freely from a compassionate God. The

Jews, who seek righteousness with great effort and determination, are left empty-handed.

Isn't this saying that while trying to do the best things, free will's efforts are in vain? That it actually makes things worse, causing people to stumble and go backward? No one can claim that they haven't tried their hardest with the full power of free will. Paul himself testifies to this in chapter ten: "They have a zeal for God, but not according to knowledge." (Romans 10:2)

So, in the Jewish people, none of the qualities we attribute to free will are missing. Yet, this doesn't lead to any conclusion; in fact, the opposite is true. In the Gentiles, none of the qualities we attribute to free will are present, but still, God's righteousness follows. What does this mean, if not to confirm through the clear example of both nations, as well as Paul's testimony, that 'grace is given freely to the undeserving, even to the least worthy of humans; while it is not obtained by any effort, endeavor, or action, big or small, even by the best and most respectable people, who passionately seek and pursue righteousness.'

SECTION 24: JOHN, A DESTROYER

Now let's also look at John, who is a powerful and capable destroyer of free will on his own. At the very beginning of his Gospel, he attributes such blindness to free will that it cannot see the light of truth, let alone have the power to strive for it. He says, "The light shines in the darkness, but the darkness does not comprehend it." And then: "He was in the world, and the world did not know him. He came to his own, and his own did not receive him." What do you think he means by "the world"? Would you exclude anyone from being part of this term if they are not created anew by the Holy Spirit?

Indeed, it's quite interesting how this Apostle uses the word "world" to refer to the entire human race, without any exceptions. So, whatever he says about the world is actually about free will, which is considered the most excellent quality in humans.

According to this Apostle, the world didn't recognize the true light. The world hates Christ and his followers. The world is unaware of and cannot see the Holy Spirit. The whole world is immersed in wickedness or controlled by the wicked one. Everything in the world consists of the lust of the flesh, the lust of the eyes, and the pride of life. We are advised not to love the world. Furthermore, he says, "You are of the world." The world cannot hate you, but it hates me because I testify that its deeds are evil. All these statements and many others like them are essentially declarations about free will, which is the main component that rules the world under Satan's control. John even speaks about the world in contrast, meaning everything in the world that hasn't been transformed by the Spirit. As Christ tells his Apostles, "I have taken you out of the world and have established you," etc. (John 15:9).

Now, if there were people in the world who tried to do good through the power of Freewill - as would be the case if Freewill could actually accomplish something - then John should have been more careful with his words to avoid including these people in the general accusations he makes against the world. However, since he didn't do this, it's clear that he blames Freewill for all the wrongdoings he accuses the world of. After all, whatever the world does, it does through the power of Freewill, which is the understanding and the will, the most important parts of a person. It follows: "But as many as received him, to them gave he power to become the sons of God; even to those who believe in his name: who were born not of bloods, nor of the will of the flesh, nor of the will of man, but of God." (John 1:12-13)

After making this distinction, John excludes 'bloods,' 'the will of the flesh,' and 'the will of man' from the kingdom of Christ. By 'bloods,' I think he means the Jews, who believed they were entitled to be part of the kingdom because they were descendants of Abraham and the other patriarchs, proudly claiming their lineage.

I interpret 'the will of the flesh' as the efforts that people put into following the law. In this context, 'the flesh' refers to those who are not spiritually-minded and don't have the Holy Spirit. They have the will and the determination, but since the Holy Spirit is not present in their efforts, they are ultimately misguided. 'The will of man,' I believe, refers to the efforts that all people, whether they follow the law or not, make to gain favor with God - be they Gentiles or anyone else. So, the message here is that people don't become children of God through their lineage, their dedication to the law, or any other human means, but only through a divine birth.

So, if people are not born of the flesh, not taught by the law, and not gained through any human discipline, but are instead born again from God, it's clear that free will doesn't play a role here. I believe the term "man" is used here in the Hebrew sense, meaning anyone at all, while "flesh" refers to the people of Israel who don't have the Spirit. "Will" is considered the highest power in a person, which is the main component of free will.

Even if we don't fully understand each word, the overall message is quite clear. By stating that people can only become children of God through being born of God, John dismisses anything that isn't of divine origin. According to his interpretation, this happens through believing in God's name. Now, human will or free will is definitely part of this dismissal, as it's not born of God or faith. If free will had any value, John wouldn't reject human will. People wouldn't be directed away from it and towards faith and new birth alone. Otherwise, it could be said, as in Isaiah 5:20, "Woe to you who call good evil." But since John equally rejects "bloods," "the will of the flesh," and "the will of man," it's certain that human will has no more power in making children of God than blood or fleshly birth. No one doubts whether being born of the flesh makes someone a child of God or not. Paul confirms this in Romans 9:8, saying, "Those who are the children of the flesh, these are not the children of God." He supports this with the examples of Ishmael and Esau.

SECTION 25: JOHN THE BAPTIST'S TESTIMONY

John the Baptist is introduced in the same way, saying, "From his abundance we have all received, grace upon grace." (John 1:16) He talks about the grace we have received from Christ's fullness, but on what basis or effort? He says it's truly because of Christ's grace, just like Paul also mentions in Romans 5:15, "The grace of God and the gift of one man, Jesus Christ, has overflowed to many." So, where is the effort of free will in obtaining this grace?

Here, John states that we not only receive grace without any effort on our part, but also through someone else's grace or merit – specifically, through the grace of one man, Jesus Christ. So, either it's false that we receive our grace because of someone else's grace, or it's clear that free will doesn't exist. These two ideas can't coexist: on one hand, God's grace is so easily obtained by anyone's minimal effort, and on the other hand, it's so valuable that it's only given to us freely through the grace of such an important person.

I also want to remind supporters of free will that by arguing for it, they're actually denying Christ. If I can obtain God's grace through my own effort, then why do I need Christ's grace to receive it? And once I have God's grace, what more do I need? But Diatribe and other scholars argue that we obtain God's grace through our own efforts and are ready to receive it, not because we deserve it, but because it's fitting. This completely denies Christ, as John the Baptist testifies that we receive grace because of Christ's grace.

As for the idea of deserving and fitting merit, I've already debunked it, showing that these are just empty words that actually mean deserving merit. These ideas are even more blasphemous than the claims made by Pelagians, as I've pointed out. So, the blasphemous scholars, led by Diatribe, deny Jesus Christ, who redeemed us, more than any Pelagians or heretics have ever done – proving that grace is entirely incompatible with even a hint of free will.

However, it's clear that those who advocate for free will deny Christ, not only based on this Scripture but also by their own actions. As a result, they no longer see Christ as a loving mediator, but rather as a fearsome judge whom they try to appease through the intercession of his Virgin Mother and the Saints. They do this through various works, rituals, superstitions, and self-made vows, all in an effort to gain Christ's favor and receive his grace. On the other hand, they don't believe that Christ intercedes with God on their behalf, obtaining grace for them through his blood – grace upon grace, as stated here. And as they believe, so it happens to them. They truly and rightfully have Christ as their unyielding judge, as long as they abandon him in his role as the most powerful mediator and savior, and as long as they consider his blood and grace to be less valuable than the efforts and struggles of free will.

SECTION 26: THE CASE OF NICODEMUS

Now, let's look at an example of free will in action. Nicodemus, I assure you, is a man who has everything that free will can achieve. What is it that this man lacks – effort or determination? He acknowledges Christ as a true witness and as having come from God; he mentions Christ's miracles and even comes at night to listen and compare the rest. Doesn't this man seem to have sought after piety and salvation through the power of free will? But look how he stumbles! When he hears Christ explain the true path to salvation through being born again, does he recognize this path or admit that he has ever sought it? No, not at all; he is so repelled and confused by it that he not only says he doesn't understand it, but even dismisses it as impossible. "How can these things be?" he asks. And it's no surprise, really. For who has ever heard that a person must be born again, of water and the Spirit, in order to be saved?

Who would have ever thought that the Son of God needed to be lifted up so that everyone who believes in him wouldn't perish, but have eternal life? Did the smartest and best philosophers ever mention this? Did the rulers of this world ever learn about this? Has anyone's free will ever tried to understand it? Doesn't Paul admit that it's wisdom hidden in a mystery? It's true that the prophets predicted it, but it was only revealed through the Gospel, having been kept secret and unknown to the world since forever.

What can I say? Should we look at our own experiences? The whole world, even human reason and free will itself, has to admit that they didn't know or hear about Christ before the Gospel came into the world. Now, if they didn't know, they definitely couldn't have tried to seek or understand him. But Christ is the way, the truth, the life, and the salvation. So, free will has to admit, whether it wants to or not, that it couldn't have known or sought the things related to the way, the truth, and salvation on its own.

Yet, even though we admit this and see it in our own experiences, we still act crazy. We argue that we have some power within us that can both know and apply itself to the things related to salvation. This is like saying that this power knows and can apply itself to Christ, the Son of God, who was lifted up for us; even though no one has ever known or even thought of such a person before.

Still, this lack of knowledge isn't really ignorance, but rather knowledge of Christ - that is, knowledge of the things related to salvation! Can't you see, and almost feel with your hands, that those who argue for free will are completely crazy when they call it knowledge, even though they themselves admit it's ignorance? Isn't this like calling darkness light (Isaiah 5:20)? God truly silences free will, according to its own confession and experience. And yet, despite all this, free will still won't be quiet and give glory to God.

SECTION 27: JOHN 14 ADDRESSED. WAY, TRUTH, ETC. ARE EXCLUSIVE.

Again, when Christ is called the way, the truth, and the life, it's done by comparison - meaning that anything that isn't Christ is not the way, but off the path; not truth, but a lie; not life, but death. Since free will is neither Christ nor in Christ, it must reside in error, falsehood, and death. So where can we find this middle ground, this so-called substance of free will? And how can it be proven? If it's not Christ (that is, the way, the truth, and the life), how can it not inevitably become error, falsehood, and death?

For if everything said about Christ and his grace wasn't meant to be compared to their opposites, then what would all the apostles' teachings and all of Scripture amount to? For example, outside of Christ, there's only the devil; outside of grace, there's only wrath; outside of light, there's only darkness; outside of the way, there's only error; outside of the truth, there's only falsehood; outside of life, there's only death. All of this might be said in vain, as it doesn't necessarily prove that Christ is essential to us (which is their main goal). There could be some middle ground, something that is neither evil nor good. It doesn't belong to Christ or Satan; it's neither true nor false, neither alive nor dead - maybe it's neither anything nor nothing - but it's considered the most valuable and exceptional quality found in all of humanity.

So, you have a choice. If you agree that the Scriptures use comparisons, then you can't attribute anything to free will that isn't the opposite of what's in Christ; you'd have to say that error, death, Satan, and all evil rule over it. If you don't think the Scriptures use comparisons, then you weaken them to the point where they don't accomplish anything and don't prove that Christ is necessary. In trying to establish free will, you make Christ irrelevant and disregard all Scripture. On the other hand, while you claim to acknowledge Christ, you actually deny him in your heart. Because if free will isn't entirely about error and damnation, but can see and desire honest and good things, as well as things related to salvation, then it's complete and doesn't need Christ as a healer; nor has Christ redeemed that part of our nature. After all, why would there be a need for light and life where they already exist?If this part isn't redeemed by Christ, then the best aspect of humanity isn't redeemed either; rather, it's good and healthy on its own. In this case, God would also be unjust in condemning anyone since he would be condemning the best and most innocent part of a person.

Everyone has free will, and even though some people misuse it, we're taught that the power of free will itself isn't destroyed in them - they can still choose to do good or have the ability to do so. If that's the case, then free will is undoubtedly holy, just, and good. So, we shouldn't condemn free will but rather separate it from the person who deserves condemnation. However, this isn't possible, and even if it were, the person would no longer have free will and wouldn't be considered human anymore. They wouldn't deserve punishment or reward, and they wouldn't be able to be damned or saved. They would be like a mindless animal, not an immortal being. So, it seems unfair for God to condemn the holy, just, and good power of free will in a bad person, since it doesn't need Christ's salvation.

SECTION 28: JOHN 3.18, 36.

Now let's look at what John says in the Bible: "Whoever believes in him is not judged, but whoever does not believe stands condemned already because they have not believed in the name of God's one and only Son." (John 3:18)

Tell me, is Freewill among the believers or not? If it is, then it doesn't need grace, since it believes in Christ by itself. However, this Christ is unknown and not understood by Freewill. If Freewill is not a believer, it has already been judged and condemned by God. God only condemns what is wicked, so Freewill must be wicked. How can something wicked attempt a pious act? I assume Freewill cannot be excluded here, as it refers to the whole person, who is said to be condemned.

Furthermore, unbelief is not a simple emotion, but a powerful force that resides in the will and understanding, just like faith, its opposite. To be unbelieving is to deny God and make Him a liar (1 John 1:10). If we don't believe, we make God a liar. So, how can a force that opposes God and makes Him a liar strive for good? If this force were not unbelieving and ungodly, it wouldn't be said about the whole person, "they have been judged already." Instead, it would say: 'the person has been judged already regarding their basic emotions, but not in their most excellent aspect, as it seeks faith or even believes already.'

So, whenever Scripture says, "Every person is a liar," based on Freewill's authority, we should say, 'On the contrary, Scripture lies because a person is not a liar in their best part, that is, in their understanding and will, but only in their flesh, blood, and marrow. Therefore, the core of a person, their understanding and will, is sound and holy.'

So, in the words of John the Baptist, "He that believes in the Son has everlasting life: but he who does not believe in the Son shall not see life, but the wrath of God remains on him." We must understand 'upon him' to mean that God's wrath stays 'upon his base desires;' but grace and eternal life remain upon that powerful force of Free Will – truly, upon his understanding and will. It seems that, in order to defend Free Will, you twist and turn what is said in the Scriptures against ungodly people, limiting it to the animalistic part of humans, while keeping the rational and truly human part safe and sound. In this case, I must thank the defenders of Free Will, as I won't worry about my sin. I will be confident that my understanding and will – my Free Will – cannot be condemned (since it is never extinguished), but always remains sound, just, and holy. And if my understanding and will are to be happy, I will rejoice that my dirty and animalistic flesh is separated and condemned – I am far from wishing that Christ be its redeemer. This is where the doctrine of Free Will takes us: to the denial of all divine and human, temporary and eternal realities, and to deceive ourselves with so many absurd fictions!

Also, John the Baptist says, "a man cannot receive anything unless it has been given to him from heaven." (John 3:27) Stop, Diatribe, showing off your eloquence by listing all the things we receive from heaven! We are not discussing nature, but grace. We are not asking what kind of people we are on earth, but in heaven and before God.

We know that humans are considered to be in control of the things below them - things over which they have power and free will, so that these things obey them and do what they want and think. But our question is this: does a person have free will towards God, so that God obeys and does what the person wants, or is it the other way around - does God have free will over the person, so that the person wants and does what God wants, and can't do anything except what God has wanted and done? Here, the Baptist says that a person can't receive anything unless it's given to them from heaven, which means that free will is nothing.

Similarly, "He that is of the earth is earthly, and speaks of the earth; he that comes from heaven is above all." John 3:31. Here again, the Baptist considers everyone who isn't of Christ to be earthly (and says that they think and speak about earthly things); he doesn't leave any middle ground between the two. But free will, for sure, isn't 'he that comes from heaven.' So, free will must be of the earth and must think and speak about earthly things.

Now, if there was any power in anyone, at any time, in any place, or in any work, that didn't focus on earthly things, then the Baptist should have made an exception for this person, and not said generally, about all those who are outside of Christ, that they are earthly and speak of earthly things.

Later on, in chapter 8, Christ also says, "You are of the world; I am not of the world: you are from below, I am from above." (John 8:23) The people he spoke to had Free Will — meaning they had understanding and will. And yet, he says they were "of the world." Now, what would be the big deal if he said they were of the world in terms of their flesh and basic desires? Didn't everyone already know this? Besides, what's the point in saying that people are of the world in the part of them that is animal-like when, in this case, animals are also of the world?

SECTION 29: JOHN 6:44

So, what does Jesus' statement in John 6:44 mean for free will? "No one comes to me, unless my Father has drawn him." He says that a person must hear and learn from the Father himself, and then everyone must be taught by God (verses 44, 45). Here, Jesus is clearly saying that not only are the efforts and struggles of free will pointless, but even the word of the Gospel (which he is discussing) is heard in vain unless the Father himself speaks, teaches, and draws us inward. "No one can come," he says. This power, which enables a person to strive for Christ – that is, for things related to salvation – is said to be nonexistent.

Furthermore, Augustine's quote, which the Diatribe uses to try and obscure this clear and powerful passage, doesn't help the case for free will. The quote suggests that God draws us like we draw a sheep by showing it a branch. The Diatribe wants this analogy to show that we have the power to follow God's drawing. However, this comparison doesn't work here. God doesn't just show us one good thing; He shows us all His good things, including His Son, Jesus Christ.

However, no one follows him unless the Father reveals something else within them and attracts them in different ways. Indeed, the entire world persecutes the Son whom He reveals. This comparison of Augustine's ideas aligns perfectly with the situation of the godly, who are now like sheep and recognize their shepherd, God. Those who live by the Spirit and are guided by it follow wherever God wants and whatever He has shown them. But the ungodly person does not come, even after hearing the word, unless the Father draws and teaches them from within - which He does by granting the Spirit. There is another internal attraction, separate from the external one; within them, Christ is revealed through the enlightenment of the Spirit, by which the person is united with Christ in a most delightful and captivating way. They experience the actions of a speaking teacher and a guiding God, rather than taking action themselves by seeking and pursuing.

SECTION 30: JOHN 16:9

I'll present one more passage from the same John, who in chapter 16 says, "The spirit will convict the world of sin because they have not believed in me" (John 16:9). Here, you can see that not believing in Christ is considered a sin. But this sin is not found in our skin or hair; it's rooted in our understanding and will. When John accuses the entire world of this sin, and we know from experience that the world is as unaware of this sin as they are of Christ himself - since it's only revealed through the conviction of the Spirit - it's clear that free will, along with its will and understanding, is seen as captured and condemned for this sin before God.

So, while free will is ignorant of Christ and doesn't believe in him, it cannot strive for or desire any good thing. Instead, it's inevitably enslaved by this unknown sin. In short, the Scriptures consistently present Christ in contrast and opposition, as I've mentioned before. They portray everything that doesn't have the Spirit of Christ as being under Satan's control, ungodly, erroneous, dark, sinful, and subject to God's wrath. Every single testimony that speaks of Christ also stands against free will. And there are countless such testimonies - in fact, they make up the entirety of Scripture.

So, if we were to judge this issue based on the teachings of the Scripture, I would undoubtedly win in every aspect. There wouldn't be a single tiny detail left that doesn't condemn the idea of free will.

Now, even though our great theologians and defenders of free will either don't know or pretend not to know that the Scripture talks about Christ in this way - by comparing and contrasting - all Christians still know and openly admit this. They know, I mean, that there are two opposing kingdoms in the world: one ruled by Satan and the other by Christ. Satan rules over one of these kingdoms, which is why he's called the "Prince of this world" by Christ and the "God of this age" by Paul. He keeps everyone who hasn't been saved by Christ's Spirit under his control, and he won't let them go unless they're set free by the power of God, as Christ explains in the parable of the strong man guarding his palace.

In the other kingdom, Christ is in charge. His kingdom is constantly fighting against Satan's kingdom. We become part of this kingdom not through our own efforts, but by the grace of God, which saves us from this wicked world and frees us from the grip of darkness. Recognizing and admitting that these two kingdoms are always battling each other with such determination would be enough to disprove the idea of free will on its own. After all, we're forced to serve in Satan's kingdom unless we're saved from it by a divine power. I'm saying that common believers are well aware of these things, and they openly acknowledge them through their sayings, prayers, efforts, and entire lives.

SECTION 31: NEGLECTS TO DEBATE THE STRUGGLE BETWEEN THE PHYSICAL AND SPIRITUAL, AS NO EFFORT HAS BEEN MADE TO REFUTE HIS PREVIOUS STATEMENTS ON THE TOPIC.

Now, let's talk about the argument from the conflict between flesh and spirit, which hasn't been addressed yet. I'm not going to discuss my strong argument that Diatribe has ignored, which is based on Romans 7 and Galatians 5. In these passages, Paul explains that the struggle between the flesh and the spirit is so intense in holy and godly people that they can't always do what they want to do. My argument is this:

human nature is so corrupt that even in those who have been spiritually reborn, it not only fails to strive for good, but it actively fights against and resists good. So, how could it possibly strive for good in those who haven't been spiritually reborn and are still under Satan's control, living with their old selves?

Paul isn't just talking about obvious, physical desires in these passages – that's the easy way out that Diatribe often takes to avoid dealing with the true meaning of Scripture. Instead, he includes things like heresy, idolatry, dissensions, arguments, and mischief as works of the flesh. These are issues that affect the highest parts of our souls, like our understanding and our will.

So, if our human nature struggles against our spiritual side in the lives of the saints, then it will definitely fight against God in the lives of the ungodly and their free will. That's why Romans 8 refers to it as 'enmity' against God.

I would be really happy if someone could counter this argument for me and defend the idea of free will. Personally, I admit that if it were possible, I wouldn't want to have free will or have anything in my control that could help me strive for salvation. This is because, with so many dangers and challenges on one side, and so many attacking devils on the other, I wouldn't be strong enough to stand my ground and hold on to it. After all, one devil is more powerful than all humans combined, and not a single person would be saved.

But even if there were no dangers, challenges, or devils, I would still be forced to struggle endlessly, uncertain of my efforts, and feeling like I'm fighting a losing battle. Because even if I lived and worked forever, my conscience would never be sure how much it needed to do to satisfy God. No matter what I did, there would always be a lingering doubt about whether it pleased God or if He required more. The experiences of all self-righteous people prove this, and I've learned this the hard way through many years of struggle.

But now, God has taken my salvation out of my own control and placed it in His hands. He has promised to save me, not through my own efforts or actions, but by His grace and mercy. This makes me feel at ease and confident because God is faithful and will not deceive me. Additionally, He is powerful, so no number of devils or adversities can weaken Him or take me away from Him. "No one," He says, "shall pluck them out of my hand; for my Father who gave them to me, is greater than all" (John 10:28-29). As a result, even if not everyone is saved, some people are – in fact, many are. If it were up to our own free will, none of us would be saved, and we would all be lost.

Furthermore, we are confidently certain that we please God not by the merit of our own actions, but by the favor of His mercy that He has promised us. If we fall short or make mistakes, He does not hold it against us, but instead, with a loving, fatherly mindset, He forgives and corrects us. This is the pride of every believer in their God.

SECTION 32: DIFFICULTY STATED AND EXPOSED

But if we find it troubling to reconcile God's mercy and fairness with the fact that He condemns those who don't deserve it - specifically, ungodly people who are born into ungodliness and have no way of avoiding it; and by remaining ungodly, they are condemned. Indeed, their very nature forces them to sin and face destruction. As Paul says, "We were all the sons of wrath even as others," (Ephesians 2:3) being created as such by God Himself, from a seed that became corrupted due to Adam's sin alone.

Difficulty exposed: In this situation, we must honor and appreciate the immense mercy of God in how He deals with those He justifies and saves, even though they are unworthy of such blessings. And we must at least make some small concession to His divine wisdom, trusting that He is just, even when He appears unjust to us. For if His justice were only considered just when judged by human understanding, it would not be divine justice, but no different from human justice. Now, since God is the one true God, and is also completely beyond our comprehension and inaccessible to human reason, it is natural - indeed, it is necessary - that His justice also be incomprehensible. Paul exclaims this: "Oh, the depth of the riches of the wisdom and knowledge of God! How unsearchable are His judgments and His ways beyond tracing out!" (Romans 11:33)

Now, His judgments wouldn't be incomprehensible if we could fully understand why they are just.

What does it mean to compare ourselves to God? How can our power, strength, wisdom, knowledge, and essence even begin to compare to His? In short, how can anything about us even come close to matching God's greatness?

SECTION 33: DIFFICULTY REPROVED AND EXPLAINED BY EXAMPLE

Now, let's just follow the natural order of things and admit that our power, strength, wisdom, knowledge, and essence are absolutely nothing compared to God's. So, why do we have this stubbornness that makes us question and challenge God's justice and judgment? Why do we give so much importance to our own judgment, trying to understand and evaluate God's decisions? Why don't we also say that our judgment is nothing compared to God's?

Ask your own reason, and see if it doesn't agree that it's foolish and reckless not to accept that God's judgment is beyond our understanding, especially when we admit that all other aspects of God are beyond our comprehension. What's going on here? We're willing to acknowledge God's divine majesty in all other things, but when it comes to His judgment, we suddenly want to deny it and refuse to trust that He is just. Yet, He has promised us that once His glory is revealed, we will all see and feel that He has always been and will always be just.

To support this belief and comfort those who might doubt God's fairness, let me share an example.

Look, God seems to govern this physical world in such a way that, when you use human reason, you're forced to say either there's no God or there's an unjust God. Like the poet said, "I am often tempted to think that there are no Gods." Just look at how true it is that bad people often prosper, while good people face misfortune. Even proverbs and experience, which give birth to proverbs, show that the more wicked people are, the luckier they seem to be. "The homes of the wicked are filled with treasures," says Job 12:6. And Psalm 73 complains that sinners are overflowing with wealth in this world. Isn't it extremely unfair, according to everyone's judgment, that the wicked should prosper while the good suffer?

However, this is how the world works. Even the most brilliant minds have fallen to the depths of denying the existence of God and pretending that everything is controlled by the whims of fortune, like the Epicureans and Pliny. Following closely behind them, Aristotle believed that the first Being, in order to avoid misery, only sees himself and not the other existing things. He thought it would be too painful for the Being to witness so much evil and injustice.

On the other hand, the Prophets who believed in God were more tempted by the idea of God's injustice, such as Jeremiah, Job, David, Asaph, and others. What do you think Demosthenes and Cicero felt when, after doing everything they could, they met their unfortunate end in a miserable death? Yet, this perceived injustice of God - which seems highly likely and is supported by such strong arguments that no logical reasoning or natural understanding can resist - is easily resolved by the light of the Gospel and the knowledge of grace. These teachings show us that while the wicked may flourish in their physical lives, their souls ultimately suffer.

So, we can sum up the answer to this unsolvable question in a simple, short sentence: "There is a life after this life, in which whatever has not been punished and rewarded here, will hereafter be punished and rewarded; seeing that this life is nothing but the precursor, or rather the beginning, of the life to come." The power of the Gospel, which comes from the word and faith, is so effective that it has put an end to this age-old question and laid it to rest.

Now, what do you think will happen when the light of the word and faith is no longer present, and the divine Majesty itself is revealed as it truly is? Don't you think that the light of glory will easily solve that unsolvable question in the light of the word or grace, considering that the light of grace has already solved a question that couldn't be solved by the light of nature?

Let's agree that there are three main lights - the light of nature, the light of grace, and the light of glory - according to the common distinction (which is a good one). In the light of nature, it's impossible to explain why good people suffer and bad people prosper. But the light of grace resolves this question. In the light of grace, it's hard to understand how God condemns someone who has no power to do anything but sin and be guilty. In this situation, both the light of nature and the light of grace say that the fault isn't with the unfortunate person, but with an unjust God. How else can they judge God? He rewards a wicked person without any merits, and He doesn't reward another but condemns them, even if they're less wicked or at least not more wicked.

But the light of glory tells us something different. When it comes, it will reveal that God, whose judgment is currently beyond our under-standing, is truly just and this justice will be clear for all to see. In the meantime, it teaches us to have faith in the certainty of this future event. The example of the light of grace encourages and strengthens our belief in this; it has a similar effect as the light of nature.

SECTION 34: CONCLUSION OF THE ARGUMENT

This is where I'll end this discussion. If necessary, I'm ready to defend this argument further. However, I believe I've said enough to satisfy those who are open to the truth without being stubborn. If we accept that God knows and determines everything in advance, and that he can't be wrong or stopped in his foreknowledge and predestination, and also that nothing happens outside his will (which even reason itself must admit) - then it logically follows that there can be no such thing as free will in humans, angels, or any creature.

So again, if we believe Satan is the ruler of this world, constantly scheming and fighting against Christ's kingdom, refusing to release his human captives unless forced out by divine power, then it's clear that there can be no such thing as free will. Also, if we believe that original sin has severely damaged us, making it extremely difficult even for those guided by the Spirit to resist the evil within them, then it's obvious that there's nothing left in a person without the Spirit that can turn towards good; only towards evil. Furthermore, if the Jews, who pursued righteousness with all their might, ended up falling into unrighteousness, and if the Gentiles, who pursued unrighteousness, unexpectedly and freely achieved righteousness, then it's evident here (as in the previous examples) that without grace, humans can only desire evil.

Finally, if we believe that Christ redeemed humanity with His blood, then we must admit that the whole person was lost. Otherwise, we either make Christ unnecessary or we make Him the redeemer of only the worst part of a person. This would be blasphemous and sacrilegious.

CONCLUSION

Luther advises, expresses gratitude, offers guidance, and prays.

So now, I'm asking you in the name of Christ, my dear Erasmus, to finally do what you've promised. You said you'd be open to learning from someone who could teach you better things. Let's put aside our personal differences. I admit, you're a great person, blessed with many incredible gifts from God, like your genius, knowledge, and amazing eloquence. On the other hand, I don't have much and am not much, except that I'm proud to be a Christian.

Also, I really appreciate and admire that you're the only one among my opponents who has focused on the core issue, the main point of our disagreement, instead of getting caught up in unrelated topics like the Papacy, Purgatory, Indulgences, and other similar subjects. Those things are more like distractions than real debates, and most of my opponents have been chasing me around them without success. You're the only one who has seen the crux of the matter and aimed for the heart of the issue. I truly thank you for that – I much prefer discussing this important question, as long as I have the time and opportunity.

If the people who attacked me in the past had done the same thing, and if those who are currently bragging about new spirits and new revelations would do so too, then we would have less conflict and division, and more peace and harmony. But God allows Satan to cause trouble as a way to punish our ungratefulness.

However, unless you can argue this case in a somewhat different style from your Diatribe, I sincerely wish that you would focus on your own strengths. Please continue to cultivate, enhance, and advance the fields of literature and languages, as you have done so far with great success and praise. Your work in these areas has even benefited me greatly, and I admit that I am deeply indebted to you. I truly respect you and consider you my superior in those fields. However, God has not yet willed or granted that you should be equal to this particular cause. Please don't think I'm saying this out of arrogance.

I pray that the Lord will soon make you as much my superior in this matter as you already are in all others. It's not unusual for God to teach a Moses through Jethro or a Paul through Ananias. If you don't know Christ, then you have missed the mark in what you're saying, and you've done so quite miserably. I believe you must be aware yourself of the kind of statement this is.

It doesn't mean everyone is wrong just because you or I might be wrong (if that's the case). God is said to be amazing in his saints, so we can consider them saints even if they're far from being perfect. It's not difficult to imagine that you, as a human, might not fully understand or pay enough attention to the Scriptures or the teachings of the Fathers, which you believe have guided you to your goal. We get a pretty good clue about this when you say that you're not making any claims, but only discussing. Someone who has a complete and accurate understanding of their topic wouldn't write like that.

As for me, I haven't just been discussing in this book; I've been making claims, and I continue to do so. I don't want to appoint anyone as a judge in this matter. Instead, I encourage everyone to accept my decision. May the Lord, whose cause this is, enlighten you and make you a vessel for honor and glory! Amen.

Made in the USA
Las Vegas, NV
17 October 2023

79235838R00190